STREISAND

The Barbra Streisand story must be one of the most remarkable of this century. Conventionally thought of as an ugly duckling, she astounded the public when she suddenly turned into a showbiz swan.
But it hasn't all been easy. This book tells of her agonizingly difficult climb to the top. It goes beyond the newspaper interviews and the press releases to discover the truth about one of the finest entertainers today. At last the forest of rumour that surrounds the star is penetrated through candid interviews with the composers and directors who charted her feverish rise to fame. René Jordan, her perceptive biographer, follows Barbra through childhood and adolescence, discovering the whys and wherefores behind the relentless ambition of a girl who made it against all odds.
Sometimes you love her, sometimes you hate her – but you are certainly never bored by her.

STREISAND

René Jordan

An Unauthorized Biography

A STAR BOOK

published by

the Paperback Division of
W. H. ALLEN & Co. Ltd

A Star Book
Published in 1977
by the Paperback Division of W. H. Allen & Co. Ltd.
A Howard and Wyndham Company
123 King Street, London W6 9JG

First published in Great Britain by
W. H. Allen & Co. Ltd. 1976

Printed in Great Britain by
Hazell Watson & Viney Ltd, Aylesbury, Bucks

ISBN 0 352 39687 3

For my father, who said that Barbra would never make it

Acknowledgments

For their help in various stages of my research I wish to thank Barry Dennen, Steve Elster, Marilyn Fried, Kenneth Geist, Linda Gerard, Garson Kanin, Mert Koplin, Arthur Laurents, Terry Leong, Gerald O'Brien, Douglas McClelland, James R. Parish, John Patrick, Al Ramrus, Harold Rome, Arnold Scaasi, Robert Schulenberg, Jule Styne, Mike Wallace

Contents

1. Facing the Lion

On a hot and humid night in June, 1960, Barbra Streisand crossed her fingers for luck, ran down three steps from the sidewalk in Greenwich Village's Ninth Street, and faced The Lion. It took courage to walk into this menacing den. The right name had been picked for the deceptive, ferocious little bar. In its crimson lair just below street level The Lion had devoured legions. Barbra Streisand walked into the circus with the almost suicidal determination of a lame gladiator. If she tamed The Lion, nothing could ever frighten her again.

In its roaring heyday in the early sixties The Lion was the most popular gay bar in New York, a dim enclave of pseudo-Bohemia where boys of all ages teetered—as the night grew older—between desperate bravado and unrequited lust. It was awesome and hilarious, often simultaneously. Moods changed mercurially, and in a second the atmosphere could go easily from Dante's *Inferno* to main deck of the *Titanic* just before the doomed started singing "Nearer, My God, to Thee." And to cue each transition, there was Patty at the piano.

Patty was a popular pianist of boundless memory and inexhaustible repertoire, who rose above his role of modern equivalent of a cathouse cleffer by tinkling away any Broadway show tune at the drop of the wildest request. When Patty was on, the boys would forsake the dubious pleasures of cruising in the front bar, flocking to the piano in the more spacious back room. Patty could go from an obscure Ethel Merman number to an even dimmer Helen Morgan ditty. Each person in the crowd remembered two or three words from the lyrics, and they cued each other, singing along between joviality and despair, postponing closing time and the grim acceptance of another empty night.

Little by little, as word got around about Patty's versatility, The Lion began to attract a mixed clientele, mainly show business types of all sexual persuasions: gay, straight, AC/DC, or tremulously undecided. They came to sing along with Patty, standing four or five deep around the corner piano. Some had better memories, better voices than others; the privileged began to stand out from the motley crowd. One thing led to another, finally jelling into the Thursday Night Talent Contest.

This nerve-racking ritual would have given Torquemada a glow. The "stars" were pale boys with restless eyes in search of a mythical producer, or smiling, mechanical girls who tapped their toes one-two-three before attacking a song as if it were their worst enemy, or balding men who brought their wives along—just in case—before they shyly confessed they wanted to give *"Un bel di vedremo"* a whirl. The talent contest was often a sick joke played on the self-deluded. The response wavered between tolerance and bitchiness, depending on the mood of a cutthroat audience. They were to be Barbra Streisand's first big challenge.

Even by the club's relaxed standards, the new contestant looked like nothing they'd ever seen before at The Lion. Her lank hair was half mousy brown, half navel orange. Her face, suffused by a layer of white makeup, was early Dracula's daughter. On both sides of an aggressively prominent nose were two piercing, close-set, slightly crossed eyes, emphasized by heavy rims of Cleopatraesque black paste. She wore a layered feather jacket that had seen better days and a paneled chiffon skirt that swirled like a crumpled parachute over her knees. Under her arm, almost holding her up like a crutch, was a voluminous red vinyl briefcase bulging at the seams.

There was a hush in the room as she walked in. Eyes rolled in mock disbelief. Drinks went from sips to gulps as the crowd readjusted itself to the sight of this creature, wilted by the heat like a secondhand rose, blinking in the reddish penumbra. Hovering between the campy and the cruel, The Lion prepared itself for the best of the worst: This was going to be one hell of a funny talent night.

Yet after the suppressed snicker there was a pang of guilt. How could one laugh at something so pitiful? The poor waif defanged the sadistic Lion into embarrassment, but not for long. Steadily, she walked toward the piano, tore some sheet music out of her bag, and announced she was going to sing "A Sleepin' Bee." This was sheer defiance; she abruptly stopped being the underdog to become fair game. You really had to have unmitigated gall to tackle a number like that one in front of this knowing crowd. The Lion licked its chops and got ready for the kill.

"A Sleepin' Bee," with music by Harold Arlen and lyrics by Truman Capote, was a hallowed song from *House of Flowers*, a lamented show that heartless critics and an indifferent public had driven to an early grave on Broadway. Who was this kid to tamper with a cherished memory and tweak her long nose at a beloved ghost? "A Sleepin' Bee" so clearly belonged to its creator, Diahann Carroll, that it had been cheated of its potential hit quality by the respect of many a recording star. It was Carroll's standard, her high point. Only a fool would try to improve on perfection.

The Lion had no patience when presumption overstepped into arrogance. This upstart deserved no pity; she had to be put in her place. Fangs bare, claws out! The circus was about to start.

Barbra Streisand closed her eyes to obliterate an audience that was prepared to laugh her off, and she retreated into some inaccessible crevice in her rock-hard personality. She opened her mouth wide and sang, not minding where the tortured, restructured notes fell, not caring whether her face was an agonized mask or her neck a ridge of strained vocal cords. She stood immobile, dead arms hanging loose at her sides, not a snap to her paralyzed fingers.

Out of this five-foot, five-inch frame came the incredible voice, sweet as molasses, tart as lemon juice. Then there were the words, savored with delight, rolled on the roof of her mouth and released in an ecstasy of clarity and pitch. Then there was the phrasing, with syllables stretching beyond the impossible, impudent like bubble gum, unsnappable, only cut short at will by a quick breath masquerading as a forlorn sigh. It was not a listening experience; it was a roller-coaster ride. High up, plunge down, crash curve, recovery, exhilarated flight, vertigo. It was no longer music, it was drama.

"A Sleepin' Bee" emerged from her as if she were inventing the song on the spot. It was taking possession of the strange kid as she took possession of it. She was not begging for attention, she was stubbornly demanding it. Then, halfway through the trance, she opened her blue eyes and never closed them again, hypnotically staring straight at the mesmerized crowd. The miracle happened for the first time; she was not ugly, she was beautiful. When the last note oozed out of her, there was stunned silence. No applause, no stagy bravos. Then the tension broke and The Lion roared in sheer animal release. The whole bar seemed to levitate in an explosion of unleashed joy: the first Streisand ovation.

It was her evening. No contest. She won hands down over a light-opera singer, a comedian, and another pop singer. The prize was fifty dollars and a week's engagement, meals included. But "A Sleepin' Bee" had been her Sermon on the Mount, and that very night the Streisand cult started. The early converts spilled onto the streets of the Village, barely able to keep the news to themselves. They called their friends, their enemies, anyone. The pages of their little black books were flipping, together with their lids. Bells were ringing. Word of mouth had turned the Lion cubs into a platoon of fervent amateur press agents, glorying in the fact that they were the first on their blocks to witness the phenomenon.

"Hey, there's this kook at The Lion. Fabulous, *not* to be believed. I'm going back tonight. Yeah, see you. She's on at twelve."

It was the witching hour. The Lion, usually as crowded as the West Side subway at rush hour, escalated into pandemonium over the weekend. The word had spread like wildfire and they were lining up Ninth Street, around the corner to Sixth Avenue, to see "that kooky kid, what's her name?" Those who were lucky enough to get in screamed, yelled, and came out raving, calling up *their* friends at three o'clock in the morning. Those left outside by the already dangerously stretched maximum occupancy limit went away only briefly frustrated. By the time they reached Eighth Street they were concocting stories about what they thought they'd seen and heard.

The Streisand legend had started. In its rich tapestry the first outrageous lies were being embroidered over early-dawn coffee mugs at the corner drugstore. It is now almost impossible to separate fact from fiction. They say she finished songs by shouting, "I'm Barbra Streisand—and don't you forget it." They swear she sang "A Sleepin' Bee" with a live one cupped in her hand, letting it fly away as the piano trilled the last arpeggio. She sat on the piano like Helen Morgan; she knelt on the floor like Al Jolson.

In fact, she did nothing of the sort. She sang as straight and as simply as possible, and most of the Lion stories are merely projections of personal fantasies of her fervent early audiences. Yet the Lion habitués preserve their dreams with the zeal of visionaries proven right by hindsight.

"I really and truly saw her there," one of them now attests, displaying a yellowing, cracked coaster like a badge of honor. "Half the population of New York goes around saying that they saw her at The Lion. It's a lie. The Lion was a smallish bar. If everyone who claims to have seen her there had actually *been* there, Barbra would have had to play for six months at Yankee Stadium."

But her friends, the ones who lived with her through the Lion experience, remember it well. The first few nights she stood close to the piano, as if it were a piece of flotsam she could hold onto in case of shipwreck. Then the admiration of her newly gained fans began to loosen her up. She ventured into the crowd, singing "Lullaby of Birdland" right and left, offering her wares like a pessimistic flower vendor who suddenly realizes the passersby are no longer brushing her away. She was exultant. The customers were in a buying mood. But she staunchly refused what they offered

Dozens of people rushed to Barbra after her turns, pleading to get her a drink. She hated the taste of liquor, she explained to a rather boozy crowd. But how about buying her an order of French fries? Her appetite was as prodigious as her talent, and after the third greasy hamburger, the twenty-third soggy potato sliver, she was on a food binge, stating the credo of her newborn career: "I'm not a singer, I am an actress who sings." Between bites her wide mouth expanded even farther in a porpoise smile while she insisted, "Every song is like a three-act play, right?"

Barbra claimed that she called publishing houses every day for free sheet music. She had heard that the suspicious heart of Tin Pan Alley was made of pure lead, so she melted leery clerks by pretending to be Vaughn Monroe's secretary. They were fooled when she faked a very nasally efficient voice on the telephone, and she got reams of songs sent by private messenger. The pianist played them and she learned them in the afternoon. No big deal, no frenzy. She had IBM memory, ESP receptivity, UHF power of selection. She told her fans that she was trusting her intuition because she'd never had a Victrola at home and had never seen a cabaret performance. Her revelations struck like lightning, electrifying the Lion coterie. She was that awesome, mysterious, mistrustful phenomenon: a natural.

The Lion audience knew nothing about her and she gloried in the enigma. paying no attention to the fables that had begun to circulate about about her. She was far better at the game. Soon she was busy filling the blanks in her past with her own brand of fantasies. One evening on the way to the club she stopped at a fruit stand on Eighth Street and saw a box of Smyrna figs. "Smyrna . . . isn't that in Turkey?" she asked a friend. That night she introduced herself as Barbra Streis, from Smyrna, Turkey. "I was born in Madagascar," she was soon telling her devotees. Next week she ventured, "I was reared in Rangoon."

She was trying myths on for size. Just turned eighteen, Barbra Streisand was detaching herself from reality, snipping a cutout and pasting it into exotic backgrounds. What lay behind the silhouette was to be blocked out, then given added stature by a tall tale. Like Scheherazade, she held her listeners in thrall, but her Arabian Nights did not extend to a thousand and one. She was at the club for only three weeks. The Lion knew a potential star had fallen into its claws, and a hand-painted sign was commissioned, silver dust on each letter: PRESENTING BARBARA STREISAND. It caused her first fight over billing. She hated the name Barbara and was sure it sounded like Bar-burr-ah. The middle *a* just had to go. She had lived with three *a*'s for eighteen years and enough was enough. She topped P. T. Barnum by arguing with the management that she did not care what they said about her as long as her name was spelled *wrong*.

By the time the name had been carefully misspelled on the sign she was gone. Barbra now had an engagement at the Bon Soir, a "name" place. Even though it was only a block down Sixth Avenue from The Lion, the move from Ninth to Eighth Street was a step up the ladder. She felt that she was launched, at least to the lower stratosphere.

Her followers decamped from The Lion and trailed her to the tonier bar. For their benefit she updated the tales about her origins, scouring the map from A to Z. Now it turned out she was born in Aruba, raised in Zanzibar. When she told these transparently fabricated stories in the nasal clamor of pure Brooklynese, she was having fun. She knew she was fooling no one, least of all herself. Yet Barbra was convinced that all that had happened to her before was completely uninteresting.

Throughout her meteoric rise to fame Streisand would show an unerring instinct for what was right, but this time she was very, very wrong. Here was one cliché she could not upturn. For in a long journey in search of Barbra the truth always turns out to be far more fascinating than her fictions.

2. *Barbara with Three* A's

"THE girl from Madagascar" was born and reared on Pulaski Street in a five-story brownstone apartment house deep in the unromantic heart of the Williamsburg section of Brooklyn. Her father, Emanuel Streisand, was a brilliant young man with a PhD in education who taught psychology and English in high school and was—according to all who knew him—on the sure path to a remarkable career as an educator.

Barbara's mother, Diane Rosen, was the daughter of a garment cutter who also functioned as a cantor in the synagogue. Diane had been graduated from school with straight A's and gone to work as a secretary in Manhattan, though she had a lovely voice, some vague theatrical aspirations, and had at one point cut a test record of Romberg's "One Kiss." All these dreams were forgotten when she married Emanuel Streisand and devoted herself to keeping a strictly kosher home for the husband she idolized.

The Streisands had a son, Sheldon, born in 1935, and they kept hoping for the little girl who would complete the required mixed couple most young marrieds felt they could afford in the midst of the Depression. But it took seven years for Barbara Joan to make her appearance, a full three weeks after her birth had been anticipated. The star who would grow to be famous for seldom being on time made her belated entrance into the world on April 24, 1942.

She was a strange baby who slept little, cried infrequently, and silently perused the world with wide-open eyes. Her head was bulb-shaped, much too big for her puny body, and not a hair grew on it until she was two years old. When Barbra later heard these often-repeated family recollections, she cast herself as a Martian. Many children express dissatisfaction with their family lot by secretly thinking of themselves as highborn creatures, stolen and misplaced by gypsies. Looking at her baby pictures, trying to conjure up erased images, Barbara's acute sense of alienation rejected not only her time and place, her home and hearth, but the entire planet. Those Martians had certainly goofed when they dropped her incognito on Pulaski Street.

By the time Barbara realized who she was and what surrounded her, she found herself almost literally in a vale of tears. In 1943, when Barbara Joan was fifteen months old, Emanuel Streisand died of a cerebral hemorrhage at the age of thirty-four. Diane, his inconsolable widow, took mournful leave of the world and spent most of her time in bed, gluttonously feeding on her grief. Relatives and neighbors tried vainly to snap her from her suffering, while baby Barbara watched, uncomprehending, from her favorite perch on the living-room sofa.

Money was scarce and there were no toys. Barbara's first doll was a hot-water bottle she squeezed until it squirted on the floor. In a flurry of annoyance, Mama shifted from weeping to spanking, offering at least a glimmer of attention. "We weren't poor *poor,*" Barbra would later describe this bleak period. "We just didn't have anything."

The family sorrow was underwritten. World War II was on and Mrs. Streisand had a brother overseas, funneling his Army paychecks to Brooklyn and keeping the household precariously afloat. The spiritually crushed widow could not force herself to confront a now meaningless world, but when her brother came back and the subsidy stopped, Diane at last faced reality and took a job as a bookkeeper.

She worked as steadily and as indomitably as she had grieved, slaving overtime, striving to raise her children into fulfilling the promise her husband had been cheated of by death. Little Barbara had had her first contact with love and loss; her boundless sensitivity had absorbed what it meant to be bereft of the one thing you cared for in life. In time her songs about a man who is irrevocably gone would ring with wails of that visceral pain oddly reminiscent of cries of desperation at funerals.

Barbara Joan grew in the shadow of Emanuel, this extraordinary man she never knew and who became the dominant male presence in her psyche. From him she had inherited her exceptionally keen mind, her intransigent pride. During her late childhood and adolescence she traced every clue about him and treasured each bit of glowing information. Even when she reached "stardom"—a term she would grow to despise—no rave review of her work would give her anything compared to the pleasure of finding her father's name mentioned in anthologies as one of the finest educators.

By osmosis she had absorbed a dream that would surface only much later. When she was four, there was only bleakness without redeeming insights and one pervading feeling: loneliness. She was parked with grandparents, relatives, neighbors until it was time for her exhausted mother to pick her up after a grueling day at the office. She played on the sidewalk in front of her grandfather's tailor shop, in constant fear that Mama would never come back because she would be run over by a car. Diane Streisand was embroiled in the task of making ends meet, but how could anyone explain such an abstraction to a painfully receptive child? Barbara felt both her parents had deserted her and that she had to fend for herself alone. Soon she became an expert at it.

She was sent to school several months before her fifth birthday and did herself proud by walking to and from PS 224 unassisted. She could stay home alone, keeping out of mischief, striving to convince everyone that she could take care of herself like a judicious adult. Paying a heavy price for her independence, she was growing up before her time.

Barbara Joan would walk up and down the corridors of the apartment house, cleverly playing the forlorn waif to cadge a snack from compassionate neighbors, assuming a role that would have shamed her mother into a furious spanking. Some of the neighbors were Jewish but did not keep kosher households; some were Italian or Irish. Barbara Joan would taste a sinful sausage, a condemned cannoli, and return home sated, ready to perpetrate the highest offense against a dutiful Jewish mama: She could hardly swallow a mouthful of her dinner

It would drive Diane Streisand to despair. This skinny child was starving to death! The kid was, in fact, gorged on unconfessable goodies, so quickly burned in excess energy that not an ounce of fat stuck to her bones. Barbara Joan loved to spend late afternoons at the home of Irving, a four-year-old friend in the building. His parents were the proud possessors of an early television set with a seven-inch screen, at which the children squinted through a magnifying-glass window, watching Laurel and Hardy demolish the world and themselves in an orgy of liberating slapstick.

Barbara suspected that the cabbage soup Irving's mother offered her was wickedly nonkosher, so she kept these meals a secret, pretending at home that she just wasn't hungry. It was her first convincing performance because she was not found out. But her lies were so believable that she was force-fed, which led to a lifelong revulsion toward what was regimentally called "the proper meal at the proper time."

Tradition was very strong at home, and like any Jewish child worth his bacon, Barbara Joan's rebellion started at mealtime. Then it grew apace, all-encompassing. Enrolled in yeshiva grade school in Brooklyn, she waited until the rabbi walked out of the classroom to shout the one forbidden nine-letter word she could come up with: "Christmas." She even tried to cross her fingers, but the family strictures were so adamant against that one bit of defiance that she only half dared. She was, of course, soon classified as an unholy terror in school, and she loved the role.

At home Barbara still kept pretense, out of deference for her mother's plight. She was respectful of grief, an obedient child, keeping her hellion outbursts at school, behind Mama's back. Her double life had started. She was sweet at home, explosive outside the family enclave. But when she was seven, a new factor upset the equilibrium: Diane Streisand brought home a very nice gentleman she wanted her children to meet.

His name was Louis Kind and Barbara Joan resented him immediately. Kind was a real estate dealer, but later Barbra described him as "a used-car salesman or something." Hostilities started on the very first visit. She felt a deep buzzing sound in her ears and quickly warned Mother. She was given a hot-water bottle as a pacifier. The buzzing persisted, but she was too proud ever to tell a living soul about it. It was her very special secret and she was going to die from it.

Barbara wrapped a woolen scarf over her ears; it would not stop the buzzing. She walked around with the scarf around her skull like a turban, in 95-degree weather. It was the summer she first gained a reputation for being "different." It was also the summer of 1949, and in the fall Diane Streisand married Louis Kind.

"When a kid grows up missing one parent, there's a big gap to be filled," Barbra would later analyze. "It's like someone being blind; they can hear better. I sensed more, wanted more, so I left myself open for life." But this painful sensitivity was intolerable in 1949. Barbara still missed Emanuel Streisand, but Diane Rosen had a very human desire to start her life again. The clash was inevitable.

Oscar Wilde said that children began by loving their parents, then they judged them and seldom forgave them. Barbara's reaction to her mother's recovery from grief was true to the aphorism. Here were the makings of one of those sad, real-life triangles in which everyone is right in his own way and wrong to the others. "He never liked me," Barbra said about Louis Kind, probably reversing gears, never having given the intruder a chance. How could a "used-car salesman" compare with Emanuel Streisand?

The rebellious yeshiva school personality suddenly invaded home and the battle started. It is time out of mind, a period to forget, to gloss over. The family moved to a better apartment on the corner of Nostrand and Newkirk avenues as Barbara Joan became very restless. She announced she wanted to be a ballerina. Eager to keep the peace at home, her mother enrolled her at Miss Marsh's dance school, but only for a short while.

After a regular checkup by the family doctor Barbara was declared anemic, and Mrs. Kind could not stand the thought of her brittle bones propped on a practice bar for such perilous calisthenics. No matter now loudly she protested, Barbara was taken out of ballet school, but she kept on dancing on her toes all over the living room, where she now slept, on a fold-out couch, every night of her new half-affluent, all-miserable life.

She was presented with sibling rivalry when Rosalind Kind was born in 1951. From her very first breath the newcomer proved the ideal child. "A great eater," her mother ecstatically described the baby. Naturally plump, with a sunny disposition, so unlike questioning and reserved Barbara: Rozie smiled all the time, lovely and contented in her crib, while her older sister pirouetted on and on, deep into her ballerina fantasy.

Barbara was growing up absurd at an alarming rate. By the time she was eleven she felt as old as Methuselah, but her body was still unformed, her emotions unseasoned. She was just about ready to forgo reality and make her home away from home at the nearby movie palace. Saturday matinee after Saturday matinee, she was swallowed like an undernourished Jonah by a whale with a non-Biblical name: Loew's Kings on Flatbush Avenue.

What a divine place! The smell of detergent, popcorn, quickly revolving frankfurters, all melded without benefit of alchemy into the magic aroma of childhood reveries. The other kids sat screaming near the screen, clustered against the left wall, sternly policed by white-robed matrons, those killers of the dream. Barbara would sneak up to the forbidden balcony and achieve Nirvana near the starlit ceiling, munching on a Melloroll. There she could escape the matrons who mercilessly shooed the children out of the Loew's Kings after each show. The balcony was her refuge, and she avoided expulsion by hiding under her seat or rushing to the ladies' room as soon as "the end" flashed on the screen. She would do anything to postpone being thrown out.

The longer the movie, the happier she felt. A rerelease of *Gone with the Wind* offered her a four-hour lease on heaven. Barbara was already a very special kind of movie fan: She did not identify with the actresses but with the parts they played. "I never imagined myself to be Vivien Leigh," she has said. "It was *me* up there and all those attractive men were pursuing *me.* " After the show was over she would lock herself for long stretches of time in the family's one bathroom, reenacting what she had seen in front of a mirror, but doing it her way.

Gone with the Wind was an ideal: Scarlett O'Hara's fury, cunning, and determination offered her an image to mold herself into, a credo to embrace. "I'll never go hungry again," she told the mirror very convincingly, though she was bloated on sticky Mellorolls. Then she would declaim, "Tomorrow is another day," alternately stressing each of the four words as the whim struck her.

Her performances took time and were often interrupted by impatient knocks on the bathroom door. Finally she would emerge and sulk around the apartment, in the grip of such fits of depression that her mother threatened not to let her go to the movies again until she learned to put a stop to all this nonsense. Barbara just lowered her eyes and moped some more; she could grimace and fake any emotion in front of the mirror, but the incipient actress still could not master the hardest trick of all: putting on a happy face for the family's benefit.

To hide the sadness she became secretive. She would go up to the roof and spend hours behind a pillar, smoking cigarettes that gave her a taste of the forbidden. She found mystery and defiance by hiding packs behind her schoolbooks. She had been told that smoking would blacken her teeth and stunt her growth, but she could not resist the temptation of doing something she might be punished for. Munching Sen Sens to clear her guilty breath, Barbara anticipated the thrill of being caught. She never was.

Diane Streisand Kind was a very basic, straightforward woman, sadly unequipped for dealing with the vagaries of a problem child. Traditionally, she had learned two staunch rules as rigorous tenets of effective motherhood. First, a brisk spanking on the *tushy* found its way up to the head and did wonders to clear it of the wrong notions. Second, whenever a kid thought too highly of himself and started to put on airs, he had to be quickly brought down by a deflating remark. Barbara's response to the treatment was a chain reaction of insecurity, resentment, and brooding.

She no longer executed *fouettés* around the coffee table, but she was still looking for recognition when she started declaiming those lines she had learned at the movies. "I'm going to be a movie star," she asserted. Mama felt this was not serious enough for spanking, so she applied method number two and told the girl she was too skinny and should come down from the clouds to eat proper, nourishing meals. Rebuffed, Barbara kept her drama confined to the bathroom mirror from then on. And her whole life turned into a series of ruses to stay away from home as much as possible.

Diane Kind had tried by every means to seal an *entente cordiale* between her second husband and her stubborn daughter, but she failed as a diplomat and the situation deteriorated progressively until 1954, when the Kinds separated. Though they never divorced, Diane and Louis lived apart until his death in 1970. But even with her stepfather out of the way, Barbara disliked the regimented life at home and envied her brother, Sheldon, who had escaped by going away to college.

The movies were her only retreat, but her allowance permitted only that one Saturday matinee at the Loew's Kings. Barbara discovered a new haven in the school library. She protested she couldn't study at home, so she stayed overtime between those peaceful bookshelves. Buying privacy at the cost of high learning, she would spend hours poring over texts on any subject, postponing her return to her cramped quarters in the living room.

Playing hooky in reverse, Barbara Joan turned into an honor student. Her average shot up into the 90's, and her innate competitiveness was fanned like the proverbial flame. She strived to be number one in each and every activity except sports: Mama was still afraid her supposedly brittle bones would crack. After being shot down from all her high-flown fantasies, at least in scholastic excellence Barbara had found a way to soar above the crowd.

She desperately needed the uplift. The sassy brat who had

heckled the yeshiva school rabbi had turned into a serious, almost dolorous preadolescent at Erasmus Hall High School. Barbara was a shy, retiring, unpopular girl with sharp bones that protruded like wire hangers under the "cute" and frilly dresses that fit only her mother's definition of "lovable." Every time Diane tied a shiny ribbon in her hair, she would untie it and hide it in her pocket as soon as she turned the corner.

The girls in her class were condescending. She always seemed to be sought after by the prettiest and the dumbest, especially a week before exams, when her cramming through courses made her into a desirable presence to have around. Barbara had inherited Emanuel Streisand's didactic knack. She could compress a whole semester into simple explanations that would win her an A and the pretties at least a passing mark.

Boys were a different problem; they shunned her like the eleventh plague. She lacked beauty and possessed brains, a parlay that doomed her to run last in the teenage sex-appeal sweepstakes. She learned to hate special occasions, when rejection was brought out in the open by formalized dating rituals. As a certified wallflower she eschewed junior proms as potential chambers of horrors; she could will herself into a psychosomatic illness whenever New Year's Eve reared threateningly at the end of the calendar, just when her ego had barely recovered from a blank Christmas.

Barbara pretended not to care; her piercing shoulders were perfecting what the world would acclaim as the inimitable "Streisand shrug." Lips puckered in a petulant pout, she fought disdain with disdain, proclaiming all those youth revels a frivolous waste of time. She set her sights on the grades that soothed her wounds and made her feel important. The future pattern was being set, right in the halls of Erasmus: She was described as arrogant when she was merely being defensive.

Barbara wore her intelligence like a shield. She was pedantic, yes, but she was fighting for some sort of identify. Nature had not been prodigal to her, but it had granted some small mercies: She had good eyesight and thus escaped the thick glasses that would have made her into a caricature of the whiz kid in the funnies. She suffered through all the humiliations of the period and stored them deep down for many a year until they surfaced in her precise re-creation of a campus freak in *The Way We Were.*

Yet, much as she pretended to scorn the transient values of beauty and charm, she longed for them. At thirteen they were her secret vice. She got thinner and thinner as she rose to the top of the academic heap at Erasmus because she was spending most of her lunch money on pathetic stabs at glamor. She wanted to be vampy like her current idol, Rita Hayworth, so she bought mad shades of lipstick and thick mascara at the Woolworth counter, then closed the curtains of photo booths and smeared all the makeup on. She opened her mouth seductively, batted a wicked green eyelid, and pressed the button. She would emerge with a four-in-hand image of impossible allure, as if she'd drawn an extra lemon in this beauty jackpot that stubbornly eluded her.

Barbara was a self-centered dot of despair with an ever-expanding radius of alienation: first the family, then the school, then the neighborhood. She brazenly asked her mother what doorstep she had picked her up at. She called Erasmus Hall "a place where they train you to marry a dentist and I'll never marry one." In a burst of alliteration, she pronounced Brooklyn to be just "boredom, baseball, and bad breath." She simply had to move, shoot out like the displaced Martian into another sphere. The immediate problem was that she had no sense of where she wanted to land.

This anguished disorientation stopped abruptly on her fourteenth birthday. All her life she had lived just a subway ride away from Manhattan, but she had never set foot on an island her mother disliked and called unclean at best and wicked at worst. But on a Saturday afternoon in April, 1956, Barbara was taken to a matinee of *The Diary of Anne Frank* on Broadway, and it drastically changed her outlook on life.

Her reaction to the play itself was a typical Streisand mixture of awe and skepticism. Hunched in her cheap seat in the second balcony of the Cort Theatre, she watched the stage with a jaundiced eye. Her idea of entertainment was conditioned by luxurious Hollywood movies and she found the set dreary, the people depressing. She also concluded she could play each part much better. She could sense when the actors were going too far, when they were holding back too timidly. The performance failed to impress her, but the fact that these seemingly ordinary people—not a Rita Hayworth among them—were down there, actually *on*, left her limp with excitement.

And then there was the attraction of Broadway, with its winking neon signs, the marquees hovering over her head, the glitter and the noise, the diffuse feeling of glory and danger. It was as if the Loew's Kings had burst and spread its innards on countless blocks of threatening magic. This was where she belonged, not Brooklyn. That night, over dinner, she announced she would become a stage actress with such vehemence that this time she did not get a snicker but a second helping of the casserole as a pacifier.

Her mother felt Barbara would get over the Broadway phase. It would pass, like those mad dreams of crashing into movies. But the girl had latched onto an obsession that had at least a minor level of sanity to hang onto. Even Barbara, in her wildest hopes, had known that conquering Hollywood was as improbable as returning to that faraway planet from which she fancied herself to be a dropout. But Broadway meant just a subway ride from home, and if those others had safely made the journey up there, why couldn't she?

As her first theatergoing experience *The Diary of Anne Frank* had been a crucial choice. She could identify with all that had happened on the stage: the rituals and the pain, the bickering and the martyrdom. The movies had acquainted Barbara with a never-never land she longed to enter, but with the lack of self-reliance of a gate crasher doomed for the bum's rush. Now she had found a more accessible target for her unfocused ambitions.

Much as she had tried in front of mirrors, behind curtains at the photo booths, she had never come anywhere near Hollywood's hallucinatory standards. She lacked Garbo's swan-like neck, Mae West's swiveling hips, Vivien Leigh's fetching dimples, Hayworth's flaming mane. But Anne Frank, her father, her sister, even the grasping neighbor Mrs. Van Daan—those people she could identify with. Strangely enough, audiences were paying good money to see their plight onstage. She, too, was Jewish and had suffered. She was sure she could persuade audiences, in time, to clamor for her drama.

Faced with the onslaught of this fervent child, her mother was sympathetic but wary. She had always discouraged Barbara from taking swimming lessons for fear she would drown in the neighborhood pool, but now the risk of going under was more imminent. Who would want to pay money to see this scrawny teenager perform? Diane Streisand Kind was an expert at propping cushions to spare her gawky daughter some hard knocks; again she tried her best to save her from disaster.

"I was so sure Barbara would be a fiasco," Mama later said, rationalizing her opposition to her daughter's career. Struggling to spare the kid from a lifetime of utter humiliation, she tried a less blunt, diversionary tactic now. She suggested Barbara should join amateur theatrics and do some plays at school. The girl rejected the peace offering with the haughtiness of a crusader in the face of apostasy. School plays were mere charades put on for drooling parents who rattled their folding chairs while shouting "Attagirl" at curtain calls. She aimed to be a professional, to belong to the Theater with a capital *T*.

Barbara wanted to enroll in Malden Bridge Summer Theater in upstate New York, near Albany. Only a tuition fee of $150 stood between her and the immediate goal. She campaigned ceaselessly for it. After all, her grades at Erasmus were the very best; she deserved the gift of a summer vacation of her choice, and in Malden Bridge she would get plenty of fresh air with none of the risks of bone-breaking sports that had always made her mother so anxious about sending her to camp.

Besides, the $150 really belonged to Barbara, left in trust at her grandfather's death in provision for "a rainy day." The conflict now was to determine what that "rainy day" meant. For Mama the kid's theatrical ambitions were no more than a passing shower, but Barbara placed them on a par with a raging Indian monsoon. The besieged mother was about to capitulate when further complications arose: There was the matter of the teeth.

Barbara's permanent bicuspids had never come down and she had two stunted baby teeth creating gaps of imperfection on each side of her too-wide mouth. The dentist told them the worst: The permanent bicuspids were lost in limbo and would never make an appearance. As soon as the offending baby teeth were extracted, however, they could be supplanted to give her a full, husband-snaring smile.

Barbara submitted, but as soon as the tiny teeth were gone, the dentist decided that, in addition, a molar should be extracted on each side. Then a year or so with braces would even out the front teeth just before the final gleaming touch was applied. That's when Barbara exploded with an earth-shaking No. She had liked her baby teeth and—in mourning for their loss—she even described them with one of her mother's favorite words: "cute." Now they were irretrievably gone, and she would not let the dismantling continue, for fear the dentist wanted to equip her with Dracula's fangs.

Furthermore, the whole process would last another year and could be paid for only with those treasured one hundred and fifty dollars. Barbara claimed the right to her inheritance with the passion of a princess about to be dispossessed of her realm. The money was hers to do what she wanted, and she'd rather go to summer theater than have her teeth straightened. Big family battles are often waged to settle the difference between what is important and what is urgent. The allocation of priorities over grandfather's legacy provoked many a tearful confrontation, but this time Barbara argued with the conviction of the doomed: She was sure she would die soon and she didn't want the money to pay for her funeral.

She had come across a brochure that catalogued seven symptoms of a fatal disease. In a burst of hypochondria she soon conjured each and every one of the unlucky seven. She had completely given up smoking when she'd turned thirteen because she could do it at school and nobody cared about her defiance. But she still had a racking smoker's cough, dark circles under her eyes, and a porcelain-pale skin that would never tan. She knew she was going to die young: Camille had become her secret heroine.

Much as she tried, every time she thought of a long-range future she would draw a blank: She could visualize no marriage, no children, nothing. She had to do something fast. For what it was worth, she had to extract the most of what little time was left before those frightening symptoms would converge into terminal illness.

The fantasy of impending death is not uncommon among the young, but Barbara Joan Streisand infused it with a special sense of tragedy. Why did she need good teeth to ensure a nonexistent future? She would not tell her mother about the dreaded symptoms because that would have meant going to the hospital for a checkup and squandering every penny of the $150 on a hopeless case. She just pleaded and cried and argued, never going beyond an enigmatic "I just have to do it."

In a last-ditch attempt to persuade her against spending the money on this summer-theater folly, her mother reminded her she would be an aspiring leading lady with two flagrantly missing bicuspids. Barbara conceded the point and started experiments with different ploys to hide her misery. She concluded that chewing Aspergum and shaping the wads into the gaps would create a stage illusion of a full, if slightly shaky, smile.

Faced with this pathetic ruse, Mama gave up. The kid could no longer be spared suffering; she had to learn the truth the hard way. She let her go, hoping she would come back chastened and tamed. Diane Streisand Kind did not know that Barbara's Aspergum bicuspids were as impermanent as her life span. The girl wanted only to pursue her dream for a summer that would perhaps be her last on earth.

Fleeing the imagined shadow of death, Barbara ran up to Albany with her $150 ransom. Never, since venal popes stopped selling indulgences on the cheap, had anyone paid such a small price to ascend into heaven.

3. *Gotta Move!*

BARBARA STREISAND arrived at Malden Bridge Summer Theatre with an impact that was described by her cohorts in metaphors reserved for meteorological accidents: She was a cyclone, a tornado. She would sweep the stage, hammer the flats, cue everyone on his lines—offering unwelcome suggestions on how to stress them for better effect. The dormant larva was awake again, but as she stealthily replaced the wads of Aspergum, who would buy her as an upcoming butterfly?

Nonetheless, she was shooting for the top with not a minute to waste. The big summer production at Malden Bridge would be John Patrick's *The Teahouse of the August Moon,* and she wanted to play Sakini. The leading part, naturally. The fact that Sakini was a man did not deter her. He was supposed to be a little guy, a runt of an Okinawan peasant, almost a gnome. The guys in the company were too big and broad-shouldered, but she was tiny and lithe enough, right?

She would be proven right in the future when Marlon Brando's screen Sakini turned into a lummox while Jean Dalrymple directed a woman, Rosita Diaz Jimeno, as a believable Sakini in a Spanish touring version. But in Malden Bridge Barbara's audacity in coveting the lead was laughable. She only got to ride a goat across the stage in a silent but spirited bit that brought the house down in each performance.

Not much, but for her it was a new lease on life. When her summer stint was over, she came back to Brooklyn, her future no longer a blank. "I'm going to be somebody," she told her classmates at Erasmus Hall. She repeated the threat at home, nurturing second thoughts about Mama's moment of weakness when she'd let her lay hands on the $150. Next summer she wouldn't have it again, but now she had a goal: She'd have her teeth fixed and her Malden Bridge enrollment money ready by spring if it killed her.

Barbara got a job as a waitress in Choy's Orient, a Chinese restaurant not far from home. She could count change like a computer and was soon promoted to cashier. After playing the Okinawan peasant, she was experiencing the first signs of identification with her parts. She felt truly Oriental and thought of the restaurant as her new home away from home. "It was the world against us at Choy's Orient," she once reminisced. The world, of course, meant her mother, who was making loud noises about the danger of school grades falling because of the added burden of work and even louder ones about Barbara eating all those nonkosher wontons.

Barbara was more scared of having to drop out of Choy's Orient than out of Erasmus Hall. She was carefully stashing away half her salary as an investment on the only future she wanted: another summer at Malden Bridge. She studied harder so that her grades would stay high, while at night she developed a working vocabulary in Chinese, plus a passion for what would become her favorite dish, moo shu pork, the mere mention of which would have brought her Orthodox household into a turmoil.

Saturdays and Sundays she took a job as an usher in the Loew's Kings, the movie palace of her childhood dreams. She always pointed the flashlight at the carpet and averted her face from the ticket buyers. She was terrified that one day, when she made it as a film star, someone would remember her and sneer at her glamour because she'd been that gawky girl who stumbled in the dark down the mezzanine stairs.

Under duress she was an honor student at Erasmus Hall, but she couldn't care less. During that year she was only buying a stake on her fancies. The straight A's she proudly brought home at the end of each interminable semester were the price. She kept insisting on an acting career, and another confrontation loomed in the wings. After the problem with the teeth there was the conflict with the nails.

Deep in her Oriental period, Barbara had let her fingernails grow to Fu Manchu lengths. They were greatly admired at Choy's Orient, and blood enamel made them worthy of an aspiring Dragon lady. Mrs. Kind, of course, felt they were outlandish because they impeded a possible career as a secretary. Against her will, Barbara was enrolled in typing school, but she couldn't manage "qwertpoiuy" without breaking her precious claws. The ring was set for the next family bout.

In her early interviews, when Barbra talks about this period, she sounds uncannily like a recitation of Laura's part in *The Glass Menagerie,* rewritten for a Salinger character, either Franny or Esme. There is the mother who begs her to take typing lessons and have something to fall back on; there is the shy daughter who pretends to heed her advice but flunks out of secretarial school because she won't let go of her crystalline illusions.

However Barbra may have dramatized these months, she was never an impractical heroine like Tennessee Williams' Laura. She fully realized the danger of becoming adept at marketable office skills: They would doom her forever to the toils of Tillie when she hankered after the perils of Pauline. Burning her bridges before she was ever tempted to cross them, she let her claws grow even longer so she would not be able to type a single word. She had, meanwhile, developed a system of punching the keys in Choy's Orient register without a crack.

Typing was out of the question, so her mother changed tactics and offered the lure of something more artistic. Piano lessons! Barbara was briefly interested, but she again infuriated her teacher by refusing to pare her nails. After all, Barbara said, she wasn't planning a career as a concert pianist, so what did it matter if the nails made a clicking sound when they hit the ivories? She had just wanted to learn the scales, with a curiosity that verged on the mathematical. Despite her impassioned plea, the heretical pupil was dropped from music school. She was back cramming courses and appeasing family misgivings by going after every academic honor in sight.

It was a clever deception. School bored her. Her main interest was the secret savings account in which she hoarded money to pay for drama courses. When she returned to Malden Bridge Summer Theatre in June, she was also displaying a newly acquired shining smile, unpropped by Aspergum, paid by her evenings at Choy's Orient. The new bicuspids improved her looks a little, her self-reliance a lot.

She played the tomboy sister in *Picnic* and the office flirt in *The Desk Set,* commanding the stage in a would-be tempting skirt, naughtily slit over her left knee so that she could dangle a skinny leg, strategically propped on a table, in a pendular motion copied from Marlene Dietrich's come-hither in *Destry Rides Again.* Her *chutzpah* was so monumental that the audience did not laugh but cheered.

Barbara incorporated all sorts of unrehearsed bits into her parts and became her director's biggest headache until the public's obvious amusement saved her from a swift demotion to stage sweeping and walk-ons. Every time she had a chance to get onstage she did her inspired, undisciplined best. Her enthusiasm was contagious; the kid was obviously having the time of her life.

When she came back to Brooklyn and Erasmus Hall, all her fantasies of early demise had vanished. She had exaggerated when she felt she was not long for this world. *This* world meant only Brooklyn, and she had to leave it behind as soon as possible. She was like a comet in mid-transit, but she still wasn't sure what role she would assume when time came for her to burst into the outside world. She had been Scarlett, Anne Frank, Gilda, Camille, and had discarded each like a worn garment. Then she met a girl named Susan.

Susan was not good-looking by any means, but she received a lot of hard-earned attention at school by being outrageously different. She slinked around in white makeup, blatantly bleached hair, and a wardrobe that seemed handpicked from a ragbag by a color-blind hobo. Susan's system was not new: In England she would have been labeled an eccentric, but in Brooklyn she was claimant to a newly minted term. She was a kook.

Barbara admired her courage, and Susan is the one person she has ever admitted to have copied. Naturally, in Barbara's case it was genius paying homage to mere brashness. When she sank her recently acquired bicuspids into the part, she outdistanced Susan by several light-years and won her special niche as the superkook. It was the year when fashion was condemning women to the horrors of the "paleface look." Barbara, with her inborn knack for hyperbole, discolored her face into a translucent pallor and walked around like a reject from the crypt. She dyed her hair into so many consecutive clashing shades that every time the sun shone on her head there seemed to be a mauve or greenish halo emanating from the mountainous bouffant hairdo. Her clothes were deliberately mismatched, and her shoes had Minnie Mouse buckles so huge that if they'd ever twirled in a strong breeze, she might have been airborne like a twin-rotored helicopter.

It was merely a tryout for the Broadway image she was preparing to launch next season, but it shocked people at school and scandalized the neighborhood. She loved being talked about, but she hated it too, in typical ambivalence. Her disdain for Brooklyn rose into active abhorrence. "I felt like a character out of Paddy Chayefsky," she has said. Everyone knew what everyone else was thinking, merely because they all thought monotonously alike. She was out of tune, and her waves were being detected and checked.

"I learned a lot in the streets of Brooklyn," she later conceded. "Out there you couldn't be dumb and survive." So she strived to be brighter than all and was graduated from Erasmus Hall in January, 1959, with an average of 93 and a shining medal in Spanish. She could have gone to college on a scholarship with flying colors, but her one aspiration in life was to get out of Brooklyn. It had become stifling and she was literally on her last gasp.

She wanted only to study drama. Barbara took a job in Manhattan as a switchboard operator and commuted to

Brooklyn, stashing sacrifice money into her savings account until she had enough for the big break. Out of a $90-a-week salary she was putting away $45 every Friday. As soon as she had amassed $750, enough to reach a head-above-water level, Barbara informed her mother that she was moving to Manhattan. Those long subway rides made it difficult to enroll in after-work drama classes.

There was another skirmish in the family war, but Barbara finally moved into a very small apartment on Thirty-fourth Street, with a girl her mother had scrutinized and found suitable. Mama kept close guard on the kids and frequently appeared, unannounced, like a master sergeant, to inspect the place thoroughly, buying her way in with two mason jars of chicken soup. These invasions of privacy made an indelible impression on young Barbara, and years later she admitted they were the basis for the best nightmarish scene in her 1971 movie, *Up the Sandbox,* when the prying mama is not intimidated by a chain lock she proceeds to destroy with a giant wrench.

Barbara had wanted to get away from home, but basically she was not lying when she had argued that she needed more time to commute among acting schools: She had enrolled in four different ones. With the suspicious instincts of a comparison shopper, she shuttled from one to another, keeping her quadruple betrayal a secret from her teachers by inventing names and personalities: Angelina Scarangella was her favorite.

She found the name in the phone book and immediately fell in love with it, to the point of having match boxes inscribed with it and distributing them in drama schools in case anyone ever got suspicious about her real identity. For a while she even toyed with the idea of changing her acting name to Angelina Scarangella, but only one thing deterred her: She wanted all those people who had known her in Brooklyn to find out it was she, rejected Barbara Streisand, who had finally made it.

From one class to the next, the bogus Angelina zoomed in her ever-shrinking spare time. Always the unwelcome kibitzer, she was the only student who asked questions and prodded teachers to give her a more solid motivation for this or that scene. At Eli Rill's acting seminar she wanted to play Greek tragedy. The teacher attempted to guide her to exploit her natural comic vein, but she persisted in being the Flatbush Duse, to the other students' snickers.

Determined to do everything her way, she was inevitably turned down by the hallowed emporium of the time, Lee Strasberg's Actors Studio. Versions of the fiasco differ. Barbra has said that she faced a standard questionnaire, and when asked who her favorite actress was, she could not come up with a safe choice like Geraldine Page or some other exalted Strasberg alumna, so she wrote that her preference was a toss-up between Mae West and Rita Hayworth. Perhaps closer to the truth is the alternate version; She got so emotional during her test scene that she burst out crying, in a display of uncontrolled emotion that proved anathema to her method-trained panel of judges.

One way or another, the Actors Studio rejection was a deep wound that took time to heal. When she wrote her program biography for her first Broadway show, she capped it with a punch line: "She is not a member of the Actors Studio." Eli Wallach and Anne Jackson, who came backstage to congratulate her on her performance, persuaded her to join them in Strasberg's private class, but she did not stay there long. The memory of that turndown, in her oversensitive seventeenth summer, was not easy to forget.

Acting schools were as skeptical about Barbara's acting potential as her mother. Yet she was unable to keep away from the living theater. Indefatigable Barbara forged on, sandwiching in chores as a scenery mover and underpaid factotum in Off Broadway's Cherry Lane Theatre during a revival of Sean O'Casey's *Purple Dust.* Anita Miller was in the cast and she was moved by the girl's dedication. She recommended her to her husband, drama teacher Alan Miller, who gave Barbara a scholarship in his acting class. To help her make ends meet, the Millers often called her to their apartment on West Seventy-fifth Street to baby-sit for their infant son, Greg.

In Miller's theater workshop on West Forty-eighth Street Barbara at last found the right milieu after her period of turncoating from one teacher to another. She played the young Italian daugher in *The Rose Tattoo* as if she were Angelina Scarangella to the manner born. In her scene of sexual awakening with a young sailor, she jumped on her bemused costudent's back, clawed at him, felt him all over with the tips of her fingers as if she were blind, discovering the mystery of male flesh by Braille. She was wild, this girl, but she was also immensely promising.

Anita and Alan Miller started as teachers and ended as surrogate parents. The Millers became a shaping force in her early development. She had been taken into a household where children were allowed to run free of the tyranny of the clock. They ate when they were hungry and slept when they were tired, never mind if it was seven or nine. After exposure to a new sort of family life Barbara was more reluctant than ever to submit to the old strictures. When she moved from one apartment to the next, in a ramshackle existence, her mother had to phone friends to locate her before making a peregrination to Manhattan with the jars of chicken soup.

Barbara was again going through the hazards of a double life. She worked as a clerk in a printing shop in the daytime, and her boss constantly objected to her humming all over the office, so she contrived to be fired and later claimed a moral victory over her employer when he came to pay his respects backstage after a performance of *Funny Girl*, reminding her of how much he had balked at her muffled singing in the file room.

Jobless, she had time—and an unemployment check—on her hands. Now she was free in the daytime and ready to try her luck at auditions. Soon she realized that what her theatrical friends called "doing the rounds" was a new, unexplored circle of hell, far worse than any she had been immersed in before. She roamed from one casting office to the next, leaving pictures and résumés behind as if she were pawning unreclaimable treasures. She had learned many a cruel phrase in her crawl to fame, but the worst was now part of her thesaurus of rejection: "Don't call us, we'll call you."

"It was degrading, humiliating," she has said. "Nobody should be forced to beg for work." So she did not beg. If they told her there was nothing for her, she would do the Streisand shrug and never come back.

Living on unemployment checks, Barbara was steps away from poverty, but she refused to go back home to Mama in defeat or—even worse—to draw on what was left of her meager savings in the bank. She was financially destroyed when her current roommate decided to call it quits and return to the safety of three square meals a day in Brooklyn. Barbara was stuck with the rent for a walk-up apartment on West Forty-eighth Street, next door to Alan Miller's Actors Workshop. She hurriedly tacked a notice on the billboard of Actors Equity. It was an SOS for a roommate. Marilyn Fried responded.

"I went over to the address Barbara had written on the card," Marilyn now says. "We decided we could get along and I moved in. We were both aspiring actresses at the time. I had no idea how talented Barbara was until I saw her do an exercise in Alan Miller's class." The students were asked to choose what they wanted to impersonate: a budding tree, a cuckoo clock, unlimited options. Barbara decided on a chocolate-chip cookie. "I had never seen anything like her expressiveness before," Marilyn tells. "She was a limp and passive blob until she was put in the oven. Then she began huffing and puffing as the dough expanded. Then she was wheezing and collapsing as she got toasted." The whole class applauded her imaginative performance, but to this day Streisand claims she has never been able to eat a chocolate-chip cookie with a clear conscience.

"After that day," Marilyn recalls, "I knew Barbara was going to be a great artist. We lived in total poverty on Forty-eighth Street. Each of us was getting thirty-two dollars a week on unemployment checks. It barely covered the rent and our fees for acting classes. Once a week when it really got bad each of us had to go to see Mama, to get the bread and the margarine and the soup. Barbara would go to Brooklyn to her mother and I'd go to the Bronx to mine. We'd both come back with the groceries and we'd take everything out of the boxes in the kitchen and put it in the refrigerator. That is how we survived.

"Barbara was devastated in class because some people said she was just so-so. Then she did a scene from a play that was exceptionally good. She called her mother and asked her to come and watch her. Mrs. Kind came down to Miller's workshop. She did not say a word after the performance. Barbara had had a hunch that she would be impressed into helping her further in her struggle. There was this terrible silence. Then, when we got upstairs to our apartment, it began. Her mother said that Barbara should get a job or find another outlet for whatever she had to offer because she did not have the ability to be an actress. We spent half an hour in the bedroom listening to this nonsense. I was heartbroken because she was not encouraging Barbara. Her mother never felt this girl's need to hear her say, 'Go ahead, do what you want to do.' And yet Barbara never felt any anger or hostility about it. After that embarrassing session, one night Barbara and I sat together wondering what we would like most to do if we ever made it as actresses and she said, 'First of all, I want to buy my mother a mink coat.'"

Barbara was always clothes-minded, but she had very little money to invest in the things she liked. She kept scouring thrift shops for the best that was available within her stringent budget and, coincidentally, giving her superkook image an added dimension. She could not afford department-store dresses, and besides, she thought the salespeople were snotty. At a thrift shop she was able to go through the hangers and choose to her Mad Hatter's content.

Her mother had instilled in her a sense of cleanliness. She figured that the secondhand stuff, in fairly good condition, had been worn by people who could afford to take frequent baths. She loved the forties styles, and her day was made if she found some thirties leftovers. Casting agents cannot be entirely blamed for shooing her away when she marched in, wearing those outlandish outfits, swearing she could play Shakespeare while looking like a high school understudy for *The Madwoman of Chaillot.*

Then, through her roommate, Marilyn, Barbara met Terry Leong, a talented young artist who began to design her outfits. "She had innate good taste," Leong remembers, "but she lacked a sense of coordination. I started to accompany Barbara in her expeditions to the thrift shops, which were a treasure trove in those days. One day we found a mauve feather jacket that had belonged to a countess. Barbara got it for twelve dollars and I designed a pleated chiffon skirt to go with it. Suddenly it became a dress and she loved it. She later wore it for her debut at The Lion. We kept finding great things: There was a lace doily I backed with satin and made into another dress. She was no longer wearing a patchwork of conflicting elements. I would create a costume around a necklace, a belt, anything we found in our excursions. It was adventurous and fun because Barbara was not afraid to wear things that would terrify or shock others."

The thrift-shop caper soon came to an abrupt end. In utter naïveté, Barbara told the Labor Department clerks that she was looking for a job as an actress. The callous bureaucrats would not forgive someone who was so oblivious of the rules of the game. She was summarily informed that her unemployment checks would be discontinued if she refused to take their offer of a job as a switchboard operator.

"She hated doing it but there was no way out," says Terry Leong. "Barbara was so bored that she began rehearsing different accents when she answered the phone. I would call and she would answer in an almost unintelligible French accent, and when she realized it was me, she'd laugh and say that she was practicing the maid's role in *The Boy Friend.*"

She was fired as fast as she had been hired. The unemployment office put her back on their rosters after a promise of looking for a real job, no acting nonsense. She was given ten more weeks; that was the absolute limit. Time was running short for Barbara Joan Streisand.

Then Marilyn Fried remembers a very special evening. "I was in the bedroom, ready to go to sleep. Barbara was with a young fellow who had come in for a cup of coffee. He was strumming a guitar. I suddenly heard this remarkable voice coming out of the living room. My immediate reaction was to go to the radio and find out who was singing so marvelously. But the radio was not on. I realized there must be someone in this tiny apartment who had this magnitude, this power. I turned around and asked Barbara, 'Who was singing?' She said, 'I was.' That's the way it all started.

"'Barbara pulled a test record out of the closet. It was a 45 rpm that she had done with piano accompaniment much earlier, when she was twelve or thirteen. She played it for us and it was incredible. Both her date and I told her she should try singing. She said, 'I'm not a singer, I'm an actress.' Out came the sensitivity, the insecurity, the shyness. She could not believe she could sing. It was amazing. But next day she was singing around the house and asking me whether it sounded right and should she go for an audition."

She was scared even to mention it, but the audition she was worrying about was for *The Sound of Music.* In her rounds of casting agencies, Barbara had circulated a highly idiosyncratic 8 x 10 photograph. According to Barry Dennen, who would soon become a decisive influence in Streisand's development, "she was all swathed in cloaks and veils and earrings and chatchkalas, looking like Ruth Draper in a moving moment. This photograph was so hilarious that Eddie Blum of the Rodgers and Hammerstein casting office called Barbara, just to see what kind of girl would send out a picture like that."

Blum asked her to audition, and Marilyn recalls that Barbara sang for three hours for Blum and his casting staff. "Then he took her to lunch, then to dinner. He spent the whole day talking to her. He was fascinated with her talent and her intelligence. Around ten thirty that night he brought Barbara back to our apartment and gave her a lot of encouragement. He told her he couldn't put her in the chorus because she was something special and there was nothing in *The Sound of Music* for a talent like Barbara's."

She was back where she'd started. Other friends were still banging on the same theatrical doors, but Barbara virtually ceased "doing the rounds." She was proud enough, astute enough to realize she did not have the Open Sesame, so she snorted, "I'm not going back to them, they'll have to come to me." She was proclaimed crazy, but her strategist's mind was already planning a diversionary tactic.

At the Rodgers and Hammerstein office Barbara had seen the first glimmer of attention from professional theater people. She told her friends that her long audition had been no more than "a lot of screaming." But the seed was planted. When her unemployment checks stopped coming, maybe she could make some money by singing for a while until she could establish herself as a serious actress. She did not relish the prospect but, after all, it was better than going back to a nine-to-five job in an office.

Before she had to face this unsavory option, Barbara had her last fling with the kind of lofty theatrical experiment she had always longed for. A group of desperately out-of-work players had banded together to form the Actors Co-Op, labeled "a nonprofit group" in case there was any doubt about their destitution. Their first and last production was Karel and Josef Čapek's *The Insect Comedy* at the Jan Hus Theatre. Terry Leong designed the costumes for the ubiquitous Barbara, who in the course of three acts and an epilogue played Apatura Clythia, the messenger, the second butterfly, and the second moth.

On Monday, May 9, 1960, Frank Aston of the *World Telegram & Sun* gave the play an amused and tolerant review, mainly because "no one in it claimed to be anything like a pro." Aston gave Barbara Streisand her first New York daily newspaper notice when he mentioned her as a denizen of "Butterflyland, where the girls assail men but get nowhere because everyone dies too soon."

The Insect Comedy lasted only three nights at the Jan Hus, but it proved a turning point in Barbara's life. On that stage she met Barry Dennen, a young actor from California, who played a cricket and a snail. Barry now remembers that "the whole production was slapped together. It was unspeakable, tacky, awful, and Barbara was hysterically funny. She was very young, endearing, and exceptionally serious about becoming a great actress." Neither of the protagonists knew it, but the saga of Barry and Barbra had started.

It began with a joke. "She was very inventive and funny," Barry Dennen remembers. "We began to make up all sorts of verbal bits. We invented a story about Mae West, who encounters a poodle which is being forced to swallow diamonds by its unscrupulous owner in an attempt to smuggle the gems through customs. Mae notices the poor little beast looking constipated and she turns to its master and mutters, 'Whatsa matta with your animal?' It became a catchphrase for Barbra and me, whenever things were going terribly wrong."

Barry and Barbara were still very good friends after *The Insect Comedy* closed. "I had an excellent Ampex stereo tape recorder and two good mikes," Dennen now says. "One fatal day Barbra asked me if she could come over with a guitarist and make a tape of a couple of songs for an agent who had requested it. We spent the afternoon taping, and the moment I heard the first playback I went insane—I knew here was something special, a voice the microphone loved. I told her she had to sing and she said, 'I'm an *ehktress.*' I had a difficult time convincing her to work on her singing, but I finally threw her a challenge. There was a club across the street from where I lived, called The Lion. They had a talent contest on Thursdays. If Barbra would actually walk in there and sign up, I would work with her on a set of songs, help her choose the material, and direct the act."

Barbara Streisand was longing for recognition and desperate for money. She was just about ready to take a shortcut to fame, but still reluctant to take Barry's dare. She went back to her apartment on Forty-eighth Street and asked Marilyn Fried and another girlfriend, Joanna Bishop, to listen while she sang. She asked them not to look at her because she'd feel embarrassed. They must face the kitchen wall. Looking at their backs, she sighed deeply and sang "A Sleepin' Bee." When it was over, there was no immediate reaction. Only ominous silence. "Well, am I any good?" Barbara half begged, half demanded. Then the girls turned and tears were streaming down their faces.

Her fate was sealed. Next Thursday, a week after her last unemployment check had been cashed, she faced The Lion and conquered it. But from then on, no matter how often she repeated, "I'm not a singer, I'm an actress," the conjure ceased to work. People nodded, applauded, and asked her for the next number. She had been sidetracked into an unexpected direction: The shortcut had turned into her road to the top.

4. *A Portrait of Barbra*

WITH the reckless instinct of a natural-born gambler, Barbra had played her ace in the hole before The Lion audience and she had won.

From her mother she had inherited the good, strong voice Diane Streisand Kind sometimes had entertained her supper guests with, trilling away à la Jeanette MacDonald through standards like "One Kiss," "It Had to Be You," and the Gilbert and Sullivan operettas. From her father she had inherited the analytical mind, and when she "put together" her tiny repertory, she had given this theatrical term a new meaning: She loved to break the songs as if they were toys in the hands of an inquisitive child bent on discovering what made them tick, then tinker with them, reconstituting the lyrics and the melodies into new forms.

The enormous talent was there, but it needed guidance. At this crucial point in her artistic development Barry Dennen came into her life.

Years later Dennen would be recognized as a brilliant performer. He would win acclaim and awards as the diabolical master of ceremonies in the London production of *Cabaret* and then create the show-stealing part of Pontius Pilate first in the record of *Jesus Christ Superstar*, then in the Broadway production, and finally in the movie version of the rock opera.

But in the summer of 1960 Barry Dennen was as unknown and as full of ambition as Barbra. He had persuaded her to try her luck at The Lion. There she had lost an *a* and gained a following. Now Barry had to fulfill his promise to polish Barbra from a diamond in the rough into a dazzling gem. Dennen now recalls how he turned into the dedicated Pygmalion to her eager Galatea:

"I was trying to make it as an actor. My father visited from California, and after seeing the dump I had been inhabiting, he insisted I move into a small but modern, clean, and cucarachaless apartment on Ninth Street. He helped me pay the rent until I could establish myself in New York. The apartment was across the street from The Lion and Barbra moved in with me. We lived together and worked together, this modern little flat crammed with fans, feathers, Tiffany lamps, clothes, recording equipment, and candles. We went everywhere together, haunting the thrift shops and junk shops and costumiers, plus the secondhand music stores, long before it was chic.

"I had my hi-fi equipment sent from California and thousands of old records I had been collecting since I was a small boy. I played countless records and tapes for Barbra: Ruth Etting, Helen Morgan, Lee Wiley, Ethel Waters, Mabel Mercer, Fred Astaire. . . . We used to play tapes of the Astaire and Rogers films which we'd recorded from television and dance around the room on the beds and the furniture. We listened to Shirley Temple, Fats Waller, Charles Trenet, and Fanny Brice. It amused me to read once that Barbra claimed she had never heard a Fanny Brice record before playing her in *Funny Girl,* but she heard all the early Brice records in my living room. Perhaps she later may have wanted to establish her genius as entirely autonomous, but she did not listen only to her inner voices like Joan of Arc. She listened to her friends.

"I had long had the idea that a cabaret act could be worked out on a series of acting problems, as if each song were sung by a different character. We constructed each number as a set piece, evolving the character of the girl as she sang all through her moods. I would work with her phrase by phrase, trying this, trying that, shaping gestures, timing, the kind of effect Barbra and I wanted. I would pick material that was excellent musically, that would show off her voice, and also songs that were unusual, forgotten, or outrageous—it was my idea to have her perform "Who's Afraid of the Big Bad Wolf?" in front of New York's cleverest and sharpest audience."

While Barry and Barbra were perfecting the material for her Bon Soir audition, another man arrived on the scene: He would eventually have a definitive influence in the creation of "the Streisand look." Bob Schulenberg, now a top illustrator, describes vividly what happened during that very special summer when Barbara became Barbra:

"It was early in July of 1960. I had just come from Los Angeles to look for a job in New York. An hour after I had arrived from the airport, Barry Dennen took me out. He was my friend from California and he was going to show me Greenwich Village. We were walking down Sixth Avenue and then I saw this apparition. She had two shopping bags to each hand and out of them were coming feathers, sequins, net, all sorts of accessory stuff, lots of it. She was like a whole photo studio on wheels.

"She had a bang of hair across her forehead and a hairpiece pinned on top of her head, wobbling like a Danish pastry. She had little wisps of eyeliner and darkened eyelids under her brows. Her wide and generous mouth was accentuated with mahogany-purple lipstick. Her earrings were glass balls that seemed to hang all the way down to her thorax. She had an assortment of necklace chains with glass interspersed and a dozen Venetian-glass bracelets on one arm, plus rings on practically all fingers of her two hands.

"As if that weren't enough, her outfit was a sort of Elizabethan top made of silver and gold lamé, the kind of fabric that existed at that time only in window displays: It turned out two friends of hers had given her the remnants of their work at Lord & Taylor's to create those square, enormous sleeves. Outside of *The King and I* nobody had looked that way ever, not even in the streets of Greenwich Village. She had a shocking-pink fuchsia skirt an inch above the knee, years before miniskirts became fashionable. She wore chocolate-brown stockings and T-strapped twenties shoes in gold and silver with accents of red.

"Barry Dennen said, 'Here's my friend Barbra.' He asked her how the show had gone; it was one of her last nights at The Lion. I had just arrived in the big city and this bird of paradise put me immediately in awe. We had a sandwich at the Pam Pam Coffee Shop, and Barbra was fascinated that I had been in Los Angeles this very day and now I was in New York. She'd never traveled and had no sense of distance. She kept asking me questions and going every inch of the way. 'You mean you had lunch in Los Angeles . . . you were in your house at noon . . . and now you're having a midnight snack here?' She frowned a lot; she found it difficult to envision this extraordinary feat. She was just eighteen, so fresh and unspoiled, absolutely captivating. She was the first girl I met in New York and she was instantly my best friend.

"Barbra did not get along very well with her family," Schulenberg reminisces. "I think I became her surrogate brother. We were so much like brother and sister that we had our astrology chart done, and all the planets were in perfect alignment. It was the closest relationship possible without any romantic involvement. To me, she was Barry's girl. I learned that Barry was preparing her for an audition at the Bon Soir. They were listening to his old records, taping and retaping songs. It was all very hush-hush, and I was never allowed to hear Barbra sing until she was ready.

"Barry was very strict with her, working on the act for hours on end. I would take her out for a breather and we became closer and closer. I think I took her to the first restaurant she'd ever been to. She had worked in a Chinese restaurant in Brooklyn, but she'd never been to one as a guest. She did not really know even to take the napkin from under her plate, so I felt it was prudent to take her to a smorgasbord. She was fascinated by this huge table full of strange food. She would feel the texture of everything with her fingers. There was this marvelous tactile experience of touching all the food and discovering the mystery of tiny Swedish meatballs and a dish that looked like solidified molasses. 'Look at this,' she'd sigh. It was wonderful to watch. It was also poignant because you realized it was such a thrill for her. Doing things with Barbra in those days was like the first time it had ever been done.

"At last Barbra and Barry were ready for the audition. The three of us picked up Burke McHugh one night. He had been the producer of an Off Broadway hit, *Greenwich Village U.S.A.*, and he was scouting new talents for the Bon Soir. It was Sunday night and the club was closed. We were practically alone in that big room in the dark. Now I was going to hear Barbra sing for the first time. Ever since I'd heard Edith Piaf I thought it was a shame we didn't have that kind of richness, poetry, and dignity in one of our singers. When I heard Barbra that night, that kind of magic was there. I was knocked out. Here was this little girlfriend of mine and she was all the things I'd postulated we didn't have in America. Burke McHugh said, 'It looks good,' and left us. Barbra was very nervous. She had put herself on the line with that audition; she had given it all she had, totally committed.

"We went again for coffee at the Pam Pam. Barbra and Barry were utterly involved in doing reruns of how it had gone, how it had sounded. I was in my own world, still dumbfounded at the instinctive power of this girl who didn't even consider herself a singer, who kept insisting she was an actress. Then she turned to me and asked, 'What did you think of it?' I started to talk but I was broken up and big tears were running down my face. She got that quizzical look, as if she were asking, 'What's this? What did I do?' She was so embarrassed that I tried to explain through my own cracking voice how wonderful I thought she was. She just shrugged and said, 'Oh, yeah?'"

The audition got Barbra a two-week booking at the Bon Soir, for $108 a week. It was more than double what she had been making at The Lion. She was elated, even if she was going to be featured only as an audience warmer for the star of the evening: Phyllis Diller.

Barbra had learned her lessons very well from Barry Dennen. From the minute she stepped into the Bon Soir she made it clear she was not going to be shaped into anybody's sclerotic concept of what a nightclub act should be. Just as she had in acting schools, she was ready to kibitz her way into originality. She would rather be a troublemaker than a copycat.

She insisted on starting her turn with a ballad and was told it simply was not done. She had to start with an up-tempo number to quieten the bar crowd with a bang. She'd rather do it with a whimper. It was better to pull her punches until the audience simmered down and dug what she was doing, she argued. "A Sleepin' Bee" had been such a lucky song for her at The Lion, so why not begin with that?

The management at the Bon Soir went along with her whim, figuring it was merely beginner's superstition, but what did she have in mind for a follow-up? "Who's Afraid of the Big Bad Wolf?" she replied, to a collective shudder. This kid was not only kooky, she was downright deranged. Anyway, very little was being ventured, so she was left alone to arrange her own funeral.

"Phyllis Diller was wonderful to Barbra," Bob Schulenberg says. "When she saw the thrift-shop outfit Barbra was going to wear for her opening, she offered her a choice of any of her dresses. 'You mean I have to wear a dress to go out there and sing?" Barbra frowned. Phyllis laughed, hugged her, and said, 'You go out and do your stuff.' Then she cracked, 'And when you come into big money, which you will, save it in Hong Kong and Tokyo banks, they're the safest.' We started laughing hysterically because nobody in our crowd had a dime to his name."

Then Barbra walked out of the dressing room, tiptoed into the spotlight, and sang "A Sleepin' Bee." A minute after she had started, the ice stopped clinking in the drinks at the bar.

Then she sang "When the Sun Goes Down" as if she were announcing the total eclipse of Western civilization and slurred "Keeping Out of Mischief" like a nasal, breathless Dead End Kid about to dip into the forbidden cookie jar of adultery. With "Big Bad Wolf" she exploded into what can be described only as surrealistic camp, screaming like a banshee, ululating like a demented Brünnehilde, laughing like a candidate for the straitjacket, and at the same time keeping the childlike spirit of the song intact, sending it up but lovingly catching it before it crashed down.

The reception was so auspicious that she invited her mother to come and see her over the weekend. For her opening Barbra had worn a four-dollar dress topped with a Persian-lamb bolero, but for Mama's benefit she wore an 1890 lace peignoir that Terry Leong had found for her. It got somewhat soggy around the edges as it trailed on the Bon Soir kitchen floor, and Diane Kind was appalled because she thought her daughter was appearing in public in a nightgown.

The audience loved Barbra. She held her notes with an intensity that seemed to go beyond human capability, and she told her stunned admirers that she relied on her Taurus willpower: She had to hold that note longer and longer, so she did. And she wasn't merely a singer but a storyteller. Every song was a mini-drama with a beginning, a middle, and an end.

"I was never a figment of anyone's imagination," Barbra later said in countless interviews. Barry Dennen winces at this statement when he reveals: "Night after night I dragged the tape recorder to the Bon Soir. We would tape her set and then take it back to the apartment and listen to it between shows, work on it, criticize it, improve it, and then back again to the club with my note pad. The running order of numbers caused us endless headaches, but we had basically hit on a format that worked. I always approached phrasing as an actor. If you don't know how to *sing* it, decide how you would *say* it. At the time, we thought the work tapes were terrible—I even erased many of them because the sound quality was poor, her performances weren't the best. 'Wait till you see her in person,' I would tell people I played them for."

Barbra was responding to the coaching, absorbing every idea, offering her own, discarding errors, plunging ahead, backtracking. The Ampex recorder whirred on and on—flash forward, rewind, stop, forward, eject—and all the time the Streisand sound was being created. Every time they hit a real blooper Barry and Barbra would burst out laughing and snarl their private Mae West joke: "Whatsa matta with your animal?" They had no idea these very tapes would cause their final, bitter breakup.

Bob Schulenberg brings this period to immediate life with a visual diary he sketched day by day at the Bon Soir and at Barry Dennen's apartment. "Barbra was enthralled with Barry," Bob says. "He has a brilliant mind. He was the first man who would ever trade jokes from Mae West or Groucho Marx movies with her and in the next moment enlighten her on art, theater, music. His influence on Barbra was tremendous. He was discovering a new world for her. Barry was thrilled with his creation, and late one night they told me they were seriously considering getting married."

Dennen was working on Barbra's style, and Schulenberg started working on her looks: "Just like Barry, I felt Barbra was extraordinary, but I wanted her to live up to her potential, to become as attractive as she should be. I didn't want to say, 'You can't end up looking that way, you're fighting too hard with the brocade and the earrings.' Barbra was very insecure and you had to be cautious not to deflate her. Then one night Barry was opening in *Measure for Measure* in the Shakespearean series in Central Park, then called the Belvedere Lake Theatre. He had saved some seats for us and I told Barbra, 'Wouldn't it be fun if we fixed you up so that Barry won't recognize you. I'll make you look like Audrey Hepburn in *Sabrina*.' She said, 'That's fantastic, let's do it!'

"At the Garden Pharmacy in the Village I got fake eyelashes and trimmed them so they'd look natural and we got all this theatrical makeup she had collected. She went to the corner deli and we had this picnic of bagels, lox, whitefish, while I made her up. I shadowed her cheeks, which were very full because she was so young. I told her to wear black, no earrings, black rings on her fingers, black bracelets. She pulled them all out of a closet; she seemed to have two of everything. By the time we were finished with the picnic and the makeup it was too late to see Barry in *Measure for Measure.*

"The tickets had been given away. Barry was furious; he had every right to be. We had stood him up, missed his performance. He didn't even comment that she looked fabulous. We came back to the Village under a pall until Barbra realized she looked incredible. People were staring at her on the platform with a kind of 'Who is she?' look on their faces. She was making a very dramatic statement and that's what she wanted.

"She was fascinated. She went out and spent all her take-home money from the Bon Soir on every eyeshade, eyeliner, and brush that the Garden Pharmacy had. We got together to do this painting. A portrait of Barbra! I'd do half her face and leave the other side empty. She would then duplicate the makeup. I was flattered that she had spent money on the experiment. She had committed herself; she wanted that look she'd had that night we'd been turned away from Shakespeare in the Park. She made herself up the way my dream said she should look. That was the Streisand face.

"We kept working at it. On her evenings off at the Bon Soir we sat listening to music at Barry's and she'd do the whole number. She'd make up one side of her face and she'd come out of the bathroom and I'd give her a critique: This was too heavy, this was too light. She still had baby fat on her cheeks, and I told her she had to model her face, highlighting the cheekbones. She would sit under a small reflector and look at the mirror closely to see what she'd done wrong. Then she'd do it again. There were nights when she must have washed her face six times, but she learned the technique very fast because she had such finesse. She could have been a painter if she had applied herself to it."

At the Bon Soir she began to look not only talented but oddly attractive. Her engagement was extended for eleven weeks and her weekly paycheck was hiked to $125. At first she had been afraid of audiences and often had to be practically thrown onstage with half her makeup on because she kept procrastinating in her dressing room, dreading the final confrontation. As soon as she became Schulenberg's ideal portrait of Barbra, she progressively gained confidence.

"Barry had liberated her talent. He had made her feel comfortable that what she was doing onstage was acceptable, not threatening," Schulenberg recalls. "Then he went to California to visit his family and I was in charge of Barbra. I took her to the club every night because she hated to go alone. At the apartment at 69 West Ninth Street Barbra had been introduced to the doorman as Barry's cousin. When he left, he indicated that if the phone should ring, she was not supposed to answer because his family should not know yet that she was living there. Which must have made her feel like a second-class citizen, but Barry and I did not realize it at the time. We were all so young. . . .

"There was a certain date when Barry was coming back. That terrible night Barbra got all the things he loved to eat and we set up a beautiful table with a floral arrangement. We even had champagne in the freezer. We went to the Bon Soir and left him a note saying, 'Eat up, we'll be back after the show.' We ran back and he was not there. Barbra was really upset. She wondered if he'd missed the plane, but she couldn't call his family because she was still not supposed to be at his place. We sat up until about three in the morning and Barry didn't call.

"She distributed the perishable food between the refrigerator and the freezer, and we prepared to wait another day. The next night we came back from the Bon Soir. The table was still set, the food untouched. We ate the things that could go bad and again we waited. Still no sign of Barry. After a week I think Barbra ate up all her emotion for Barry. Finally he came back and she was very cool. All our smorgasbord was gone and he never even knew it had been there. She just said, 'Hi, how was your trip? Is your family well? Great! I'm still singing at the Bon Soir. Well, glad to see you, nice you're back.' That was all. But this had been so hard on an eighteen-year-old kid! There was this joyous welcome and then nothing. Barry and Barbra were together for months after that, but I am convinced that was the real ending."

When her engagement at the Bon Soir was over, she was restless and expressed a desire to get out of town and think things over. Schulenberg did an idealized sketch—she looked like Audrey Hepburn in *Sabrina*. She made glossy copies, and her first agent, Ted Rozar, circulated it through agencies. She got a booking in Detroit's Caucus Room for early 1961, to be followed by a stint at the Crystal Palace in St. Louis.

"She had become willful and impatient," Schulenberg says. "Around Christmas I invited her to a cocktail party in a very elegant town house off Park Avenue in the Seventies. Only I was wrong and it wasn't a cocktail party but a very formal dinner party. We arrived and she was wearing one of her most outrageous outfits: a dress only half zipped in the back, a monkey-skin hat, and a huge Mexican woven bag hanging from her shoulder. The butler said the guests were already at table and we panicked. I knew that Barbra was not yet ready for the restrictions of a stylized dinner party. We were ushered to a dining room that looked like a movie set. I was very distressed about her. She ended up eating the carrots and celery in the centerpiece, and when she decided none of these people had anything in common with her, she tried to strike up a conversation with the butler by saying that he reminded her of her brother. I'm afraid it embarrassed the man terribly."

As the date approached for her Detroit engagement, she was a mass of contradictions. One day she said she was going to plead she was sick and cancel it, then the next she was consulting guides to find out where the good Chinese restaurants were. "With Barbra, you never knew what was coming," Schulenberg tells. "She was half exhilarated, half scared. It was her first time out of New York. Finally we packed her bags into a taxi and rode to the train station. Suddenly she asked if she could stop the taxi to get something at a drugstore. I wondered if she needed a laxative, sanitary napkins, or something she was shy about telling me. She was late and I knew she would miss the train if we stopped, so I asked her point-blank what it was she *had* to get. She blurted out, 'Do you think they have toothpaste in Detroit?' I assured her they did and got her safely to Pennsylvania Station."

Once she arrived in Detroit, Barbra was shaky but self-assured, putting on an act for the local press: the same one she had tried on her admirers at The Lion and the Bon Soir. On March 6, 1961, she told an interviewer from the Windsor *Star* all the favorite stories and was hailed as "the Turkish-born, Brooklyn-raised songstress in a big hurry, with a totally untrained but remarkably true voice." Another Detroit paper also swallowed the bait and proclaimed she was born in Turkey and that her name had been spelled Barbra all her life. The headline, predictably, was SHE STARS AS SINGER BUT YEARNS TO ACT.

"She was like a ten-year-old in Detroit," Schulenberg proves, riffling through a trunkful of Streisand memorabilia. "She went to see Mae West and she went horseback riding and took her first driving lessons." But by the time she got to St. Louis and the Crystal Palace the thrill was beginning to wear off. The Smothers Brothers, who shared the bill, were wonderful to her. "They became her surrogate family on the road," Schulenberg reminisces, but she still felt very lonely and confused away from "her crowd" in New York. "For me it's strange," she wrote Schulenberg in a postcard. "I'm sort of depressed. Forgive me. . . ."

From the Crystal Palace in St. Louis she wrote Barry Dennen about how great the food was. She asked him to send her the guitar chords that Barry had worked out for "A Taste of Honey" because they were so beautiful and no one could figure them out on the road. She also asked Barry to suggest a substitute for "Lover, Come Back to Me" as the closing of her act. Barbra was still relying on Barry's expertise, but her absence dealt the final blow to their relationship.

"When she came back to New York, we ceased living

together," Barry says. "She had brought back tapes of local radio shows she had appeared in during her tour. We went over them as we had at an earlier time. I told her how to improve her performance, what songs to include in her repertoire: They were basically the ones she would later do in her first album. In May, 1961, she came to my apartment one afternoon and we recorded "A Taste of Honey," with me playing the guitar. After that I saw her less and less as she made it more and more."

Barbra went back to the Bon Soir. She had learned a lot on the road; she had acquired not only more poise but also a sense of theatricality. When she did "My Coloring Book," she was perched on a high stool, shoulders hunched, hands dangling between her knees, like a forlorn child being punished and having to sit in a corner, the class dunce who had flunked at love. She told this story of diminishing passion as the spotlight got smaller and smaller until it focused only on her face. It went out and left her in the dark as she moaned that her disappearing man was gone.

In Detroit and St.Louis she had been in command. She gloried in an ability to learn the right by fighting the wrong. At the Bon Soir the instant they told her a baby spot should be pink, bang! she just knew it had to be blue. The infuriating thing was that her effects proved invariably correct. By now she was sure she never wanted to inherit anything, even the earth, if the price was to be meek. The willfulness was ingrained. It had become a part of her forever.

"Barbra loved Barry, but it was much more than that," Schulenberg explains. "She respected him as a teacher, a driving force. When it didn't work out between them, she was terribly hurt. She reacted by refusing to take advice from anyone. I remember one night we had dinner at Marta's, a small restaurant in the Village. I asked her if she could have a glass of white wine with her meal before going on at the Bon Soir. She hesitated and I said maybe she shouldn't because she never drank anything but sodas. She was immediately defiant and had three sips of the wine. Well, she was not used to it and she blew the whole show. She could not remember the lyrics of 'Big Bad Wolf.' She giggled. Afterward I told her it was a lousy performance and she said, 'They're coming to see me. They have to take the good with the bad. That's me, that's what I do.' I told her I'd been to the club every night and I knew who she was and what she could do, so she owed me five dollars because this particular show wasn't worth it. I said I felt cheated, and that slowed her down. For the rest of the run she was faultless." More than ever before, Barbra was attracting attention. Important show-business figures were filtering down to the Bon Soir to watch the newcomer. Dorothy Kilgallen gave her a good notice in her *Journal American* column. Liberace expressed some interest in using her as part of his Las Vegas show, but his entrepreneurs thumbed down the choice because she had a reputation for being kooky and unmanageable.

No matter how the skeptics might have carped at her unconventional approach, she was making converts twice a night at the Bon Soir. She was giving the audience the truth and no baloney, she later said. "At the Bon Soir I got special satisfaction out of performing. In real life I felt people paid no attention to me. All of a sudden, singing, I could say what I felt and I was listened to."

And then one night she sang "Cry Me a River." In Julie London's plaintive, lovely version it had been a late-fifties hit: a lament of lost love and impossible retaliation. When Streisand sang the lyrics, it became something else. She was telling a story about a repentant lover who had come back for a second chance. And here was the once-scorned woman ready to put him to the test. Holding her ground, not budging an inch, she sneered in total triumph between tightly repressed sobs.

Her thin long hands shot forward, with clawlike, beckoning fingers. "Come on, come on, cry me a river," she taunted, demanding those tears that had been denied her for so long. "When I sang that," she said long afterward, "I was thinking of one particular person," and admitted she had never done the song full justice later because she no longer felt about "that man" so vehemently. But while the fury boiled, she was Medea, ready to punish her Jason.

"When I heard Barbra sing 'Cry Me a River' the first time," Schulenberg recalls, "I was stunned because I knew exactly what she meant with those lyrics, but it took me awhile to gather up courage and tell her."

The saga of Barry and Barbra continued, on and off, for a few more years. Barry recalls that "in 1962, when she was going to do the 'Pins and Needles' record for Harold Rome, she called me again. By this time I had broken up financially with my father and determined to make it on my own. I was living in high poverty in Little Italy on the fifth floor of a really slummy building and working in a bookshop to pay the rent. I was glum and didn't want to help her anymore, but she tempted me with a free lunch at Sardi's: Food was always a major issue between us. There, at the table, she brought out the sheet music and we worked on it together. There was a second work session and several phone calls. She used all my bits of direction and ad libs on that record. There were vague and ultimately unrealized promises that I would work on her first album. At one point I swallowed my pride and called her to ask if she would introduce me to some people in the business. She did nothing.

"I didn't see Barbra for ages, and then, while waiting for a bus on Central Park West one afternoon, her chauffeur-driven limousine pulled right in front of me. It was really just like a Warner Brothers movie. She mouthed 'Hello' and waved her poodle's paw at me. I was about to say, 'Whatsa matta with your animal?' The car pulled away."

But Barbra had not forgotten Barry Dennen. After a couple of years in Europe Bob Schulenberg came back to find Streisand as the star of *Funny Girl.* He visited her in her dressing room: "I was amazed. The paisley walls, the black leather chairs, the plants . . . it seemed that I was back at Barry's apartment on Ninth Street. It looked exactly the same. The first thing Barbra wanted to know was whether Barry had seen her play Fanny Brice. I said I'd find out."

"Bob Schulenberg called me," Barry says, "and told me Barbra was put off because I hadn't seen *Funny Girl.* I told him I couldn't afford the ticket, which was true. Soon after, I got a call from Barbra inviting me to see the show free and to come back and say hello afterward. I fought my way through the stage-door crowd because she had forgotten to inform the doorman I was coming and there was some embarrassment.

"When I got to see her, she seemed very wary. I told her she was very good in the show and thanks for the seat. We chatted and then she asked me if she could have copies of the tapes I had. I told her I would play them for her anytime she liked, but although she was now very rich and could afford to buy almost anything she liked, she did not, and could not, *own* those tapes. I felt very manipulated and we both got upset. Our meeting was not a success."

Bob Schulenberg shudders when he thinks of that night in the dressing room: "I had engineered that meeting, and I felt terrible hearing Barbra tell Barry that the tapes belonged to her since her voice was in them and Barry very calmly countering that they had great sentimental value for him, that they were the only thing he had left from their past."

"Years later, when Barbra was preparing one of her television specials, *The Belle of 14th Street,* she wanted me to do some graphics for the show. I went to her apartment and we started reminiscing about things. At one point I tried to reestablish the old intimacy and said, 'You know, Barbra, after all these years, the only thing I'm really grateful for is that every time I hear you sing 'Cry Me a River' I'm so pleased I'm not Barry Dennen.' She looked into my eyes and said, 'How do you know about that?' I jumped up. 'How do I know about that? I lived through it with you.' And then she said, 'Well, it was nice to see you, but now I have to run.'"

5. *Tiger at the Gates*

IN the spring of 1961 Barbra's sap was rising. She could now make it alone, with no one to shape her, help her, prod her. Her willfulness was soon to be nipped in the bud. The management of the Bon Soir informed her that in a few weeks her contract would not be renewed. They were ready for a change, and another of their regular performers, Felicia Sanders, was coming back.

"Barbra felt at home at the Bon Soir," Schulenberg says. "When she heard that, she really went into a panic. It was end-of-the-world time. She had expected to be the resident singer at the Bon Soir as Mabel Mercer was at the Roundtable. I had to repeat what I had been telling her for the past year: 'You've got to have another agent.'"

All her friends rallied together to get her one. Her ex-roommate Marilyn Fried talked an artist's representative into going downtown to listen to Barbra. The man was impressed, but Barbra told Marilyn it was no go: "He wants me to change my name and there's no way I'll do that." Another agent suggested that she try a repertory of popular tunes of the day; still another one politely recommended plastic surgery on her nose.

According to Schulenberg, Barbra was never happy with Ted Rozar. "They never hit it off," Bob recalls. "I saw him sometime later when they had parted company and he told me that 'my little friend' was not going to make it because she thought she was hot stuff but was too undisciplined for big-time show business."

Through Rozar, however, Barbra got her first chance on television on the *Jack Paar Show*. One week when Orson Bean was substituting for Paar, Phyllis Diller was booked as one of the guests. She put in a good word for Barbra, who made an appearance on the *Paar Show* on April 5, 1961, on the same bill with Diller and writer Gore Vidal. Streisand was warmly applauded, but nothing substantial came out of it. She was back at the Bon Soir, counting the days until her stint was over.

The last night at the club came, and by morning she had nowhere to go. She would not walk back in defeat to her mother's in Brooklyn. Neither would she seek haven at Barry Dennen's on Ninth Street. Both doors were open for her, but she was an expert at closing each phase of her life with a resounding turn of the lock. Barbra became the sixties equivalent of a nomad, crashing pads before the term was even coined. She collected keys and added them to an enormous key ring: They were her right of entry to friends' apartments. She lugged a portable cot on her back, always depending on a sliver of kindness from whoever was willing to put her up for a night, three days, a week.

She was down and out, but she still had her charisma. Before ever singing she could make converts to the Streisand cult. The next one in line for the irresistible spell was Al Ramrus, one of the writer-producers of Mike Wallace's television program, *PM East*, who now recalls:

"Our show was syndicated, low budget, and, I'm afraid not a very successful rival to Jack Paar's, so we generally had to scrape pretty close to barrel bottom when it came to booking talent. One day I needed a singer to round out an upcoming show, and our talent coordinator suggested Barbra Streisand. 'Barbara who?' I asked. 'She's a character,' I was told. 'Fine, bring her over,' I said, figuring on being saddled with another loser.

"I always preinterviewed guests in order to prepare Mike Wallace for his own on-camera interviews. But Streisand, I was told, did not have a phone . . . she'd have to call me. Two or three days later, about midnight, the phone rang. 'Hi, Al,' came a nasal voice that sounded like one of my Brooklyn aunts. 'This is Barbra.' I had completely forgotten about that girl we'd talked about, so she explained she was Barbra Streisand.

"I thanked her for getting back to me and suggested, since it was so late, that she might want to set up some other time to talk, but she said she did not mind talking now. I remember she was calling from a bar because not only did she not have a phone but she had no apartment. 'I sleep in friends' apartments,' she said. 'Whenever I get tired at night I call a few numbers. When I find a place that's not being used or that has extra room, I go there. I carry around a bunch of keys my friends gave me so I can get in anywhere. I don't make much money singing in little places but I have a typical Jewish mother. She waits outside wherever I'm singing till one or two in the morning with frozen steaks.' She said something about her father, very vague, that he was a genius who had traveled around the country, a wanderer on a bicycle, and that she was a bit like him.

"She talked about being unhappy, an outsider in high school, and how much she wanted to be a singer. The voice was pure Brooklyn, and having been born there myself, I recognized the type. . . . Unhappy, full of *chutzpah,* full of 'unrealistic' ambitions. But there was something about her, even over the phone, that was unique. She was like the *essence* of every confused, not-very-attractive girl who wanted extravagantly more out of life than birth or circumstances could possibly give her. Her voice, her life-style, were almost fictional, they were also so right for the role that I told her—by now it must've been past 1 A.M.—that whether she could sing or not she was going to be a star.

"The next afternoon she breezed into the Dumont studios for rehearsals, chattering like some adolescent yenta, carrying her giant ring of keys and a few old dresses slung over her back. Her appearance, the Streisand nose, the crooked teeth, were a bit startling at a time when singers were supposed to be Doris Dayish pretty. The songs she had selected were not exactly in the top forty: 'A Sleeping' Bee' and 'Lover, Come Back to Me.'

"It was an incredible moment. She purred through the first one and belted the second one with almost arrogant confidence. The Brooklyn accent disappeared. Her phrasing was immaculate, every word and every idea crackled with excitement. It sounds like a bad Twentieth-Century Fox musical, but virtually everyone on the set, sound men, lighting men, secretaries . . . they all stopped and listened. The night before, I'd told her she'd be a star. Now I was sure of it."

Mike Wallace came in an hour later and he recalls that "everybody in that studio was carrying on about how great this new girl was so I said, 'Okay, she's on tonight.' Barbra was there only for an audition and she had not expected to be actually on television that night. She was very nervous. I said I was not going to interview her, she did not have to talk, all she had to do was sing. 'Oh, then it's all right,' she said, and quieted down. I was busy with the other aspects of the show, but when she came on and sang, I knew Al Ramrus had made the right decision. She was terrific."

It was one of the first nights that *PM East* was on the air. The early programs were developed around a theme, and this particular show revolved around glamour. The guest roster included photographer Milton Greene, model agent Candy Jones, and beauteous models Theodora and Suzy Parker. And then there was Barbra, singing "A Sleepin' Bee" on a stool and then "Lover, Come Back to Me" after she had climbed on the piano.

She made a definite impact on everyone but herself. Steve Elster, the talent coordinator who had seen her at the Bon Soir and recommended her for the show, sneaked Barbra in the next day to watch the videotape. She had no idea how she had looked and was displeased with the results. Those models were dressed to kill, with every hair in place as if they'd been carried on a stretcher from the beauty salon to the Dumont studios. All she had been able to wear was her simple sleeveless black dress, a pin in the shape of a thunderbird, and her hair piled up in a beehive topped by her "Danish pastry" postiche.

She certainly could not compete with the glamorous ladies. Furthermore, she didn't want to. After watching the tape she told Steve Elster, "What's the big deal? Should I go out and buy a new dress for every program? Forget it, I can't afford it!" Just as in high school she had rebelled against the image of the "sweet young thing" by inventing the superkook, she now decided she would not sulk for her lack of conventional appeal.

The horoscope said it was a great year for Taurus, and she

would get her big break when Mert Koplin became executive producer of *PM East* a month after the program had been foundering in low-rating shallows.

"Initially," Koplin tells, "the show was as stodgy as a BBC panel. To compete with Jack Paar we needed something alive, human. I had seen Barbra at the Bon Soir and I felt her appearance at that glamour bash was all wrong. When I called her back, I wanted her to be herself. From the first day I talked to her at the studio, she knew she was going to be a superstar. That kind of brashness annoyed some people but not me. I also knew it, though she was wearing a basic burlap bag and looked like a disreputable Judith Anderson.

"The problem was to convince others about her. In the beginning only the musicians liked her. The camera crew always had her in long shot, and when I asked why she was not given close-ups, they complained she was too ugly. These were the same guys who ended up saying she had a strange kind of beauty, but by the time she got to that plateau it was an uphill climb.

"Barbra was discouraged by people who kept telling her she had to have her nose fixed if she wanted to succeed. One day she told me she was seriously considering it. I told her the story of Everett Sloane, a very fine actor with a hook nose, who had made several great films, including Orson Welles' *Citizen Kane.* Sloane had had his nose fixed and then he found he could not get the exceptional parts he had been playing. He had had a nervous breakdown and had even attempted suicide. I told Barbra, 'You go ahead and do it if you want to, but think first. . . . Can you become a new person with a new nose?' I knew I had to scare her to change her mind, so I did not give her an empty talk but a concrete example. After that she never gave that nonsense another thought."

This pep talk was all that Barbra needed to forge on. On *PM East* she proceeded to vindicate the abused term "stunning" by giving it a literal, almost knockout meaning. She deliberately made herself plainer and stranger than she really was. Audiences had no idea what to make of this tiny girl emerging from yards of cloth like a disheveled bedouin looking out from a tent to see if the simoo had blown over.

Mert Koplin changed the show's format into a harbinger of today's talk shows, with personalities expressing opinions and exchanging quips. The public needed a minute to get adjusted to what Barbra looked like. When she started talking, disbelief mounted into riproaring amazement. Once she launched into such a venomous tirade against the evils of drinking milk that the dairy-industry lobby would have sent a stampede of mooing cows to trample her if she could be taken seriously. But could she? Barbra was fervent, seemed to believe her words, and at any given moment only the brave would bet their lives on whether she was joking or telling the truth. She was a past mistress of the put-on.

People watching her on *PM East* suddenly sat up and looked hard into the screen. They started calling others to come out of the kitchen and watch her. "Hey, come see this, there's this kook on TV." Few remembered her name, but she was readily identifiable as "the kook on that late show." She became one of the program's regulars, more outrageous every week. She had a swashbuckler's curiosity to see how far she could stretch her image without snapping.

"She was always against the grain," producer Koplin recalls. "One night Burt Lancaster walked out on Mike Wallace in a tantrum about Mike's persistent questions about his temper. After the commercial, with Lancaster gone, everyone on the panel was commiserating with Wallace and telling him that Burt shouldn't have done that. 'Well, I don't blame him,' Barbra said. 'You kept asking him about his temper so he showed you he had it.'

"Then there was that memorable night with David Susskind. He had proposed a show built around the cast of a movie he was producing, *Requiem for a Heavyweight.* We didn't want the show to develop into a publicity puff for the picture, so I suggested 'the sweet smell of success' as a theme. Barbra would open it as a young performer aspiring to glory, and then Susskind's famous people would come in. Mike Wallace started by spending ten minutes with Barbra, who was telling him about all the frustrations of an unknown actress.

"Susskind then marched on with Rod Serling, the writer of his film, plus the stars, Anthony Quinn and Mickey Rooney. Serling and Rooney were very sympathetic toward Barbra, but Quinn ignored her as if she had just crawled from under a rock. Susskind was annoyed because we'd given that much time to a nobody like Barbra, and he made no effort to hide his dislike for her. Well, she let him have it. She interrupted him in the middle of his peroration and asked him if he knew anything about struggling for success. She said she'd spent endless hours in his office trying to see him and when she finally did he'd looked through her. She told him it was people like him who were ruining show business because they would not let new talents emerge, it was their duty to stifle them. Susskind was so taken aback that Barbra had to let him off easily by cracking, 'I scare you, don't I? I'm so far out I'm in.'"

Koplin's audio tapes from *PM East* are a treasure trove of early Streisandiana. She would not be put down by anyone. After Barbra sang "A Sleepin' Bee," Eartha Kitt was trying to get a word in edgewise and facetiously inquired what happened when a bee lies sleeping in the palm of your hand. "It stings you dead," Barbra retorted. She would not be cajoled either. When Mike Wallace remarked that his show helped Barbra attract attention from theatrical producers like David Merrick, she said, "Now, let's be honest. Those people don't watch television, not the ones that do the hiring. A show like this just gets the public interested in paying the minimum to see me at places like the Bon Soir."

Streisand looked so odd and acted so cool, brilliant, and detached that producer Koplin felt he had to humanize her, fearing that "the public might think she's just come down from the planet Saturn. We had a little celebration for her, with a cake and flowers. Her mother and her sister were in the show. She had despised the idea to begin wtih, but once the program started she was moved by it. Barbra hugged her mama with true affection and there was not a dry eye in the studio. Then she came back the next day and told me, 'I hated that. What are we running here, the late-show version of *This Is Your Life?*' "

Television and nightclubs had given Barbra self-assurance. It vanished as she prepared to go back to the theater. Barbra was one of the young hopefuls in an Off Broadway revue, *Another Evening with Harry Stoones,* and she spent the first day of rehearsals vomiting uncontrollably in the ladies' room. She soon recovered, and by the end of the week she was giving her all, with unrelenting determination, as if this little show were the glittering resurrection of the *Ziegfeld Follies.*

She insisted on writing her own biography for the program, and it read like a potpourri of hopeful fact and hopeless fiction:

> Burma born (Rangoon) and a graduate of Yeshiva of Brooklyn and Erasmus Hall High School, Barbra Streisand has had a remarkable success in her short professional career. Although she is making her Off Broadway debut, her singing at the Bon Soir led Dorothy Kilgallen to refer to her in her column as "a rising star." She has been seen on the *Jack Paar Show* and on *PM East.* She has played niteries in Canada, Detroit, and St. Louis.

Another Evening with Harry Stoones was a showcase for newcomers that included Dom De Luise and Diana Sands, the latter fresh from a Broadway hit as the pugnacious daughter in *Raisin in the Sun.* Jeff Harris, a bright twenty-six-year-old, had written the music and lyrics for a hearty but sophomoric romp that stretched its cuteness pretty thin over a staggering total of thirty-eight sketches.

Barbra ran through a kaleidoscope of impersonations. She did a takeoff on ballet dancing; she was an Indian maiden in a spoof of Columbus' discovery of America; she sang with bite-your-tongue fury about life in New Jersey and slyly crooned "Values," a hilarious number about an amatory turncoat who could not decide whether she loved Harold Minget, Arnie Fleischer, or their respective cars.

Harry Stoones started with the eight aspiring young players running onstage to sing "Hello, Goodbye, and Thanks." The number proved prophetic because the show opened on October 21, 1961, and closed the same night. The New York *Times* said it was "not exactly unbearable but none too stimulating." The *Post* called it "puerile, flat and in bad taste." The *Journal American* blasted it as "sophomoric and on the dull side."

Barbra got some good personal notices. *Variety* called her "a slim, offbeat comedienne with a flair for dropping a blackout gag"; the *Village Voice* said she "could put across a lyric melody and make fine fun of herself at the same time," and the *World Telegram & Sun* found her "outrageous and delightful." The influential *Times* saved all its praise for Diana Sands and completely ignored Barbra. Even worse, most reviewers who mentioned her misspelled her name and called her Barbara.

She was crushed. All her hopes for theatrical recognition had foundered in one night. She had made her bid for Broadway—even if the small Gramercy Arts Theatre qualified merely as Off—and she had been slapped down. She had to go back to being just a singer, a term she felt had "all the connotations of a second-class citizen."

And even as a singer she had problems. No record company was interested in launching her career because her appeal was deemed "too limited." On March 27, 1961, she'd had an inconclusive audition at the Blue Angel, but by the fall the management was ready for her—with reservations. The initial problems were identical to the ones at the Bon Soir. The Blue Angel was a classier place. It meant moving up from Greenwich Village and facing tougher, more demanding audiences, but she would come in only on her own terms. She would not be a finger-snapping automaton with a gift for belting out a song.

"I could never understand a performer getting involved with his audience," she explained. "I'm busy with my own reactions, my own thoughts. When I sing, I go inside myself." This self-absorbed, almost onanistic style made the entrepreneurs wary. She would not smile down on the customers, she would not move around on the small podium, she would definitely not start with an up-tempo number.

Barbra had only one peace offering: she would close th act with a Cole Porter tune. There was a sigh of relief: Maybe at last she would sing something easily identifiable, like "Night and Day." But her choice was an obscure ditty from *Aladdin,* one of Porter's few flops: "Come to the Supermarket in Old Peking." In a paroxysm of consumer frenzy she took the audience for a mad tour of that wondrous emporium. At breakneck speed she did the number as a perverted parody of a Gilbert and Sullivan patter song, her eyes glazed by all the exotic goodies on the shelves.

She was a hit, and in two days she was packing them in on the strength of solid reviews and ecstatic word of mouth. The Blue Angel folded its wings and conceded the bout. She was left alone to do what she wanted. Her repertory was still small, and when the public shouted, "Encore," she learned to quip, "I don't have an anchor, I'm not the *Queen Mary.*" One night a drunken heckler shouted at her, "Aren't you from Brooklyn?" and she brought the house down by coolly retorting, "Aren't we *all* from Brooklyn at some time or another?"

She was winning every battle, but still she had to fight them. That took time and energy. She needed someone to fight for her: an agent. Mert Koplin remembers one afternoon that proved another turning point in Streisand's career:

"Barbra was taping one of her *PM East* appearances. The Clancy Brothers were in the same show. They were managed by Marty Erlichman. I told Marty about this girl and brought him into the audio booth with me as she was about to sing. He sat there with his mouth open, unable to say a word. I knew he was hooked."

Marty asked to see Barbra in her dressing room at the Blue Angel between shows. She called her friend Bob Schulenberg and asked him to be there and advise her on a very important decision: Bob had always insisted that she get an agent and there was this guy who was interested in representing her. Schulenberg asked Barbra the three basic questions: "Does he want to change your style, your name, your e only wants to take care of the business end yself," she said. "Then what have you got to ied.

igned with Marty Erlichman as a client. Soon he d all the other acts in his roster; she was too absorb- g. "She was like Chaplin. She had a quality that made you want to protect her," Erlichman would say a decade later after she became the driving force behind a hundred-million-dollar business. "He doesn't love me for the money I make, he loves me as a person," Barbra would rejoin. A powerful alliance was born that night. Erlichman sensed that behind Barbra's brashness there was a painful vulnerability. He became her shield against troubles and gave her the strong, brotherly affection she craved. Marty soft-talked the miscreants, hard-talked the chiselers, fended away the importuners. He was more than an agent: The budding princess had found a paladin.

At *PM East* her group of stalwarts was also pushing her—without much success. Al Ramrus recommended Barbra to a Hollywood television producer who was planning a half-hour documentary on a rising young singer: Streisand was turned down because she was "too New York and too Jewish," and Joanie Sommers did the show. Mert Koplin suggested Streisand for a role opposite Cesare Siepi in a Broadway musical, *Bravo Giovanni*, but producer Phil Rose decided against her.

"At the time," Koplin says, "we thought the problem with Barbra was that she only sang songs nobody ever heard of. One night Richard Rodgers was going to be on *PM East* with Diahann Carroll, the star of his new show, *No Strings*. Carroll had agreed to be present but would not sing. I felt it was a great opportunity for Barbra to catch Rodgers' attention. I persuaded her to take care of the musical interludes, singing a batch of Rodgers' standards. The composer was too busy talking to Diahann Carroll about what they would say on the show: He never once looked up at Barbra. A few years later, in the liner notes for the *Simply Streisand* album, he wrote that she had brought him laughter and tears. I wish he'd said it that night at *PM East*, when she really needed the boost."

The more Barbra realized conformity did not help, the weirder she became on *PM East.* She wore dark orange lipstick that made her ample mouth look black and greedy on the strongly contrasted black and white TV sets. Her gingham tent dresses were so floppy that she was often suspected of being six months pregnant under the folds. "It was a defense, a defiance,"she has said about this period. "But at that time it was theatrically *right* for me."

It was also romantically wrong. Steve Elster, the talent coordinator on *PM East,* was about her age and could put up with her kookiness, but he admits nobody else on the show would dare be seen with her outside the studio:

"We started dating steadily and I had no idea what she would wear. She had a horrible monkey-skin coat and she'd taken a fancy to wear a long sweater that looked exactly like a man's underwear buttoned at the collar. One night I took her to see Ella Fitzgerald at the Basin Street East, and when I realized she had the undershirt on under the monkey coat, I begged her to keep it on, so she sweated through the whole show. As far as I can remember, only two other guys dated her then: Tom Smothers of the Smothers Brothers and Danny Meehan, who later played with her in *Funny Girl.* It was all very intellectual, a lot of talk about art and philosophy. Nobody was getting to first base with Barbra. She went through an Anna Magnani phase with heavy black makeup on her eyes, terribly Italian. When you took her out, you had to be as brave as she was because people kept looking at you."

Her evenings at The Blue Angel and *PM East* were shining, but her days were glum. Steve Elster recalls that Barbra briefly stopped lugging around her cot when she found a tiny apartment on West Fifty-fifth Street. She had sublet it from a man who had it on a sublet. When the original tenant returned, he was annoyed to find Barbra camped in his living room. She was ordered out on the double and had no place to go. Again she relied on the kindness of friends. Don and John Softness, who had a public relations agency, let her move into their office until she found a place to park herself. She kept her clothes in bags in the closet, left promptly before nine in the morning, and returned after five, when the business day was over. Again she was sleeping on the ubiquitous cot.

The guys at *PM East* got together on a crash program to find her an apartment. She was a regular on the show, and without an address or a phone it was impossible to contact her and tell her when she was scheduled to appear. After some hectic scouring for a suitable bargain they found her a rent-controlled floor-through on Third Avenue and Sixty-sixth Street, just around the corner from the Dumont studio. The rent was only $62.70 a month. The reason for the low price was that the flat was perched precisely above the kitchen of Oscar's Salt of the Sea Restaurant. The fumes of frying flounder and baking scallops pervaded her quarters, but as soon as she got used to the odor she applied herself to a job of redecoration that could best be described as demolition. With awesome stamina she knocked down plaster all day and then got ready for a couple of shows every night at the Blue Angel.

On Thanksgiving Day in November, 1961, Barbra went to dinner at Bob Schulenberg's Gramercy Park apartment. She stayed so late that she had to sleep on the living-room couch. In the morning Bob gave her a paper bag with three sandwiches stacked with slices of last evening's turkey and sent her on her way to audition for a new musical, *I Can Get It for You Wholesale.* Then and there the Streisand legend takes another spin.

According to one version, playwright Arthur Laurents had seen her at the Blue Angel just as he was about to branch out as director of *Wholesale* and then persuaded producer David Merrick to come to the cabaret to watch this promising girl. According to another version, it was Merrick himself who discovered Barbra at the Blue Angel and asked her to audition for the show.

Arthur Laurents now sets the record straight by saying, "Nobody asked Barbra to audition. The day she walked into that theater I had never seen her before in my life. She came in with a bagful of turkey sandwiches, was very talented and funny, but that was all. I know she disputes me on this but it is the truth. There was no part for her in the show. The ingenue role was cast with Marilyn Cooper. The part she eventually played, Miss Marmelstein, was written for a much older woman. I thought she was so talented that I sent her to Columbia Records with a special recommendation for the president of the company, Goddard Lieberson, who rejected her because she was 'too special.' Then Barbra came back to audition again because the composer, Harold Rome, and the writer, Jerome Weidman, liked her very much. That's how she got to play Miss Marmelstein."

Harold Rome, composer and lyricist of *Wholesale,* corroborates Laurents' version about what happened in that fabled audition:

"Barbra was never asked to come to the theater. Least of all by Mr. Merrick. The fact is he never liked Barbra, never trusted her potential, and was on the verge of firing her several times. We had called for an open audition and she literally came in off the street."

Then Rome goes on to tell about that post-Thanksgiving day when the show's creators gathered in the darkened St. James Theatre and Barbra Streisand erupted, unannounced as a volcano, right in the middle of the stage:

"We were all sitting there, tired and weary, after having auditioned at least fifteen unknowns. Open-call auditions are terrible. I feel sorry for those hopefuls that come in, one after another, do a couple of songs, and are waved away. But it is also terrible to sit there watching one impossible performer after another. You wish someday a kind of miracle will happen and someone really talented will walk in and light up the stage. It is such a rare occasion in the theater . . . but that afternoon it happened.

"This little girl came onstage and—no doubt about it—she was something different. She had on a ratty thrift-shop fur coat of about seven colors that came down to her ankles and seemed to be shedding all over her purple sneakers. She carried a huge, unwieldy plastic bag, and as she tried to pull some sheet music out of it, the whole thing exploded all over the piano. She shouted, 'Excuse me,' got down on her knees, picked up the sheets, selected one, and thrust it at the pianist.

"Then she sang a song from a one-night show she'd been in, *Another Evening with Harry Stoones.* It was something about being in love with a guy named Harold only that midway through she realized she liked Arnie Fleischer better. It was so funny and a little pathetic. Just what we wanted for the part of the secretary, Miss Marmelstein.

"We asked her if she had a ballad. '*Do* I have a ballad,' she shouted back into the dark theater. She rummaged through her pile of sheet music and threw another one at the pianist. She sang 'A Sleepin' Bee' marvelously. By then we were asking her for songs and it had stopped being an audition. We just had her there, singing for our pleasure. She sang six numbers in all and topped them with 'Too Long at the Fair.' Well, the miracle had happened. The theater had lit up and we were in the presence of talent, great talent.

"We told her to come back next Tuesday and then next Friday. I think, all in all, she auditioned on five different occasions. Then we could not hold out any longer, so we did something that's hardly ever done in auditions. We told her right there, while she was onstage singing, that she had the part of Miss Marmelstein. 'Goody, goody,' she screamed. 'Now I can pay for my telephone. I just got my first one, you know?'"

Jerome Weidman, author of the book for *I Can Get It for You Wholesale,* remembers one of those auditions almost exactly as Harold Rome remembers it. There was the strange fur coat out of Michael Strogoff and Barbra announcing there was no third *a* to her name because "who needs it?" When asked if she could sing, she replied in mock annoyance, "If I couldn't sing, would I be here wearing this coat?" Then she asked *what* she should sing, protesting that even with a jukebox you made a selection before pushing down the button. When she sang about her wavering love for Harold and Arnie, Miss Marmelstein materialized in a flash from the writer's creation into a living and breathing person.

But soon Harold Rome was full of uneasiness and doubt. "She was an accident," the composer explains, "and in the theater even the best accidents can spell disaster." The role of Miss Marmelstein was initially very small, and Rome was worried that this very peculiar girl might attract too much attention. The audience would surely be waiting for the explosion of a talented time bomb and would feel cheated if she just sputtered away in the background. When Rome voiced his misgivings to writer Weidman, he was surprised to find out they'd been thinking along the same lines.

"When you have a talent that large onstage," Weidman said, "you just can't let her wander around. You have to give her something to do or she'll kill you. She'll steal scenes, make up business, throw people off cues." "So Jerry and I got together," Rome says. "We realized her part had to be expanded or we were in trouble."

Little by little, during the weeks in rehearsal, Miss Marmelstein moved from the wings and started taking stage center, until the final splash on the Broadway opening night when Streisand stopped the show. But between that first audition and her night of glory there was a long, devious road with many detours. In each and every one there was someone to turn to. Ironically, it was the man she was stealing the limelight away from. Theatrical tradition was reversed. The young star Barbra was overshadowing did not hate her but fell in love with her. His name was Elliott Gould.

6. *Enter Miss Marmelstein*

AFTER a street accident stunned pedestrians often mutter, "I never knew what hit me." The cliché would have served Elliott Gould if he had ever tried to explain his first feelings when he watched one of Barbra Streisand's auditions from the back of the St. James Theatre. He was on his way out for a snack but suddenly he was not hungry. He stopped and stared in a daze, watching the feat of the girl onstage.

The incurably romantic may call it love at first sight; delvers into the occult will explain it as psychic predestination. The fact is that Elliott Gould stayed at the scene of this hit-and-run artistic accident, unable to tear himself away. Then he started collecting the data.

After her last song for the show's high echelon Barbra was wandering around backstage, handing everybody pieces of paper with her newly acquired telephone number and pleading, "Hey, give me a call, even if I don't get the part. I just want to hear it ring." Elliott got the number from one of the boys who was about to discard it in a trash can. That night he phoned her and said, "You said you wanted calls, no? You were brilliant today. This is Elliott Gould." And he hung up.

Gould was the male lead in *Wholesale* and Barbra was impressed by the compliment but not too much. She had learned to be painfully wary of people. When she met Gould face to face, on the day the full cast assembled for the first reading, she was polite but rather diffident toward him. Brashly he offered her a cigar. Silently and philosophically she puffed twice on it before returning it with a noncommital smile. He was convinced she was the most innocent, defenseless creature he had ever seen, but he admitted he was somewhat scared of her mind. There were things going on in it, things no one yet suspected.

During that first reading Jerome Weidman saw her taking notes frantically on a pad of paper. He was touched by the dutiful, very professional way the kid was approaching his libretto. After the reading ended, he asked her if he could clarify some aspect of the character she was to play. Then he found out what all the scribbling had been about. Barbra had been writing her capsule biography just the way she wanted it printed on the programs once the show opened. The first lines were: "Born in Madagascar, reared in Rangoon. . . ."

This was merely the first quirk of an egocentric talent that was to amuse, confound, or annoy the *Wholesale* troupe for many a day. During rehearsals she seemed to be playing a different Miss Marmelstein every time around. She was experimenting with the character to get at its inner core, but her groping with the role was disorienting to all—and doubly irksome because her instincts so often proved correct.

She had a running battle with one of the stage managers who objected to her going onstage chewing gum. Pretending to spit it out, Barbra would flatten the wad and go through her songs with the secret proof of her defiance pressed against her palate. If she could do her job just as well with the gum in her mouth, who cared? Besides, she argued, it was very possible that Yetta Marmelstein actually chewed gum in the office and had learned to hide it from her cantankerous boss.

"Barbra was so stubborn that I liked to taunt her to see how far she would go," director Laurents now remembers with a smile. "I knew no one could sing like she did with a wad of chewing gum in her mouth. One day when the stage manager insisted, she pretended to take it out and press it on the bottom of her chair. After she finished her number, I upturned that chair and there was nothing there. I then asked her to spit it out and she was silent for a moment. Then she said she'd swallowed it. I know she disputes me on this too, but I'm sure there never had been any chewing gum in the first place."

Hypersensitive Barbra was still complaining to Laurents about recording executive Lieberson calling her "too special." He told her not to worry, but Streisand never forgot that cutting remark and would often repeat it to interviewers after Columbia Records relented and signed her for a multimillion-dollar, long-term recording contract.

It was just a temporary setback: She was in good hands with the *Wholesale* creators. Miss Marmelstein was growing and breeding resentment in the rest of the cast. The more the upstart got away with, the tenser the backstage situation became.

The headliners in *Wholesale* were a group of waning luminaries trying for a comeback on Broadway: Lillian Roth, the famous torch singer whose battle with alcoholism had been dramatized by Susan Hayward in *I'll Cry Tomorrow;* Harold Lang, the versatile hoofer who had a big hit with *Pal Joey;*

Bambi Linn, the now mature little girl the critics had loved in *Oklahoma!*, and Sheree North, a fine actress whom Hollywood had criminally misused as little more than a glorified chorine. Each had a big professional stake in the show; all were bravely fighting to hold their own in a fragmented book in which no one had a predominantly starring part. Every minute onstage counted.

The newcomers were Barbra and Elliott Gould, who had been recently upped by David Merrick from the chorus of *Irma La Douce* into a make-or-break starring role. On somewhat hostile ground, both tyros were fated to gravitate toward each other, but it took some time. As much as Elliott tried to be friendly, Barbra held back. Then one day, while he was rehearsing "Momma, Momma" in a baby-blue sweater, she noticed how the hair curled in the back of his turtleneck. She fell in love with his nape, she later proclaimed. After that they were inseparable.

A show on its pre-Broadway tour is very much like an army preparing to lay siege to an impregnable fortress. The situation is fraught with hope and anxiety, a breeding ground for undying friendships and equally undying enmities. Barbra and Elliott became buddies. They shared minor victories and comforted each other in moments of despair. As they approached opening night in Philadelphia, Barbra needed Elliott's crying shoulder more than ever: Her blackest hour was about to close in on her.

The first performance did not go well. Critics were cool and the company needed a scapegoat. Barbra had been withdrawn and unresponsive onstage. She had committed the capital sin of not playing to the balcony and had instead retreated into her inner depths, just as she had at the Bon Soir and the Blue Angel whenever audiences were sending the wrong vibrations.

"Merrick wanted to fire her on the spot," Harold Rome recalls. But Rome had written a number for her, "Miss Marmelstein," and he felt no other girl would be able to sing it as well as Streisand. Director Laurents—no matter how sorely she had tried his patience—had great faith in Barbra.

Together with author Weidman, Rome and Laurents formed a triumvirate; Merrick was prevailed on to wait for the final decision. Maybe a good bawling out would make the kid toe the line.

When the cast was assembled for the postmortem after the Philadelphia debacle, the director had to do the dirty work and assume the role of stern parent to the wayward child. In front of the whole company Laurents let Barbra have it in no uncertain terms. The poor waif sat there, head down, eyes fixed on the tremulous fingers on her lap. After the ordeal was over, Rome recalls that he went over to Laurents and told him he had gone too far and should let the kid alone for a while; she would shape up and learn to communicate more immediately with the audience.

Weidman, equally shaken by the dressing down Barbra had suffered, went over to comfort her. He expected to find tears in her eyes as she looked up from her lap, but her baby-blue eyes were clear, although troubled. Then she showed him what her fingers had been twitching over. It was a floor plan of her apartment over the seafood restaurant and she was wondering what to do with it. Weidman concluded that their find had "genius plus the one other ingredient necessary for stardom: She was made of copper tubing."

Not really. Barbra was just concentrating on her apartment to avoid being too hurt by her troubles with the show. Back in New York her friend Steve Elster was in charge of dismantling the flat, and she was sending him endless lists of instructions on how to knock down partitions and not let Carlos, the superintendent, overcharge her. She wrote Steve to bargain to the end, using his "Yiddisha kup," and to call her if there was any trouble, reassuring him that it took only sixty-five cents to ring her backstage in Philly.

"That apartment was the weirdest place," Elster remembers. "There were actually windows indoors, separating the living room from the sleeping area. I spent a whole afternoon getting them unstuck. Then there were about eight coats of paint to be stripped off. Barbra wanted everything *natural*-looking, especially the marble on the fireplace. She wanted the bathroom papered with old sheet music she'd gotten hold of. And you had to do all that without scratching the thrift-shop furniture she'd been buying. Instead of a chest of drawers she had an ancient dentist's cabinet with a marble top and very narrow drawers to keep instruments in. It was beautiful but impractical. She could keep only a pair of gloves or panties in each drawer. I was protecting it with a tarpaulin while Carlos, the handyman, was knocking down partitions. A scene out of the Marx Brothers!"

Down in Philadelphia Barbra was creating her own pandemonium. Her performance was still raw and Merrick kept talking about firing her at the end of the week, but she was indestructible. Laurents remembers that at her worst moment of crisis she came up to him. "I thought she would ask me to keep her in the show, but what she wanted was the ingenue part. She felt she would be much better in that role than as Miss Marmelstein. I just told her to hold onto what she had and pray."

Barbra was never on time. She had a fear of the audience that made her procrastinate and postpone the confrontation to the very last minute. She had insisted on singing Miss Marmelstein's lament on a swivel chair because she knew from experience that secretaries spent most of their time sitting. Once, explaining her tardiness, she said she wished she could be thrown onstage. Laurents had a directorial insight. Just before her big number she would be pushed into the proscenium and make her entrance rolling on her chair, literally dumped in front of an audience. It worked wonders, and her solo turn began to get increasingly big hands on the pre-Broadway tour.

There was no longer any question of firing her. Harold Rome had bailed her out with a potential show stopper, and the company had to bear with Barbra to the bitter end. Some of the principals started to understand her well-hidden insecurity and to give her a helping hand. Lillian Roth took her under her wing and gave her motherly lectures about acquiring discipline and tact. Barbra was grateful, appreciative—and went on doing things her own way.

There was still animosity toward Streisand, especially among the lesser players and the chorus. Some of these people had spent half their lives striving for a chance, and here was this nobody who had landed not only a good role but possibly the best song in the whole score. Blinded to her talent, they saw only an element that theater folk are seldom tolerant about: sheer luck. Her trespasses were not about to be forgiven—and there were many.

She kept being late for rehearsals while she made long-distance phone calls, plunging rows of coins into the pay telephones in the theater lobby as they moved north to Boston: The masterminding of her new dwellings was still the motivating force that kept her mind off the tryout agonies. Harold Rome recalls a day when they were shouting for her all over the theater and a girl from the dancing ensemble piped in venomously, "Try Elliott Gould's room." It was the voice of jealousy and envy.

The young, handsome star of the show had obviously fallen for this skinny-legged girl who could never have aspired to rotate a dimpled knee even in the third row of a fly-by-night chorus. Backstage the standard question was: "What does he see in her?"—especially since the swaggering, cigar-smoking Ellie had a reputation as a ladies' man and was rumored to be shacked up in New York with the most luscious feathered and sequined blonde on the Latin Quarter front line. Nobody seemed to understand that the attraction between Elliott and Barbra was not the usual tryout romance. It was taking roots because it was the real thing.

Or maybe because it was the unreal thing, marvelously and impossibly sweet, right out of the movies Barbra had gobbled in the Loew's Kings, together with the Mellorolls. They learned together, breathed together. They could not be apart for more than a half hour, Barbra later told, blissfully recalling this period of their relationship. While everyone was sweating out the tryout anxieties in Boston, they were watching horror movies, buried in an avalanche of buttered popcorn, at the double-feature fleabags three blocks from the theater. Or having poetic snowball fights that needed only a Technicolor camera to be embalmed into a fantasy of love, Hollywood style.

It is significant that they referred to each other as Hansel and Gretel, for they were really swapping childhood traumas in a perennial loving battle to the tune of "my past can lick your past." Barbra had discovered that Elliott's brashness was a front and he was as much a scared kid as she was. Born Elliott Goldstein in the Bensonhurst section of Brooklyn, he was the son of an office manager in Manhattan's garment district and his dissatisfied, show-biz-oriented wife. Bernard wanted Ellie to go into his chosen field, but Lucille had fantasies of the child becoming a famous performer. Elliott had grown up in no-man's-land between their marital skirmishes.

At seven little Elliott had chopped down the cherry tree, in a lopsided white wig, as George Washington in a pageant at Brooklyn's PS 247: Lucille Goldstein was sure she had a star in the family. He was enrolled in a professional children's school, where he danced in bow ties and cute straw hats. By the time he was eight he was doing kiddie spots on television shows like Milton Berle's and the *Colgate Comedy Hour.* When he was informed, just before going on TV, that his name had been changed from Goldstein to Gould, he closed his eyes and started walking, to see how far he could get away without looking back: He hit a telephone pole and broke a tooth. He could not escape his destiny, and by the time he was eleven he was tap dancing at the Palace Theatre with vaudevillian Jimmy Callahan. Ellliott remembers it all as the most humiliating period of his existence.

He finally hit his stride as a chorus boy with enough personality to attract attention in *Say Darling* and *Irma La Douce* prior to his bid for stardom with *Wholesale.*

At twenty-two his success both in the theater and with women had bolstered Elliott's self-confidence, but he was far from the braggart and lady-killer he was taken for. Secretly, he needed Barbra as much as she needed him. And Streisand had met her match. If she remembered how her mother had squelched all theatrical ambitions by pronouncing her too skinny, Elliott could counter with a shuddering tale of how *his* mother had pushed him to be a baby stand-up comic. If Barbra moaned about the early loss of her father, Elliott could upstage her by relating such disagreements between his parents that he had sighed with relief when they had finally filed for divorce.

The good life is usually the opposite of the one you have led, and these harassed children found they had so little—and so much—in common that they could form a symbiotic relationship, each feeding on what the other had, facing the world as an indivisible, all-powerful unit. Their spiritual needs dovetailed; if they could hold fast, shutting out the world around them, nothing and no one could ever separate them.

The first crisis was just a week or two away. As *Wholesale* approached that definitive phase so aptly and frighteningly described in theatrical lore as "freezing," an unavoidable fact was emerging: Elliott was miscast in the lead. He was playing Harry Bogen, a Garment Center hero-heel who claws his way to the top by hook or crook. Years later Gould would become a movie idol by playing amiable boobs in many a good performance, but he was only twenty-two and no X-ray could have detected that as a star personality he did not have a mean bone in his body.

The drive and ruthlessness of Harry Bogen escaped him: His performance was getting closer to an impossible compromise between the *schlemiel* and the Wolf Man. Barbra, on the other hand, was right on target as Miss Marmelstein. Each night her round of applause was getting stronger; his, more perfunctory. In *Wholesale*'s divided lot there was room for only one striking debut: The rest of the praise would be allotted among the old-timers. It was simple arithmetic on the level of fourth-grade division: She was leaving nothing for him. The inevitable showdown came on the night of March 22, 1962, when *I Can Get It for You Wholesale* opened at the Shubert Theater in New York.

Barbra was the first person onstage, singing "You're Not a Well Man," a duet with Jack Kruschen, who played the grumpy boss to her frumpy, harassed Miss Marmelstein. She was odd and funny and she got a big hand, but still no fireworks. Then she was part of the chorus in a couple of numbers, "The Sound of Money" and the first-act finale, "The Ballad of the Garment Trade." She was, again, duly noticed, but hardly a topic of conversation during intermission.

Then came the second act and her big solo number. Quivering in her swivel chair, she was pushed onstage, rolling until she stopped. She let out a sigh so profound that her very soul seemed to be leaving her body in a final exhalation. She sat there, deflated, for an instant, and then she began to sing a rejected girl's lament that touched a sensitive chord.

She was the girl everyone called Miss Marmelstein, the one who never got on a first-name basis with the boys in the office and was never asked for a date. Efficient and resourceful Yetta Tessye Marmelstein could get anything done in the filing department, but in the man-hunting department she was an arrowless Diana.

It was the first dramatic statement of the Streisand charisma. To this hypercritical, unforgiving Broadway audience she was declaring outright that she was not pretty, had little sex appeal, and that she was Jewish. She had been singing for only one minute when there was an audible rustle in the theater: Seven hundred programs were being opened at the same time to find out who this girl was. It was clearly the hum of success, but Barbra panicked when she heard it because she thought that ominous *woosh* meant that people were leaving their seats.

Undaunted, she went on. If she had faced the circus at The Lion unscathed, no Neronian audience of snobs was going to give her a thumbs down this late in the game. Like a masochistic St. Sebastian, she stabbed a pencil into her beehive hairdo and showed them Miss Marmelstein to the last bleeding ego wound. In three minutes she made the song into a character study, a psychiatric test, a fever chart of an ailing soul.

She was alternately naughty and naïve, defeated and courageous, furious and plangent. She muttered asides as if she were getting ready to be carted away to intensive care at

Bellevue. She lifted the end of phrases with a questioning lilt that had the pungency of a kosher pickle. Finally, exhausted after Miss Marmelstein's painfully hilarious orgy of self-revelation, she broke into a giggle, stifled a sob, and then gathered her voice like a clenched fist, ready to hit an unfeeling world right in the kisser as she pronounced herself ready to bust.

It was like a cue for the audience to explode with her, releasing the tensions of the last three minutes of heightening amazement. The show stopped dead in its tracks and the Shubert Theatre went wild with applause, bravos, or just plain old rude stomping on the floor. This was not a performance, this was an event. And in the midst of hysteria there was this girl, frozen in her swivel chair, clutching its wooden arms, trying not to roll down to the orchestra pit.

"After the show was over, it was the biggest crush I've ever seen in a theater lobby," Steve Elster remembers. "The crowd wasn't moving because dozens of people were reading the Playbill biography to find out where Barbra had come from."

What they read was the biography Barbra had been scribbling during that first reading, an updating and embellishment of her initial one in the *Harry Stoones* program and even wilder in its fantasies:

> Barbra Streisand is nineteen, was born in Madagascar and reared in Rangoon, educated at Erasmus Hall High School in Brooklyn, and appeared Off Broadway in a one-nighter called *Another Evening With Harry Stoones. Wholesale* is her first Broadway show, although she has appeared at New York's two best-known supper clubs, the Bon Soir and the Blue Angel. She has also appeared eight times on Mike Wallace's *PM East* and twice on the *Jack Paar Show.* She is not a member of the Actors Studio.

The Playbill had Elliott Gould, Harold Lang, Bambi Linn, Lillian Roth, Marilyn Cooper, and Ken LeRoy on the cover. Barbra was way below on the credits and her biography was the very last one on the cast list. The night, nonetheless, was hers. At the post-opening-night party at Sardi's theatrical gossips were eagerly expecting her confrontation with the stars she had overshadowed.

"Sardi's was abuzz with suspense," recalls Gerald O'Brien, who was present at the gala. "Everyone was waiting to see who would come in first, Elliott or Barbra, and how he would take it if her ovation turned out to be bigger than his. Elliott had been assigned to Table Number One with the bigwigs while Barbra was to sit at something like Table Thirty-Three. Her mother was already there, in a shiny blue dress, telling everyone, 'That crazy kid of mine! I can't get over it!'"

Steve Elster, who had finally finished reconstructing Barbra's new apartment, had been summoned backstage: He was supposed to escort Barbra into Sardi's, but at the last moment there was a change in plans. The gossips had waited in vain for a showdown because when Elliott came into the party, Barbra was at his side and he had a protective arm around her shoulder. As it turned out, they shared the ovation, just as they had decided to share everything from then on.

Even that early in their relationship the world would not leave them alone. Her enemies at Sardi's, disappointed at being cheated of melodrama, venomously insisted that Elliott had brought her along deliberately, to be spared the embarrassment of getting less applause. It was an omen of what they would be up against for the next seven years. But that night of March 22, 1962, they were oblivious to envy and evil: Hansel and Gretel were together, discreetly holding hands under the white linen cloth of Table Number One.

7. *The Kids in the Tree House*

AFTER the success binge came the morning after. Reviews for *Wholesale* were a hangover headache for Barbra Streisand. Somehow they failed to convey the excitement Miss

Marmelstein had ignited at the Shubert Theatre. The critics were appreciative of her gifts but shied away from all-out personal raves. No one would go out on a limb to proclaim her as a potential superstar. She was too odd, too atypical, with all the earmarks of a flash in the pan.

Worst of all, reviewers made comments on her physical appearance, and however highly they praised her performance, in her oversensitive epidermis the wallflower of Erasmus Hall felt the sting like a stab. "One guy calls me an oaf, another one a frump, one says I was rude, another one that I have a classical Assyrian profile, yet *Variety* advises me to get my nose fixed if I want to get into movies. It's all a lot of guff," she fumed.

The nose, of course, could not be mentioned at the time. Not if you wanted to be on good terms with Barbra. She kept saying that if she had wanted to have her nose fixed, she would have done it when she was seven. Later in the star game she would make jokes about her proboscis like a rueful disciple of Jimmy Durante, but it was still too early: Barbra was a nineteen-year-old kid with no real sense of her special kind of beauty.

The prominent, crooked nose was still a disconcerting feature she had not learned to accept. She'd had dreams about becoming a high-fashion model and done series of poses in her outlandish monkey-skin coat and cloche hats. At this stage of her career it was rumored she had again toyed with the idea of plastic surgery to correct the nose to a stereotype of bland perfection, but she had been warned that it might change the quality of her voice. That buzz she had been hearing since she was a child was possibly caused by a deviated septum; it gave her songs the priceless tremolo of anxiety that made people compare her to Judy Garland. In plain commercial fact, she could not afford conventional prettiness at the risk of losing her one claim to success.

So there she was, after a smash of sorts in *Wholesale,* maybe doomed by Miss Marmelstein to becoming an ethnic comedienne. Perhaps she would never rise higher than the fine but ultimately forgotten Alice Pearce, who had briefly wowed the public in *Fallen Angels* and the movie *On the Town*. When a couple of chroniclers compared her to Pearce, it was enough to make her shudder; she didn't even want to be compared to Fanny Brice. Barbra dreamed of playing Shakespeare as the sublime Juliet of her generation, but she was already being strapped into a restricting borscht belt.

The *Wholesale* cast could not understand why she went around "like a *forbiss*, kind of depressed," while the *Herald Tribune* was calling her "the evening's find." When they asked, she replied that she had to be great, she couldn't be medium, "because my mouth is too big." It was the kind of remark that sounded like the perverse antithesis to a Dale Carnegie lesson on how to make friends and influence people. For those who envied her nightly ovations her disdain was a provocation, mainly because most theater folk live by the day and thrive on the moment. Barbra Streisand was different; she held onto impossible dreams.

The measure of success she had achieved was not enough. It was dangerously confining. Where could she go from here? She kept coming back to one of her favorite words, the one that haunts her through the interviews she gave at this period: What she had was not *tangible*, and it was a pity success was something you could not hold in the palm of your hand "like a hard-boiled egg."

In search of something tangible, Barbra bought an old Singer sewing machine for her apartment. She planned to do herself proud by making doilies with flowers on them, but she gave up after two afternoons of pedaling and stitching. She needed something more visible and corporal to hold onto. There was Elliott Gould.

"She was frail, vulnerable, she needed someone to take care of her," he said. "She was like a flower that hadn't blossomed yet. I think I was the first person she liked who liked her back." No matter how sexy the girls who threw themselves at him, he was hooked on Barbra and her fantasies. Their disposable doily of a love affair was expanding into an awesome floor-to-ceiling tapestry of forlorn maidens, stalwart princes, and even a unicorn or two in the crowded fringes. Outside her dream world everything looked so tarnished and prosaic. . . .

During the first weeks of the *Wholesale* run Barbra and Elliott's story curiously begins to resemble the tale in the *Arabian Nights* in which a wayfarer is moved by pity and offers to carry a helpless beggar on his shoulders. Quickly the stray becomes a powerful jinn who tightens muscular thighs around the wayfarer's neck, forcing him to take the stubborn genie for an endless piggyback ride. Barbra had been waiting for someone like Elliott for a long time. Now she would not let him escape. She loved him totally, possessively, and lived in constant fear of losing the tiny parcel of paradise she had cornered.

She severed connections with friends and told Steve Elster that she had eloped to Baltimore and married Elliott during the Philadelphia run. Barbra asked him to keep it a secret because it was too early to tell. She surprised Steve further by alleging she had not wanted to marry Gould in New York because the state law required adultery as the only grounds for divorce. Barbra was planning to move Elliott into her apartment, and she needed an excuse for a way of life that was an eyebrow raiser in 1962. Despite her highly exaggerated news about the elopement to Baltimore, almost two years elapsed before she and Elliott finally said "I do."

She wanted to see no one else and demanded the same fidelity from Gould. A strikingly beautiful theatrical agent, who was twenty and flirtatious in 1962, now laughs when she remembers an incident that she considers typical of the Barbra-Ellie menage of those uncertain days:

"I was at a party, one of those bring-your-own-bottle things for the young theater crowd, and I went to the kitchen to see if someone had been mooching from the pint of scotch I'd brought. Elliott was there and we started chatting casually. Not three minutes had gone by and Barbra was at the door telling him to bring back some ice for her soda. She didn't drink, get it? She was pure. And she wasn't asking him, she was *telling* him, mind you, to come back to the living room on the double. You know, I don't blame her. Since she'd started going around with Gould, this girl we all thought of as homely was actually becoming beautiful. He was doing wonders for her and she had to protect it, protect herself."

Barbra was counting her blessings one by one, hoarding them like pennies in that piggy bank back on Pulaski Street. People who knew her during this phase remember her as "a mousy, frightened thing, always hiding behind Elliott's pants." There was, for example, the night of April 8, 1962, three weeks after the *Wholesale* opening, when the Academy Awards ceremony was being telecast from Hollywood and they attended a private "Oscar party."

"They came late," Gerald O'Brien remembers, "because they couldn't get away until the show broke. They were just in time to hear the announcement of those big winners they save for the end: best picture, best actor, and all that. It was the year *West Side Story* got practically everything, and Barbra had some opinion or other about who should or shouldn't have won. She voiced it within earshot of a high-powered theatrical lady, somebody's influential wife. The woman corrected her but Barbra insisted. Well, all hell broke loose. The important lady shouted at Streisand, 'You don't know a thing. How dare you go around talking like that? You are nothing! You'll never get anywhere in the theatre.'"

Famous last words, indeed. Extra pungency is added by the fact that the theatrical wife later branched out as an agent and tried—unsuccessfully—to sign Streisand for a couple of projects. Yet that night the little girl did not fight back. She shriveled, walked away without a sound, and sat on a sofa, holding Elliott's hand for moral support until her tormentor left.

Barbra had more than her share of put-downs in that indecisive year, 1962. Joe Franklin recalls that she used to follow him around, practically begging him to put her in his show. He finally scheduled her on the same program with Rudy Vallee. "I'll never forget that," Franklin tells. "He told her she'd probably never make it in show business."

As in the thirties song, everything she did was a buildup

for an awful letdown. The worst came with the Tony Awards. Barbra had won the *Variety* Poll of New York Critics as best supporting actress in a musical and was considered a shoo-in for the Tony. In the *Wholesale* group she was the only person to have garnered a nomination. It was a source of friction considering that one and all, including Elliott, had been ignored by the Antoinette Perry Award committee. No other performer in her category had received such good notices and she was expected to win over Elizabeth Allen in *The Gay Life,* Phyllis Newman in *Subways Are for Sleeping,* and Barbara Harris in *From the Second City.*

Yet, on the night of April 29 there was an upset, and Phyllis Newman got the coveted plaque. Barbra came back to *Wholesale* on Monday. Commiseration was being hung on her like so many leaden funeral wreaths. She had been resented as a winner, but now she was being hugged into warmer bosoms as a fellow loser. She swallowed bile and sympathy and went on, holding to her tower of strength, her Elliott.

Once through this period they came very close to a breakup. She accused him of carrying on with a chorus girl and left the theater in a snit. All through the night she kept ringing his number and hanging up. He would call her back, knowing very well who was sending the SOS, but she wouldn't answer. The argument, as recalled by Gould, is oddly reminiscent of the scene that Barbra would play superbly with her reluctant lover, Robert Redford, more than a decade later in *The Way We Were.* All was resolved when she made a tearful appearance at Gould's door, with her piebald coat slung over a nightgown in the middle of a rainstorm. He patted her back, reassured her she was loved, put her in a taxi, and dropped her back home in her apartment over the seafood restaurant. Even faithful Elliott refused to visit her in her aromatic quarters, but in time he got used to the pervading odor of churning sole and he moved in. For better or worse, they called it home.

"They were like kids in a tree house." This is the way a friend describes the idyllic mood of their first months together over Oscar's on Third Avenue. Hansel and Gretel had found a secluded abode: The world at large was the Wicked Witch. Visitors were infrequent in their fishy place and they were left alone. Their best friend was a hungry rat that made periodic forays in the kitchen. It became their pet and they named him Oscar, after the restaurant below.

The sewing machine, now abandoned as an ineffectual stab at vocational therapy, became their dining table. Off it they ate Swanson's frozen fried chicken and Breyer's brick coffee ice cream in the glow of a couple of Woolworth's candles that precariously sustained a romantic atmosphere. Barefoot and beflowered like an aspiring Isadora Duncan, Barbra taught Elliott the sweet geometry of truth and beauty as converging lines. She read aloud from the classics she had learned in acting school. Instead of canasta or Scrabble they played Lorca, Molnar, and Chekhov. They toyed with the idea of learning Greek or Latin so they could communicate with each other without being understood by interlopers: Like delinquents, they were groping for a secret language, an argot that would set them apart as an impregnable unity, safe from detection and imprisonment in bourgeois cages.

Barbra craved the peace of her tree house with Elliott because she was again on the warpath at the Shubert. *Wholesale* was frozen to the last step, but she kept thawing out her Miss Marmelstein. She now had new insights into the character but found it hard to convince anyone that a good thing needed improvement. They yelled at her because she would not repeat the same gestures. Harold Rome recalls she would disconcert the conductor by changing her pace and inflections without notice.

"Just give me the music and I'll make it work," she insisted. She did and they left her alone, but not for long. There was the dispute about her apocryphal Playbill biography. She was asked to change it and stick to the facts. Instead she offered even more exotic birthplaces, from Aruba to Zanzibar. "The Playbill people want facts," the harried press agent exploded. "Then let them print a blank," Barbra retorted. "Luckily, the show closed before the argument got settled" is her final comment on the matter.

The management had to go along with her irrepressible whims because she had become one of the show's major assets, possibly its greatest. David Merrick had signed her tentatively for $165 a week, yet he had to escalate her salary when her original contract expired. Her wages were hiked to $200 a week, every bit as much as Elliott was making as leading man. Her pride was soothed—temporarily—but not her sense of professional stagnation.

The routine of mouthing the same lines every night was getting her down, so Barbra came back to the Bon Soir in mid-May of 1962, a couple of months after the *Wholesale* opening. Miss Marmelstein's severe coiffure had turned into a constricting helmet and she wanted to let her hair down again. At the Bon Soir she attacked "I Stayed Too Long at the Fair" in a paroxysm of *angst.* She had sung it before, but never like this. The words were acquiring new layers of meaning. She was the artist trapped in a deadening treadmill of a Broadway show that would run for nine months. She stressed the word "successful," devouring it and spitting it out immediately as if she had found a bitter taste in the deceitful bonbon.

Barbra had reached one of the many plateaus of dissatisfaction in her career. Again Harold Rome came to the rescue. He had gone to Sheila Chang's Chinese Restaurant on Eighth Street for Barbra's birthday celebration at midnight on May 10, 1962, three weeks after she had turned twenty. Barbra sang a couple of thirties numbers that she was considering for an appearance on a Garry Moore show based on music of that period. Rome walked out of the party with the unshakable conviction that only Streisand could reproduce the vintage sound he needed for the record he was planning.

It was to be a twenty-fifth-anniversary tribute to *Pins and Needles,* a musical revue that had become a legend. The WPA project, first staged in 1937 with a cast of amateurs from the garment district, had run four years and contained some of Rome's finest words and music. He suggested Barbra as the indispensable singer to do the key numbers, but Columbia Records again thumbed its collective nose at her. Five alternate vocalists were proposed, but Rome was adamant in his choice of Streisand.

Barbra was fully prepared when she came to the recording session. "We had to do the whole thing very fast," Harold Rome says. "There was no time to perfect the sound and Barbra was unhappy. She wanted retakes but we had the studio for a very limited number of hours. She broke up once in a giggle while doing "Nobody Makes a Pass at Me" and pleaded to do it over again to get it right, but I wanted that laugh there. She has such a wonderful laugh!"

The record was truly the work of a fine actress who just happened to express herself in songs. Streisand sang the unwanted girl's woes in the Miss Marmelstein vein: In a conspicuous-consumer frazzle she wondered why she wasn't amorously accosted after eating the right brands of food and dabbing herself with the most advertised deodorant. Then she proved her ample range by "Doing the Reactionary" like a shocking-pink menace or by turning uppity to admonish the unruly masses that it was "Not Cricket to Picket." She topped it all with "What Good Is Love," a proletarian diatribe about the impossibility of romance on sore feet and fallen arches: One could picture her collapsing against a tinkling piano like Helen Morgan doing an impersonation of La Pasionara.

With the *Wholesale* album and the versatile *Pins and Needles* performance selling briskly, Barbra's agent had enough bait for the hook. Marty Erlichman did the rounds again, trying to persuade recording companies that his client was a talent to be reckoned with. There was some interest, but there were also concessions Barbra had to make before she signed a contract. If only she would sprinkle her repertory with a few current hits and go easy on those cockamamy songs. . . .

Streisand said no. She would make it her own way or not at all. All the numbers suggested to her had stupid lyrics that meant nothing. She could not put any dramatic feeling into their vacuum. The battle to browbeat Barbra into a standard mold now raged on a different front. She would not budge, and a year elapsed between the opening of *Wholesale* and the day she recorded her first solo album.

Most of that year was spent in helpless fury. She had grown to hate that eight-performance-a-week grind in *Wholesale.* There was nothing to win and she'd stayed too long at the fair. Barbra was late thirty-six times and was reprimanded twice by Actors Equity during the nine-month run. It seemed she was provoking the management into firing her so she could go into a very profitable nightclub tour arranged by Erlichman. But in her initial insecurity she had given her pound of flesh to *Wholesale* and was bound by an ironclad run-of-the-play contract.

Half irritated, half amused by her antics, producer Merrick called her "a flibbertigibbet with no technique, no discipline, but enormous talent." Translated into Broadway terms, those words were the equivalent of a life sentence. Miss Marmelstein was keeping the show alive and she had to stay on the job, no matter what.

Barbra's span of attention has always been as intense, as creative, and as perilously short as a child's. Bored with what she was doing onstage at the Shubert, she began to perform for the benefit of amused reporters in frequent, endless, and maddeningly contradictory interviews. She did it mainly because she wanted to have splendiferous lunches at restaurants she had never before been able to set foot in. "I could be bought for a chocolate mousse," she later quipped. She hated the interviews when she saw them in print: They cramped her volatile personality and impinged on the feminine privilege of changing her mind.

One day she would say—on the spur of the moment—that she loved rubies and hated diamonds. Then, when she decided she liked diamonds better, she found herself codified in black and white. She began to protest she had been misquoted and to fear the working press her ego and stomach fed on.

There are a few constants in that rash of early Streisand interviews. One was her obsession with the Statue of Liberty, which she seldom failed to mention, claiming never to have visited it because it awed her: Barbra would get back at the giant lady in her movie career, once by upstaging her in the first-act finale of *Funny Girl,* later by actually bombing it to smithereens in *Up the Sandbox.* There was also the dominant preoccupation with the evanescent and unattainable: She repeatedly said she loved gardenias "because their fragrance can never be captured in a perfume," avocados "because you have to eat another one to remember how they taste," and almond tea "because you can't begin to describe it."

The interviews were sometimes used as a valve to let off steam in her personal life. She once announced to the New York *Post* that she would enroll in Dartmouth University as soon as it became coed in 1963 because she felt she had to complete her education in order to be a fine actress, and besides, she would enjoy being around all those fellows on the small-town campus. Of course, she never went to Dartmouth and the announcement was considered by friends as "just a way to get back at Elliott after a fight."

Yet their fights were infrequent. Sheree North, who shared Barbra's dressing room in *Wholesale,* called them a "mutual-admiration society": They gave each other sustenance during difficult times. Barbara was champing at the bit backstage, but Elliott calmed her down, told her to be patient, and gave her secret tokens of affection: Her favorite one was a blue marble egg he had found in a musty antique shop. No one was allowed to snoop into their private world. When her mother asked what he'd given her for her birthday, she just muttered, "A check."

Barbra and Ellliott had an almost magical rapport, but it was doomed to change. "I was like godfather to their union," Arthur Laurents says. "It was a pleasure to see them together. But she was becoming too embroiled in her career. I came to their apartment over Oscar's Restaurant one Sunday afternoon in a convertible. We were going out of town to go 'antiquing.' Barbra was conferring with three men in black suits—agents or entrepreneurs—and they were discussing business. We had to wait for an hour before we left on our weekend drive. I said, 'Barbra, you're getting corny with all this entourage.' She didn't answer."

Barbra came back to the Blue Angel in the summer of 1962. This time Arthur Laurents coached her. It was not an easy job. Laurents remembers one rehearsal when he told her, "Don't look down, Barbra, always look up." She looked hurt and mumbled, "It's the nose, isn't it?" "No, Barbra," Laurents said, "it's the chin." From then on, Streisand learned to look up, pointing her chin so that her Modigliani neck and perfect shoulders would be shown to their best advantage. Everyone who collaborated on the emergence of Streisand agrees: She had to be told the unflattering things, but only once. After that, they were easily assimilated.

At her second run at the Blue Angel Barbra's greatest hit had been pretested. On Garry Moore's television show she had done a sketch about an elegant lady who had just crashed down with the market in 1929. She ordered champagne, and when the waiter presented her with the bill, she removed her diamond earrings and placed them on the tray before she mournfully sang "Happy Days Are Here Again." By the time she opened at the club the song had been purged of all parodied elements into a brilliantly atypical interpretation.

Streisand took a beery, convention-hall ditty, widely associated with the fake enthusiasm of political campaigns, and transmuted it into an ominous dirge that forecast even deeper depression. She turned the song like a glove and slapped the audience with it until they helplessly turned the other cheek. Then she let them have it with a final, piercing scream that could mean only that the sky was falling and Apocalypse was just around the corner.

The ovations were thunderous. She could go anywhere from the Blue Angel as soon as *Wholesale* closed. Her nightly ordeal as Miss Marmelstein ended on December 8, 1962. Composer Harold Rome went to the last performance and describes it with regret: "She seemed even more withdrawn than at the beginning of the Philadelphia run. She played the final show for the first twelve rows of center orchestra and gave the impression of counting every minute until she was out of it."

Rome had given Streisand her first toehold on Broadway, but he now ruefully comments, "After that night she never sang a song of mine. I sent her a whole batch when she emerged as a top recording star and she didn't even acknowledge getting them. I called up and a very fake secretarial voice answered and asked, 'Harold who?' I hung up. I can understand Barbra's point of view. She runs away from the past and she was trying to put that period out of her mind."

Her only link with the *Wholesale* experience was Elliott Gould. As soon as the musical closed, they were in trouble. She was at last free to do all the things she had postponed, and had offers to play the best nightclubs from coast to coast. All Elliott had was an offer to stage a cabaret act for Anna Maria Alberghetti. No matter how they kidded about it, the truth was staring them in the face. She was going up; he was going nowhere.

The first tearful separation between Elliott and Barbra took place when she went to Los Angeles to tape an appearance on the Dinah Shore TV show. After that there were no more tears: Separations were par for their diverging courses. Barbra sang at the Hungry I in San Francisco, at Chicago's Mr. Kelly's, and, in a blaze of triumph, at New York's Basin Street East, making $5,000 a week. Liberace came to see her there, and by then he had enough arguments to convince his manager to book Barbra at $7,500 a week as a second stringer for this forthcoming show at the Riviera in Las Vegas.

"My mate was making it and was very happy about it," Gould would reminisce about this period. "I had to deal with it and I did." But something far more important had happened, and Streisand was past the point of no return as a superstar. She had finally signed a recording contract with Columbia for her first solo album. It took merely one session to complete it, but those few hours changed her future. The LP was a Whitman's sampler of delectable goodies, an anthology of all the mad and glorious things she had done till then, with clear indications that there was no stopping her.

The Barbra Streisand Album includes the tried-and-true standards: the haunting "Sleepin' Bee," the grievous "Happy Days," the covetous "Much More"; "Big Bad Wolf," in which she camps her blanket somewhere between Beatrice Lillie and Anna Russell; "Cry Me a River," with its rise from an understated sneer to a cataclysm of spite; "A Taste of Honey," murmured as a sea chanty of sugar and brine; "Right in My Honey's Loving Arms," done to a crisp with the mockery of a trouper who had found the devil in the middle of vaudeville.

Then there are revelations like "I'll Tell the Man in the Street," a psychoanalysis of a pop tune that escalates Streisand from the neurotic to the psychotic because her phrasing and tempo indicate that anyone who shouts from the roofs about a sweetheart is a candidate for electroshock. She closes the record with "Soon It's Going to Rain," a tree-house elegy for lovers in jeopardy that echoed the current anxieties of the Streisand-Gould ménage.

It was a dazzling multiple performance, endorsed by an ecstatic jacket blurb by Harold Arlen—composer of "A Sleepin' Bee"—who compared her to Beatrice Lillie, Helen Morgan, Fanny Brice, and the paintings of Modigliani. Everyone who listened to advance copies predicted the album would be a hit. Right then, in March of 1963, Barbra and Elliott were offered the leads in the London production of Comden and Green's *On the Town.* It was the first real break Gould had had since the *Wholesale* closing and he naturally jumped at it. Marty Erlichman felt that it was the wrong move for his client: Barbra's salary was skyrocketing in nightclubs; her record would be out any day. Why did she have to go and play an aggressive lady taxicab driver on the other side of the Atlantic?

March of 1963 is a nebulous month in the Streisand-Gould calendar. He went down to Miami, where she was appearing at the Eden Roc, to convince her to do *On the Town* in London with him. It was impossible, she was already signed for other commitments. At least she would be with him on opening night, but that meant traveling to another country, and as coed roommates and lovers they were experimenting with a life-style: Things just weren't done that way by public personalities in 1963, even if they were whispering to friends that they'd been married last year in Baltimore.

Gould told the press that they had been married during

his visit to Florida, by a justice of the peace somewhere, but the ceremony would in fact be delayed for another six months. After the announcement it would look respectable for Barbra to visit him in London while he prepared for *On the Town*. So he left, alone and depressed. Soon they were spending a fortune in transatlantic calls because Barbra just couldn't get away. Something terrific had come up unexpectedly.

John F. Kennedy had loved her in the Dinah Shore show and personally invited her to entertain at a White House dinner for foreign-press correspondents. On May 13, 1963, while Elliott was deep in rehearsals in London, Barbra was charming the President and his guests. "You're a doll," she told Kennedy when they were introduced. When he asked how long she had been a singer, she replied, "Just about as long as you've been President." She made a distinct hit, her picture was in all the papers, but her mind was elsewhere. Elliott was about to open in London and she insisted on being there even if it meant canceling a couple of engagements.

On May 26, 1963, *On the Town* had its London premiere at the Prince of Wales Theatre. Much better cast than in *Wholesale,* Gould made a good personal impression as the beleaguered sailor, Ozzie, yet the show's overall notices were mild and polite, with no real selling magnet for the public. On his first Sunday off Elliott and Barbra motored through quaint villages in the countryside, trying to put up a brave front for each other. They really knew the musical would not run through the summer.

Barbra came back to reap the first harvest of raves for her just-released album. The reviews were excellent and the sales a surprise even to her partisans. By June, just four weeks after it came out, it was Number One best seller on the long-playing list, safely on its way to win Streisand her first gold record. Thousands bought it and then confessed it was troubling, not easy listening: Its compressed emotions were dangerously communicable. It was not a party record, not dinner music. Devotees preferred to play it when they were alone. Barbra admitted, "I'm sorry if I put my audiences through the wringer but I can't help it." She was hitting an exposed nerve and her public loved the treatment. She seemed to be singing *for* them, *about* them, and especially *to* them. Even as a disembodied voice she could achieve instant identification with the listeners. Her stardom was certified.

Prophetically, in July of 1963, she was telling reporter Pete Hamill that she would win every award: the Grammy for records, the Emmy for television, the Tony on Broadway, the Oscar for movies. That was what everybody told her and she firmly believed it. All the major television shows wanted her as a guest star, and she was scheduled to appear with Bob Hope, Judy Garland, Bing Crosby, and Ed Sullivan. She wanted to be known by everyone, "including the cowboys."

That would take awhile. Barbra was still far from becoming a household word, and she was actually barred from the studio entrance the day she was due to tape the Sullivan show, when doormen thought she was a gate-crashing teeny-bopper looking for autographs. She brushed away the incident with more amusement than pique. In show buisness 1963 was shaping into the Year of Barbra Streisand. She clinched it with her second album.

It contains her two fabled ballads from the Bon Soir-Blue Angel days: "Too Long at the Fair" and "My Coloring Book," plus a forlorn, waiflike "Who Will Buy?" from the stage hit *Oliver!* But these are exceptions to the mood of the whole performance, which is of a nervousness bordering on hysteria. It was as if her inner restlessness had dictated her selection of songs and her tense interpretation. Peter Matz, Streisand's musical director, had written "Gotta Move," the first number, which sets the tone for the album: She sings it as if her frenzied voice were running away from pursuing furies.

After that she goes through a catalogue of songs about rootlessness and flight, from "Like a Straw in the Wind" to "Every Place I Hang My Hat Is Home." There is repressed anger as she eviscerates "Lover, Come Back to Me," turning this bland, moony valentine into a quick order for sex with no trimmings. She converts "Down with Love" into a raucous parody of the "mushy" songs she detested, adding a barbed potpourri about "hating the spin I'm in 'cause I don't stand the chance of a ghost with you."

The *Second Album* underlines the mocking, impish quality of the first, but with a pen dipped in acid. She had complained of not having enough time to polish her debut record. This time, with another best seller looming in the wings, the perfectionist in Barbra started to act up. She insisted on rerecording numbers until her keen ear was satisfied. Equipped with earphones, a frown knitting her brows over the wrinkled nose, she seemed to be able to smell what was wrong and prove—despite no technical knowledge of music—that the brush was hitting the drums a fraction of a second too early.

The Second Barbra Streisand Album was not released until October of 1963, but it created a sensation before it hit the stores. The girl sounded even better this time, and she was sure to top the already astonishing sales of the first one. Nightclub shows began to turn her off. On the floor she was beholden to the competence of a hastily assembled group of musicians, to the reaction of the public, to the vagaries of her own capability to give of herself totally, in sickness or in health. She still fed on her Taurus willpower, but in a cabaret she could never manipulate the result as she did in a recording studio.

Money was pouring in, though, and she began to cuddle in the lap of luxury. She was alone while Elliott was in London, waiting for the faltering *On the Town* production to grind to a halt. She thought of surprising him with a new, sumptuous tree house as soon as he came back. She gave up the fishy apartment on top of Oscar's Restaurant and rented a spectacular Central Park West penthouse, once the home of lyricist Lorenz Hart, and began filling it with choice antiques no longer exhumed from thrift shops. Yet she would roam around the terrace, wryly commenting that New York was as sooty way up on the twenty-third floor as on the pavement below.

"Success can never come up to your dreams about it," she

confessed to *Life* magazine as its pages heralded her acquisition of "a $12,000 skunk-skin coat, a penthouse apartment and a husband." The "husband" returned in mid-August to catch her show at the Coconut Grove. At the tune of $5,000 a week she had literally all of Hollywood at her feet as she quipped from the center platform, "If I'd known there'd be people on both sides of me, I'd have had my nose fixed."

Elliott returned from a London flop to find Barbra as the top young female vocalist in America. He followed her from Los Angeles to Lake Tahoe, where she was due to sing at Harrah's. Everyone thought they were married and they decided it was time to take the plunge. In secret, with a couple of trusty witnesses, they went to a justice of the peace and finally made it legal in Carson City, Nevada, on September 13, 1963.

Signing a paper meant little to them; they had felt married for months. The only difference was that she was now a "name" and Elliott was being called Mr. Streisand when they registered at hotels during her tours. It hurt less because Elliott knew Barbra loved him and had faith in his talent. Besides, as a bulwark against humiliation, he had an offer to do *Once Upon a Mattress* in early 1964 as a color television special with Carol Burnett. Barbra was sure the show would definitely turn the tide for him. But Gould was furious when it was printed that he was her business manager. "I advise her on career choices merely as her man," he bristled. "I am *not* Barbra's manager."

Early in October *The Second Barbra Streisand Album* came out and all predictions proved true. Her fans had been waiting for it so avidly that it sold out in many stores twenty-four hours after the first shipment arrived. The fans again turned out *en masse* for her one-night stand at the Hollywood Bowl with Sammy Davis, Jr. She went on to pack the Arie Crown Theatre in Chicago for two evenings at $8,000 a performance.

At this rate—including royalties from her records—she could have the solid basis of a small fortune in less than a year, but, abruptly, she broke the pace. Basically, she had always wanted to be an actress. Those numbers she dramatized in nightclubs were at best a series of disconnected monologues that would never amount to a complete characterization. There was no chance that anyone would offer her the role of Medea. She was ready to settle for Fanny Brice.

Ever since she had broken audiences up as Miss Marmelstein, pundits had started calling Barbra "the new Fanny Brice." The Gag Writers Association of America had given her the Fanny Brice Award as the best comedienne of 1962; she had received the diploma in Mike Wallace's *PM East* show. After that Billy Rose, Brice's last husband, had come to see Barbra backstage in *Wholesale* and dubbed her the only performer who could possibly do justice to a stage or movie biography of Fanny. Rose later backtracked and told the press that no living actress could ever play the Brice role. By then it was too late: Barbra was already trapped in the fantasy of many influential theatrical personalities as the reincarnation of Fanny.

When Barbra Streisand signed a run-of-the-play contract to play Fanny Brice in an upcoming musical then entitled *My Man*, people in show business politely commented she was making the wrong career choice or impolitely whispered she had flipped her lid. She was walking away from hundreds of thousands of dollars in the nightclub circuit just on the chance of making it as a Broadway star for considerably less money. If the show failed, it remained to be seen whether Streisand could regain her status after a thorough put-down by those notorious grave diggers, the New York drama critics.

Streisand feared success even more than failure. In the new musical she would be playing a Jewish comedienne of such charisma that she could be trapped into a mold if the audience accepted the impersonation. There was also the threat of a long run—and after *Wholesale* Barbra kept saying that she could not even sit in a theater orchestra without feeling trapped.

The odds were against her, win or lose, but she could not refuse the bet. In the fall of 1963 she hopscotched to fulfill her last obligations in cabarets and arenas. Her first starring role was waiting. When she turned up for rehearsals at the Winter Garden Theatre in November, all she found was an unformed, barely palpitating embryo of a show. It did not matter. She would give it spine and marrow, flesh and blood, until it was finally born, five months later, as Barbra Streisand's baby, alias *Funny Girl.*

8. *The Making of a "Funny Girl"*

FUNNY GIRL was almost the show that never happened. Producer Ray Stark had originally wanted to make a movie about Fanny Brice, but, however fictionalized, her story had always been in the worst kind of trouble: family trouble. Stark was married to Frances Arnstein, Fanny's daughter. It was not easy to tell the true drama of Stark's mother-in-law, especially since his father-in-law, Nicky Arnstein, had been convicted of embezzlement, done time in Sing Sing, and was still alive and ready to sue if he felt the picture maligned him.

In the late forties Stark had commissioned a screenplay from Ben Hecht. After reading the first draft, tough, lucid Fanny had demolished it with a quip: "You write it a little fancy, kid, but at least you've got some of it straight." The job was then offered to Henry and Phoebe Ephron, who wrote another abortive version. Brice then decided to tell the story her way and was dictating an autobiography when she died in 1951.

When Stark read the finished memoirs, he did not like the manuscript and bought the plates from the publisher for $50,000; the book was never published. Maybe the true Brice story could never be told. All through the years Stark had failed to interest Hollywood studios in making a movie out of it. There was a bad precedent. In 1939 Twentieth Century-Fox had cast Alice Faye and Tyrone Power in a barely disguised retelling of the Brice-Arnstein episode, called *Rose of Washington Square.* Fanny and Nicky had sued Fox: she for $750,000, he for $25,000. Both settled out of court for undisclosed amounts. After that no studio was ready to go through a similar hassle just to finance another stale backstage musical about a star only old-timers remembered.

Finally, in 1960 screenwriter Isobel Lennart came up with a script entitled *My Man* that pleased both Frances and Ray Stark. But when he circulated it, Hollywood moguls read it with a mixture of wariness and apathy. Stark then decided that the Fanny Brice story had a better chance to be produced as a movie if it was presold to audiences as a stage version. A Broadway production was planned. Stark referred to it as a "dry run," an appropriate term for what would soon become a long trek through a Sahara in which every oasis dissolved into a mocking mirage.

Stark was a successful actors' agent who had represented such stars as Marilyn Monroe and Richard Burton. Through his Seven Arts Company he masterminded such films as *The Night of the Iguana* and *Reflections in a Golden Eye.* For a formidable stage venture he needed the collaboration of a man with the solid theatrical experience he lacked. David Merrick was brought in as coproducer. Thus began what *Funny Girl*'s composer, Jule Styne, calls "a very strange chapter in the Streisand story."

"The original thing," Styne recalls, "was that I was going to do the music, Stephen Sondheim the lyrics, Mary Martin was the star, and Vincent J. Donahue the director. Steve Sondheim and I had our first meeting with Stark and Merrick. A week later Sondheim told me he was not interested in the show if Mary Martin was the choice to play Fanny Brice because although he thought her talents were tremendous, she had not the remotest connection with the Fanny Brice style. When Sondheim bowed out, I never heard from Stark for three months. He then came back and said, 'I have Jerome Robbins to direct and he has been fortunate enough to get us Anne Bancroft. She has read the play and she wants to do it.'

"Frances Stark had loved Anne Bancroft in *Two for the See-*

saw and had her heart set on this fine dramatic actress to play her mother. But Merrick was never in favor of Anne Bancroft. He asked me to go down to the Bon Soir and see Barbra Streisand. I had seen the girl in *I Can Get It for You Wholesale,* in which she had a secondary part. Very funny, but it didn't look like she had the quality one would require for a romantic story like the one Isobel Lennart had written.

"Merrick insisted and I went down to the Bon Soir. It was the first time I'd seen Streisand perform in a café, and I saw a tremendous star dimension that had not been onstage in *Wholesale.* This girl had so much, she tried to do so much that sometimes she did too much. I discounted that because she was so young. I returned to the Bon Soir twenty-seven nights out of twenty-eight in a row. I took several of my friends to see her and got opinions from all sides. They were all in awe of her gifts, not knowing that I already had her in mind to play Fanny Brice.

"It was wishful thinking on my part because even if she had never been announced officially for the role, we already had Anne Bancroft. She was a star and didn't have to do it, but she is a terribly nice person and she came to my apartment to sing twenty songs so that I could get used to what she could do, to what her voice was like. But after watching Streisand three times, I could not put her out of my mind. I was writing the score for someone with that range, that dynamism, that sense of fun. I must say it was all David Merrick's doing. He had suggested Barbra to Ray Stark but Stark would not listen to him. Merrick was now in on my secret. He knew I would be writing in my mind for Barbra Streisand and he loved the chicanery. He knew I agreed with him and we both wanted Barbra.

"I had no clear idea of what sound to use for the songs because we weren't going to bring Fanny Brice back to life. We would just try to persuade an audience that Anne Bancroft was Fanny Brice, using her talents, which are more dramatic than musical. But I was in a bind, compelled to write the score for this tremendously talented sound I had heard out of Barbra Streisand while we still had Bancroft, a great actress but not a great singer. Barbra's voice drew things out of me and Bancroft's didn't. So I told Ray Stark that I would go down to Palm Beach for a while and think it over.

"Sondheim was out and we had no lyricist, but a clause in my contract gave me the choice of a replacement. Several names were suggested, but I felt no chemistry. I was mulling the decision when I met Bob Merrill on the street in Palm Beach. He told me he was there for the summer. I hardly knew him, but I had a hunch. I asked him if he would write words for the four songs I had written, using Isobel Lennart's script as my text and Barbra's voice as my inspiration. I told Bob he might not get the job, that this was being done on speculation, but he agreed. In a period of three weeks he finished the songs: 'I'm the Greatest Star,' 'People,' 'Don't Rain on My Parade,' and 'Who Are You Now?'

"We went to California to meet Jerome Robbins, Anne Bancroft, and Ray Stark at the Beverly Hills Hotel. I told Robbins and Stark that Merrill had written lyrics for those first four songs. We played them and they loved them. I was congratulated on picking a fine lyricist. Merrill got the job before Anne Bancroft arrived at the meeting.

"She was turned off, for several reasons. Part of it was that Robbins had suggested changes to make it less of a drama and more of a musical, but I think most of her reluctance was based on the music she heard that afternoon. It was too difficult for her voice. After she left the show, Stark asked us to change the music because it might frighten off other potential stars, but I said no. The script kept changing every day and those four songs were the only tangible thing we had."

Those four Styne-Merrill songs were the first transfusion of real blood to an anemic show. Isobel Lennart had written a clever fantasy, admitting that she had "avoided digging into the past, which would produce history but not theater." Jule Styne had met Fanny Brice in 1930, when he played the piano during her appearance at the 225, a Chicago gambling club that a gang war closed after one night. He admired the no-nonsense Fanny and felt that the antiseptic libretto did not do justice to her salty personality.

Isobel Lennart confessed she went through hell for a year

with Merrill and Styne, who wanted to inject more realism into the fable. After many a heated discussion they reached a somewhat unstable compromise. The show, of course, would carry no mention of Fanny's first unhappy marriage at age fifteen to a barber. Her passion for gambler Nicky Arnstein would be the squishy center of the candy plot, and Arnstein's conviction for embezzlement would be presented as the result of his pathetic stab at making some quick money so that his wife's fame would not overshadow him. The underlying theme, Ray Stark declared, would be that "men resent women who place themselves on an equal footing with them." Despite the softened premise, Stark still took the precaution to give the eighty-one-year-old Arnstein a sizable sum to keep him quiet.

The musical, nonetheless, seemed to be jinxed. No sooner had its creators gone over one hill than the Himalayas loomed ahead. As it progresses, the *Funny Girl* story becomes a maze of conflicting versions that makes *Rashomon* look as simple as tick-tack-toe. Playwright John Patrick, the author of *The Teahouse of the August Moon*, had been approached originally by Stark to do the screenplay for the Fanny Brice story, but he had instead chosen to write the script for Stark's production of *The World of Suzie Wong*. With that solid hit Patrick won Stark's undying trust and became his consultant on all the trials and tribulations of the Fanny Brice story, in its transition from the embryonic *My Man* to the full-grown *Funny Girl*.

"Throughout the years," Patrick remembers, "Ray Stark asked me to read all of the Fanny Brice scripts that were done. I repeatedly pointed out to him that he was casting the role 'pretty.' I also tactfully reminded him that his mother-in-law had been a rather unattractive woman. He had cast Anne Bancroft, but he told me he wasn't sure about her. I pointed out that she might turn it down, which Ray found ridiculous. As we were talking, the phone rang and it was the lady in question turning it down. Ray then had the script rewritten, and the role came out so exaggeratedly unattractive that I had to advise him to pull back from that extreme."

With the "unattractive" script in one hand and the four excellent Styne-Merrill songs in the other, Stark went looking for a replacement for Anne Bancroft. Styne clearly recollects the ordeal:

"They went looking for girls. I didn't mention that Barbra Streisand was my choice, but I called her agent, Marty Erlichman, and told him that Bancroft was gone and I had a strong feeling that Barbra could do it, but to cool it and let me do all the work. They went first to Eydie Gormé, who turned it down because she did not want to break away from teaming with her husband, Steve Lawrence. They went to Carol Burnett, who was very honest and told them, 'You need a Jewish girl to play this. It's a whole different quality.' They tried many other people, whoever they might be, with no luck.

"Finally, when I thought they were very vulnerable and at a dead end, I said to Jerome Robbins, 'I want you to go down and hear Barbra Streisand sing at a club.' He said, 'Don't go with me, you'll try to persuade me.' Then I took Ray and Frances Stark. He thought she sang well but Fran hated her and told me, 'I'll never let that girl play my mother.' So Ray went along with her and said Barbra was a slob and this and that. Jerry Robbins still had not seen her, so I phoned Arthur Laurents and asked him to give Jerry a call and do some more persuading.

"Robbins was knocked out by Barbra. He said, 'My God, she has many bad habits, but there's never been anybody in my time who sings like that.' He had her come over and read a portion of the play. I can't tell you how horrible she looked. She wore a Cossack uniform kind of thing she'd picked up at a thrift shop. She was freaked out on those clothes then. In the scene she read she was supposed to get emotional and weep. She didn't. Robbins said, 'Barbra, that was not what we worked on.' She sighed and shrank in her chair. Marty Erlichman heard Stark say, 'She's terrible, look at that chin, she'll never play my mother-in-law.'

"Barbra came back for another try and this time she provoked Robbins. He said, 'That isn't it, Miss Streisand,' but she turned on him. 'Mr. Robbins,' said she, 'I can't cry with those words.' Isobel Lennart stood up and applauded. Barbra tried again and every time she couldn't do it. Ray Stark would say, 'See, I told you, I will never allow her to play Fanny.' But Jerome Robbins knew he was dealing with honesty. He couldn't make anybody cry unless the words made it. And Barbra got the job from Robbins, but then he didn't last.

"There had been many changes in the book, and Robbins did not like them. He quit, and when he did, the show was off for about three months. I was involved in producing another musical, *Something More,* and I tried to put Barbra in it, but she said no. She wanted to wait until the Brice story was definitely canceled. For the moment she wanted that or nothing.

"Then we got a new director, Bob Fosse, and the Brice show was on again. Fosse worked four months on it, fashioning the book and the score with us. We loved his ideas, but then, for some unknown reason, Ray Stark wanted to make sure whether Bob was good for it. He went and asked Cy Feuer, who is Fosse's friend and had worked with him on several shows, whether Bobby was really *that* good. Whereupon Feuer called up Fosse and said, 'Gee, boy, your producer has a lot of faith in you! He just asked me if you could bring it off.' Well, Bobby Fosse was hurt and he left us to work on *I Picked a Daisy,* which later became *On a Clear Day You Can See Forever.*

"The Brice show fell apart again. We met a couple of times with Sidney Lumet. We talked about it, but he was dismissed. Barbra didn't like him and Isobel didn't consider his thinking was correct. He had come in after Robbins and Fosse, who thought musically, and Lumet's talent was more along a dramatic line. Nobody liked his ideas and he was gone after a week."

Then both David Merrick and Ray Stark got together on the phone and called Garson Kanin. "They asked me if I would be interested in collaborating on the book with Isobel Lennart," Kanin recalls. "I said no simply because I loathe collaborating. I'm no good at it. I collaborated in four films with my wife, Ruth Gordon, very successfully, but neither of us enjoyed it so I gave that up. As far as directing was concerned, I told the producer I had to know a little more about it, whether it was the kind of show I could do.

"They sent me what they had, and it was a sort of treatment for a screenplay that Isobel Lennart had turned rather quickly and haphazardly into a libretto at Stark's request. Isobel was an excellent screenwriter, but she had no experience in the lyric theater. When I met with Stark and Merrick, I told them their difficulty was not that they had a bad book but that they had no book at all.

"Jule Styne—irrepressible salesman of his own music—turned up at my house with Bob Merrill and they let me hear what they had of the score. I thought it was very good. Not so much the ballads but the musical bridges, the surrounding material was terrific. I still was unprepared to take the job because I had done a previous musical, *Do Re Mi,* with Jule Styne, and I know he is as difficult as he is gifted. I had to consider being involved again in what I knew would be a conflictive situation.

"At that point the star had yet not been definitely chosen, and Stark seemed to be favoring Shirley MacLaine. Several other names were mentioned but only one attracted me: Barbra Streisand. I had seen what I think was Barbra's first performance before an audience in her first Broadway musical, *I Can Get It for You Wholesale.* When that show was about to begin its tryout period in Philadelphia, I was there directing Henry Fonda and Olivia de Havilland in *A Gift of Time.* My whole company was invited to watch a run-through before their opening night. She was magnificent. Hank Fonda had never heard of her, and after the performance all he could talk about was 'that girl, she's fantastic. What's her name?'

"Fanny Brice was a beloved friend of mine, and I felt Shirley MacLaine had none of her special attributes. Here was a story about an unlikely creature from the Lower East Side of New York without anything except talent and a drive that propelled her to the top. I knew Streisand was the ideal choice, so I told Merrick if he could achieve this and convince Ray Stark about Barbra, I would be very tempted to sign for the show. Stark heard about my decision and called me up to say, 'But she's only twenty-one, she's nobody. How do we know she can act? How do we know she can make it?' I told him, 'If you're worried whether she can play the part, that's what I'm here for. She's young, ambitious, she wants to do it, she has the energy. I think I could pull it off.' 'Before we talk any further about this,' Ray said, 'I'd like you to meet Barbra and talk it over with her.'

"We had a very funny kind of lunch because of course I came to it thinking the purpose of the whole thing was for me to make absolutely sure that I wanted her for the role after meeting her face to face. Yet I think Barbra's impression was that *she* was looking *me* over to decide whether she wanted me as director of the show. I liked her personally at once. She was funny, relentlessly ambitious, nothing was going to keep her down. I felt those qualities were very important because they were principal aspects of the Fanny Brice I knew. She didn't seem to be too interested in Brice, and in a way I thought that was right because we were not going to do a documentary but a musical show about a character, a certain type of girl.

"But even after that auspicious lunch Stark kept procrastinating. I think Barbra's diffidence about Fanny had a lot to do with it. Ray Stark was Brice's son-in-law and, to be perfectly candid, Ray was not one of Fanny's favorites. It would have been different if Fanny had lived long enough to observe Stark's success as a power in show business. But when her daughter, Frances, married Stark, he was just a minor agent, and in Fanny's scale that didn't carry any kind of status. He adored her and she made the best of it. Stark had conceived the show as a posthumous tribute to his mother-in-law and he would not allow anyone to spoil it.

"No final decision was being made about a star, and Merrick called me and said, 'Let's go see Barbra at the Basin Street East. I'm inclined to think you're right about her for the show, and if Stark keeps fussing about, it will never get done. You go for her, Jule Styne loves her, and we should all say, let's make a deal with her.' That night we sat through two of her shows at the nightclub. I wanted to see her flexibility, her malleability. Even a trained seal can do the same trick a number of times, but I wanted to see how Barbra reacted to different audiences and whether her ad libs were truly hers or written by a gag man.

"I was convinced she was unique, and we pressed the point with Ray Stark. He conceded and said, 'If you all feel so strongly about her, we'll sign her.'" The official press release about Streisand's selection differs vastly from this version. Ray Stark announced that a friend had shown Frances Stark a picture of Barbra as Miss Marmelstein in the *New York Times Magazine* and she had immediately sensed the resemblance to her mother. But even after all those crucial decisions Streisand's stake in the show became shaky indeed.

"Then the whole show was off," Garson Kanin remembers. "David Merrick and Ray Stark had some kind of disagreement and Merrick was out. Through some technicality at Actors Equity Merrick had signed the contract with Barbra because he was an established Broadway producer and Stark had never had a show on Broadway. Barbra was no longer bound to Stark, and Ray was so fed up with all the wheeling and dealing that he was ready to give up, go back to California, and do the Fanny Brice story as a movie. I stayed on the phone all night—literally—trying to appease both parties. I couldn't let this show fall apart—I owed that girl her big chance. Finally Stark had to negotiate the contract with Barbra from the beginning, and by this time she had Styne and me behind her so she was able to get a much better financial deal."

"That problem was out of the way," Jule Styne recalls. "We were at last getting close to rehearsals. Now comes the day when I play the songs that I had for Barbra Streisand. I went to Chicago, where she was doing a two-night stand in the Arie Crown Theatre. Something very funny happened. She did not like 'People' and she did not like 'Don't Rain on My Parade.' I had to convince her, and they became the two biggest hits in the show. She did like 'Cornet Man,' 'Who Are You Now?' and most of all 'I'm the Greatest Star.' We elaborated on the songs. If she asked for a note to be higher or something changed to suit her comedy style, I would do it. I did not want to restrict her. I wanted the same girl I had flipped over at the Bon Soir."

Back in New York Garson Kanin was busy with the casting. "For the supporting players," he says, "I chose all the people I knew and trusted. Kay Medford, Jean Stapleton, Danny Meehan. Stark especially objected to Kay Medford because she insisted on a six-month contract and I had to tell him very frankly, 'The show is going to stand or fall on Barbra Streisand. The book is not very good and will never be great. The score is fine but it's not *Guys and Dolls* or *West Side Story* or even *Gypsy.* But you have a nova, the astonishing theatrical adventure of the birth of a star. If we can explode Streisand in the Broadway sky, we have a hit.'

"Observing Streisand from the first day of rehearsals, I knew she was one of the great theatrical talents around. That angel, that genius of a girl was so marvelously naïve. She truly was an innocent. If you had told an experienced singer like Ethel Merman or Mary Martin, 'Now you do this terrific song and then you do three choruses of dancing and then you finish another chorus of the song and then you do a dramatic scene,' Merman or Martin would have said, 'Whoa! Wait a second, I'll be out of breath.' Barbra didn't know that. It didn't occur to her. She just had to do it so she did it.

"Ray Stark was producing a film, *The Night of the Iguana,* in Puerto Vallarta, Mexico, and *Funny Girl* on Broadway at the same time. I told him it was impossible to do them both properly. He said, 'Oh, I can spend four days a week in Mexico and the remaining four days of the week in New York with this show.' 'You're giving yourself an eight-day week right there,' I replied. 'Don't worry, I'm very organized,' he assured me.

"So what happened was that Ray came back from Puerto Vallarta on our third day of rehearsals and immediately wanted to fire Barbra. He thought she was not projecting enough, but the truth is that at that time he was an amateur in the theater. What he saw looked drab to him, which indeed most rehearsals do without the sets, costumes, lighting. Worst of all, he kept protesting that Barbra did not look like Fanny.

"Stark was bearing another difficult cross, which was his wife, Fanny's daughter. My original choice for the part of Nicky Arnstein was Jerry Orbach, a fine musical-comedy actor who had done *The Fantasticks* and *Carnival.* I had him learn a couple of the songs, put a mustache on him, and he gave one of the best auditions I've ever seen. I was then told he was not acceptable. Frances Stark had come to the audition and she didn't want Jerry playing her father because she did not like his posture. That's how we ended up with Sydney Chaplin, whom I never wanted for the part."

With all the planets in astrological opposition, Barbra Streisand began to draw on her Taurus willpower to seize the opportunity and move the show into her orbit. The Starks' love for Fanny Brice had dictated the creation of a fairy tale, with Fanny as Cinderella and Nicky Arnstein as Prince Charming. Well, if it was not going to be the Fanny Brice story, at least she could turn it into the Barbra Streisand story.

From the very first day Barbra had refused to study the Brice personality. She did not want to do a cabaret impersonation of Fanny and insisted on inventing the character from scratch. Ray Stark had been unable to clear the rights to "My Man," the Maurice Yvain song that had been Brice's musical signature, so David Merrick had given the show a new title as a parting gift: *Funny Girl.* It cued Barbra's invasion into Brice territory.

Twenty-two-year-old Barbra did not resemble the early Brice at all, though her wide smile and prankish attitude as Miss Marmelstein had brought recollections of Fanny as the mature comedienne who had been radio's Baby Snooks for a decade. The young Brice, though by no means a beauty, had hidden her plainness with makeup; photographs of the twenties show her as an attractive, somewhat vampish woman whom Florenz Ziegfeld discovered in an obscure show, *The College Girl,* and elevated to stardom in his *Follies.*

As Barbra played her, Fanny was an ugly duckling discouraged by her mother from attempting an artistic career. More and more, *Funny Girl* sounded as though it were happening in Diane Streisand Kind's apartment on Newkirk Avenue rather than in Fanny Brice's mother's saloon four decades before. Jule Styne swears a song like "I'm the Greatest Star" was written by Bob Merrill with no inkling that Streisand would play the part or that she even existed. If so, this is a case of theatrical premonition bordering on ESP because the lyrics sound oddly like a musical adaptation of the early Streisand interviews. The relentless drive to succeed, even the obsession with playing Camille, are there.

"Of course I adapted all I could to fit what Barbra did best," Garson Kanin insists. "That's what a competent director does." Despite the many conflicting versions, one thing seems clear: A hitherto rudderless show was taking a direction and becoming Streisand's. The script was crumbling, and into every chink some private anecdote, some unconfessed agony of Streisand's would work itself into the plot and hold a scene together. Her anxiety about Elliott Gould's gambling proclivities gave dramatic substance to Fanny's suffering over Nicky's wild schemes. When Fanny and Nicky parted before the final curtain, she poignantly thanked him for giving her a blue marble egg, just like the one Gould had given Barbra on their first anniversary together. Streisand had Kanin's ear, and the touches she proffered were being added, to everyone's chagrin.

Scenes were being rewritten, changed,. Most of the changes favored Barbra, and the rest of the cast was restless. Allyn McLerie, the ingenue the critics had loved as Amy in Ray Bolger's early-fifties musical *Where's Charley?*, was making a comeback in a featured role in *Funny Girl*, but her part as Georgia was written out and she was let go two weeks before the Boston opening.

Leading man Sydney Chaplin threatened to quit because he wanted a happy ending that would make Nicky Arnstein less of a heel. He was appeased with a promise of some rewrites as soon as the show got on the road. It was an understatement: Before the musical opened on Broadway, he played no fewer than forty different versions of that disputed last scene.

As that dreaded Boston opening approached, John Patrick joined the company in an advisory capacity. He agreed to travel for a while with the show as a favor to Ray Stark, helping out with revisions of the script. "From the beginning," he recalls, "there was great dissension in the group. Everybody seemed to have a quarrel with someone and the atmosphere was electric with hostility." "Garson Kanin was fighting with Isobel Lennart about the libretto," Jule Styne says, "so we had a thing going there." "There was a lot of acrimony," Kanin counters. "There were endless fights between Styne and the choreographer, Carol Haney. It was a bloodbath."

After nearly three years in the works *Funny Girl* had its first public performance in Boston on January 13, 1964. That night the curtain fell at 1:45 A.M. The show had started late because a blizzard was raging, but even allowing for the delay, it was at least an hour overlong. "After the performance," according to John Patrick, "we all sat around a large table in a restaurant and for some reason I was chosen to read the reviews. They weren't good. Barbra was depressed. Isobel Lennart bowed her head on the table and cried. It was not the happiest of evenings."

Elliot Norton, Boston's most influential critic, wrote in the *Herald-American* that the show had a spineless libretto and that the characters of Fanny and Nicky were idyllic to the point of dullness. Norton diagnosed the ailment that would plague *Funny Girl* in all its subsequent versions. The leading man dissolved into a puff in the second act. Nicky Arnstein could not be truthfully presented onstage. He was still alive, and despite all the assurances to Stark, there was still fear that he might sue as soon as a drop of sourness curdled the custard-sweet image Lennart had created.

The real Arnstein is supposed to have inspired the image of the acidulous sport W. C. Fields played so effectively. Hardly the prototype of the romantic hero in a melodrama of doomed passion. Each effort to make the character more realistic clashed both with Lennart's conception and with

Sydney Chaplin's matinee-idol interpretation. "Garson Kanin kept asking for rewrites and we tried everything," Jule Styne says. "We had the denouement with the trial, the lawyers, the whole thing, even a scene in a hospital. That way the second act came on stronger because we showed Nicky's shortcomings, but Fran Stark did not want us to present her father in that light. We lost five songs that way, including a very moving lullaby Arnstein sang to his baby daughter. After a couple of tries the second-act songs for Arnstein had to be discarded. I don't regret the loss because Chaplin could not sing them, he just lacked the range."

"It was not only the songs we lost," Kanin affirms. "There was a lot of dramatic stuff for Barbra in the second act and it all came out in Boston." They started to make up for them with production numbers. John Patrick says, "Stark started to spend money lavishly on quite tasteless things. There was a number in which the chorus girls dressed as babies and spread out in a line on their backs. Then Barbra, dressed in diapers, sang something called, I think, 'How Do You Tell Little Boys from Little Girls?' The number opened and closed in one night at a cost of some ten thousand dollars in discarded costumes, scenery, and orchestrations." According to Kanin, the song was called "Something About Me Is Different." "It was a charming number, but it was sabotaged by those who hated it: Bob Randolph, who did the scenery, and Irene Sharaff, who did the costumes. They never came up with the right look for the number." Among the powers that be in *Funny Girl*, the bloodbath was getting bloodier.

"Garson Kanin's wife, Ruth Gordon, was with him and sat in on all conferences," John Patrick explains. "At one of them I remember Gar looking cautiously about the hotel room and saying, 'This musn't go beyond these walls but I want to tell you what my wife, Ruth, said about Streisand: "She is great, but she is not yet good."'" It was a shrewd assessment of a budding talent. The Kanins had realized Barbra's endless stamina had to be shaped into a coherent performance. Garson concentrated his efforts to bring "sensuality and elegance"—the two qualities he considered essential in Brice—into Streisand's still undeveloped performance.

Barbra had hated the backstage politics in *I Can Get It for You Wholesale,* but the intrigues surrounding *Funny Girl* made her previous show look as bland as a PTA meeting by comparison. Day by day she learned to fight back. She could no longer be the wide-eyed innocent and survive. The *Funny Girl* tour provided the finishing touches to her education as an invincible warrior.

The company thought they had reached the nadir with that terrible opening night in Boston. The show had nowhere to go but up. They were mistaken. Everything that could go wrong went wrong during that hellish Boston run, including one night when Streisand's microphone began to receive radio signals from police cars cruising around the block.

"She did not need that microphone, and how she hated it!" Kanin says. "She could easily fill the theater with her voice, but they strapped it to the inside of her thigh. One day some instant cuts were made, and at the last minute we realized that Barbra could not possibly step out to her dressing room for a change of costume. It was too late, and I told her we had made a terrible blunder that we'd correct the next day, but would she mind stepping into the wings to make a quick change there? She looked a little apprehensive, and I said I'd fix it so nobody would be around to watch. 'I don't mind if anybody sees me bare-assed for ten seconds,' she said. 'I just don't want them to see that damned body mike.' That was so endearing to me that I hugged her because I knew that was her professional pride speaking. Her feelings were hurt that people would assume her voice needed amplification to be heard in a theater."

All those changes in the show further disconcerted her She was a quick study and could learn a dozen pages each day, but there were also new songs and endless reorchestrations. Boston audiences sensed she certainly had something but. . . . was there enough of it to sustain a three-hour show? In the midst of chaos Streisand started trusting her instincts and suggesting her own changes.

There was a seduction scene in which Nicky swept Fanny off her feet during a rendezvous in a restaurant's private dining room. It was initially played in all seriousness as a sexy interlude, but Streisand could sense the audience withdrawing. She began to hoke up the material with a hip-swinging strut, coy giggles, and some hilarious business with a fan she used like a rapier in her duel between the eager rake and the weakening virgin. A new facetious tone grew out of her cheeky improvisation, and the audience started laughing instead of squirming.

The show improved in Boston, but only minimally. Exhausted and demoralized, the company arrived at the Forrest Theatre in Philadelphia on February 4, 1964, for another three weeks of grueling tryout. Director Kanin was complaining to the press that there was not enough time to put "this huge, complex thing into viable shape." Barbra's manager, Marty Erlichman, was lamenting that *Funny Girl* was not a gamble but a suicide risk for his client, who had turned down one million dollars' worth of nightclub and arena work to get into this endless predicament.

Jule Styne can smile now when he recalls: "We had to fight for everything. It may sound incredible, but we had to fight for a song called 'People' because it was the one the director did not like. Bob Merrill, who is a very quiet man, suddenly stood up and he was nine feet tall. He would not let 'People' be deleted. He shouted, 'I'll let you know why this song's gotta stay in. Because it's a great song and Barbra's just made a great record of it.' He told Kanin that if we did not get a big hand for 'People' in Philadelphia, we would take it out and write a replacement. But by then Barbra's record broke through as a tremendous hit. They were recognizing the tune and applauding it even in the overture. It stopped the show, and that rarely happens with a ballad. We even had to have an encore for 'People.'

At the Forrest Theatre the show was beginning to jell, but slowly, slowly. It was a case of too many cooks spoiling a thin broth. John Patrick explains the worsening situation. "In the first conferences, when the director, composer, or producer would turn to me for an opinion, Isobel Lennart burst into tears as she felt ignored. By the time we reached Philadelphia I had learned always to stay *behind* Isobel so that it would appear the question was directed at her."

Patrick could not stand the strain any longer and left. Then Kanin recalls that Stark brought another of this trusted writers, Norman Krasna, all the way over from Switzerland to hole up with Lennart and rewrite the script. As if they didn't have enough troubles, Stark was regretting that he hadn't let Chaplin go when he first threatened to quit. He wanted to replace him, but the male lead had a run-of-the-play contract and firing him was financially hazardous. Kanin remembers Hal Linden came down to Philadelphia to audition for the Nicky Arnstein role and also Darren McGavin.

"This is a very tense group!" had been John Patrick's parting shot. No one was more tense than Streisand. Tom Prideaux of *Life* magazine came down to catch the show in Philadelphia and thought she was "skittish, insecure, and oddly indifferent towards her audiences." With all the discarded scenes, props, and arrangements, *Funny Girl* was steadily rising to a record cost of $650,000, at that date the most ever spent for bringing a show to Broadway. Any other musical in similar straits would have closed out of town, but curiosity about Streisand was so strong that even rumors of an impending fiasco could not stop *Funny Girl.* It was selling out in Philadelphia and had almost a million-dollar advance in the tills of New York's Winter Garden Theatre. "People" was playing on the radio as fast as disc jockeys could spin it. Whatever catastrophe they were all heading for, theatrical tradition had to be honored: The show must go on and it did. On and on and on until desperation set in.

Something odd happened in Philadelphia. This is Jule Styne's version: "The truth is that Garson Kanin, in a very human way, became so fascinated with Barbra's talent that it caused blind spots. It's happened to me too; all you see is the good things. A lot that she was doing was brilliant and a lot of things were wrong. She didn't know where she was in a certain passage. 'Where am I supposed to be?' she pleaded. "Sydney is getting closer in this scene. Where should I move?' Nothing she did was being knocked down because Kanin and Ruth Gordon were so taken with her performance. We had three more weeks to play in Philadelphia and a week of previews in New York.

"So Barbra came to Ray Stark and she said, 'I don't know what I'm doing up there. I know I could be better if I understood what I was doing. I think I'm not being directed enough. I need a lot more direction.' All she heard was how wonderful she was. She used to say, 'But what did I do *bad*?' No one would tell her. I used to go backstage and tell her, 'Gee, Barbra, when you hold onto that chair during that song, it weakens it. You look like a little old lady.' She took up all suggestions; she was eager for some sort of criticism."

Conspiracy was afoot. "I sensed something was wrong," Kanin says with a wry smile, "because all of a sudden Stark and Styne started sending me little presents like a set of antique china for my wife." Styne describes the period as panic time: Ray Stark went back to Jerome Robbins and told him, 'You started this show, now the show needs you.'" Garson Kanin took it philosophically: "My agent called me and said Stark thought he was on the verge of one of the biggest hits ever but that everyone was so fixed in his position that nobody was budging an inch. The time had come for a fresh eye. I said nothing was more welcome, depending on who it was. When I heard it was Jerome Robbins, I said it was a sensational idea. I would have objected to a hack, but Jerome Robbins is one of the three or four authentic geniuses of the American theater and I couldn't be more pleased."

Styne says that Kanin walked out in a huff, but Garson denies it fervently. "I was in on the show at a considerable royalty. I daresay mine was higher than anyone else's, so the success or failure of the show meant a great deal to me from a financial point of view. I stayed with *Funny Girl* through its opening in New York and sold my share of it after it had been running a month or so. The only thing I ever objected to was a codirector credit for Robbins because it would not have been fair. He had worked on the show for only a few weeks, but I'd done all the casting, the basic work. I was given full credit as a director in posters, programs, everything, and Robbins was listed as production supervisor."

After Robbins came in, Styne was elated. "One move that Robbins made improved the first act enormously. He called Bob Merrill and me and told us that the rendezvous scene would never score as Sydney Chaplin's solo. He was singing 'You Are Woman' while Barbra was breaking the audience up with her pantomime. 'You have to make her sing along with him,' Robbins suggested. 'That accompaniment you got is very good and her gestures are funny, but there have to be words for Barbra to tell the audience what she's feeling at the moment.' Merrill and I worked from four o'clock in the afternoon, and by seven we intercepted Robbins in the hotel lobby and asked him to come and listen to what we had. After eight bars he said, 'It's going to be the biggest song in the first act and it's the funniest number I ever heard.' That's how that duet was born, the one in which she is about to be seduced and flutters all over the private dining room. Once we had it the first act leaped from good to smashing.

"That was the kind of thing Robbins contributed," Styne declares, "though most of the fine things in *Funny Girl* are Kanin's ideas." Robbins' greatest job was to stop the squabbling, put the show into perspective, and control Barbra. On February 19, 1964, Robbins was officially announced as production supervisor. It was obvious that *Funny Girl* could not open in New York by February 27, as scheduled. The show moved to the Erlanger Theatre in Philadelphia for three weeks of additional tryouts. The Broadway debut was postponed to March 14, the first of four changes. It was later set for March 22, then moved forward to March 26, then back to March 24. All this scramble with dates puzzled the thousands who had bought their tickets in advance. The consensus was that the producer had a bomb on his hands and was just hesitating about when to set it off.

Funny Girl started previewing at New York's Winter Garden Theatre on March 14. Streisand was chronically late for rehearsals and arrived with no makeup, a bandanna tied around her hair, looking like the Wicked Witch of the West and with just about the same grumpy disposition. She balked at suggestions and argued every fine point, but Robbins was handling her with a tight rein.

"She taunts you with her childish stubbornness, impetuosity, and conceit," Robbins would later say of her. "She concedes you are right without admission and balances all with artistry and grace. Fighting is fun; losing, a camp; winning, the best." It was the ideal working condition for Streisand. She and Robbins were a made-in-heaven match of sparring partners. No mayhem was meant, but no punches were pulled. Barbra was better every day, but the countdown was inexorable. They had to have the critics in before the end of March.

Even in the last week of previews *Funny Girl*'s future was cloudy. Broadway soothsayers predicted that it would be panned by the reviewers, play out its advance, and never recoup its staggering cost. The theatrical crowd whispered that David Merrick was washing his hands a la Pontius Pilate and waiting for the musical to be crucified. At least he had been lucky to get out in time. But backstage at the Winter Garden the true believers forged on heroically.

"Twenty-two songs had been eliminated," Jule Styne says, "and more than twice that number of scenes. On the very last day things were being changed around. We had a seven-thirty curtain for the New York opening. At ten minutes to seven Jerry Robbins was still rehearsing a new version of the last scene. Streisand and Chaplin had learned it that evening around six. When the critics saw that finale, it had never played before an audience before."

Preview audiences had been very receptive, but it was the critics everyone feared. Yet it was impossible to hold back any longer. On March 24, 1964, at 7:43 P.M., the curtain went up, thirteen minutes late. Ready or not, here came Barbra Streisand. As the overture ended, she crossed the stage from left to right, stopped midway. Her shoulders jerked up with the Streisand shrug and she moved on with a here-goes-nothing smirk. She got an ovation. She had feared that first-night tough customers would be hoping for her to fail, but now she realized they wanted her to be marvelous. The first walk-on through the stage was Robbins' psychological ruse to put her at ease. She knew she was not among enemies but well-wishers. She inhaled the admiration, and it set her going like a whiff of pure oxygen. They wanted Streisand? She'd give them Streisand!

The play began with a chorus of misgivings voiced by a group of skeptical card-playing Jewish ladies who warned Fanny Brice's mama that this homely girl could not possibly make it in the theater.

The self-deprecation game was set, and Barbra crashed full tilt against those show-business windmills. In an ill-fitting sailor dress she took the spotlight in stage center and shouted "I'm the greatest star."

They knew it, yes, they knew it, those in the privileged audience at the Winter Garden. The first song transcended itself to become musical autobiography. They saw her cough like Camille, vamp like Hayworth, finagle like Scarlett O'Hara. It was the full repertoire of childhood dreams. She was not afraid to reveal them in all their laughable impossibility. This girl was shameless. She had the knack of releasing the public's repressions like a madwoman suddenly pulling her finger out of the dike.

She laid it straight on the line. She was a misfit all right, but she had not an ounce of self-pity because she was destined to make it to the top. Her frustration erupted into rage because she felt ignored. She was honest to the point of megalomania. She was pugnacious and vulnerable, pathetic and hilarious, delicate and coarse.

They watched her with fascination, torn between a desire to hug her or strangle her, spank her or pet her. Out of such contradictory emotions love is born between mother and child, between man and woman, between audience and star. The waves of applause melted Streisand's diffidence, and soon she was having a love-me-or-leave-me affair not only with Nicky Arnstein but with each spectator. As the first-act curtain fluttered down, she was singing "Don't Rain on My Parade," arms shooting straight out, fingers shaking like a puppeteer's, an invisible string hanging from each of them. The public was responding to every twitch.

The second act was still the problem to lick. All the sentimental fakery about Fanny and Nicky had accumulated in those forty-five minutes. In pure Streisand style she got ready to apply a torch to a marshmallow. As Mrs. Arnstein she became "Sadie, Sadie, Married Lady," glorying in the ownership of an icebox with a five-year guarantee, yet somewhat hurt that her groom was prettier than the bride. She melted the stickiness with a humorous portrait of a woman who had suffocated her husband by loving him not wisely but too well.

After a rousing stage turn as Private Schwartz from Rockaway Fanny kept her uniform on for a meeting with Nicky in her dressing room. In male garb she pleaded to him: "Who Are You Now?" This tear-jerking device had worked beautifully when Judy Garland had had her climactic crying jag in clown's makeup in *A Star Is Born.* Barbra did not weep. In her outlandish Private Schwartz costume she knelt before Arnstein and begged him to face reality. It was uxorial psychoanalysis minus the couch and the Kleenex. The audience responded to the adroit manipulation. Married couples were rubbing knees in the darkened theater; Barbra was more than singing a song, she was playing a recognizable emotion: the fear of not really knowing the one you love. The quiet interlude got audiences ready for the knockout finale.

It had taken years for Isobel Lennart to translate the very special emotional tangle between Brice and Arnstein into domestic terms that millions could identify with. In her final version Nicky had tried so hard to equal Fanny's success that he had failed at one of his get-rich-quick schemes and been caught with his hand in the till. He had been sent to jail and now he was back. It was time for her to be brave enough to stop the emasculation and let him go. The whole charade was unbelievable, but it was shrewdly rigged and Streisand made it compelling.

Since the rights for "My Man" had never been cleared, Styne and Merrill had written "The Music That Makes Me Dance," a substitute torch song that was far more effective for the kind of show *Funny Girl* was. As Nicky faded from her life, Fanny bade him good-bye with this sorrowful tune, but right after it she burst into a reprise of "Don't Rain on My Parade," indicating that Brice was closing up a chapter and going on with her life as a born survivor. The swift transition was schmaltzy but dramatically potent. If Fanny could not have her love, she would have her art. If she could not be Mrs. Arnstein, she would be the greatest star.

In those last five minutes of *Funny Girl* the Streisand-Brice magic fused together. She started singing "Don't Rain on My Parade" haltingly, almost sobbing, then she gathered momentum, burying her past, whamming into her future with a Walkyrian cry. Her arms sprang up to embrace that world, that audience, with an intensity that brought the theater to frenzy. The illusion was complete. Perhaps this Fanny-Barbra had nothing else, but she need not worry. They were there, from front row to top balcony, ready to fill that void, to satisfy that voracious hunger for love.

They cried and yelled and whistled and roared. They would not let Barbra go, for a final count of twenty-three curtain calls. But who can be sure how many there were? How can such adoration be measured? Barbra had just given a superb performance, but the audience felt that she had bared her soul before them. Maybe she was too proud to admit it, but she needed people. Whether she wanted it or not, she would be smothered in the affection she craved in those songs. On the night of March 24, 1964, a dangerous thing happened: The audience adopted her.

For better or worse, like all idols, she would forever belong to this putative family she had just acquired. They would grow in geometrical progression from coast to coast, from continent to continent. They would love her, chide her, forgive her, then disown her and adore her again. And like all families, through all these irrational zigzags, they would ask themselves—in regret, anger, or fear—"Whatever happened to our 'Funny Girl'?"

9. Twinkle, Twinkle, Grumpy Star

THE morning after the opening, predictably, the joy had gone out of the funny girl. In the tritest tradition of backstage musical dialogue, people came up to her and said, "Kid, you've done it again." She froze the fawning entourage with an answer Ruby Keeler would never have uttered in *42nd Street.* "Yeah, what have I done?" she asked.

The *Funny Girl* reviews were good but far from delirious, pointing to the hearts-and-flowers second act as the show's serious flaw. Not even Streisand's energetic performance had been able to convince the critics that a strong marital drama could be sculpted out of spun sugar. Though reviewers were personally favorable, she felt damned with faint praise when Walter Kerr of the *Herald Tribune* wrote, "Everyone knew that Barbra would be a star and she is," or when Howard Taubman of the New York *Times* qualified his approval by saying, "She goes as far as any performer can toward recalling the laughter and the joy that were Fanny Brice."

Barbra moped around backstage, just as she had after the *Wholesale* opening, asking people, "Well, what do they mean? Am I great or am I lousy?" In that second reading with Jerome Robbins she had declared abruptly that she coldn't cry with those lines. By superhuman effort, she had made the audience cry, but critics were made of sterner stuff. They had refused her the tears she had milked out of the first-nighters.

She was skeptical when friends tried to convince her that her notices were exceptional. She cringed when they said

Funny Girl was "an audience show" and was further dejected when assured that it would run at least two years. She had given her all, and now it would be demanded on schedule, eight times a week. Once again she was on a treadmill.

Her *Third Album,* released to coincide with the *Funny Girl* opening, gave her more professional satisfaction than the ovations she was getting nightly. She listened to the record all the time, nit-picking here and there, but generally soothed by its aura of relaxed perfection. It caught Streisand in an exceptionally mellow mood, as if she had used it as a tranquilizer for all the tryout jitters.

Except for some flurries of anxiety in "Never Will I Marry" and her jazzy variations in "I Had Myself a True Love," the *Third Album* was her first unqualified "party record," the one that could be listened to while carrying on a conversation. In its quiet, unobtrusive way it was also her first bid at performing in the vocally supine, cabaret manner of a *chanteuse.*

Close listening reveals it as much more than background music. In ballad after ballad she alters the basic rhythm and makes each song indisputably hers: "Melancholy Baby" becomes a lingering lullaby for adults, and "Just in Time" is almost a church hymn, in a Leonard Bernstein special arrangement based on Gounod's *Ave Maria,* played by a distant harpsichord. Once again Streisand was changing direction. To breathe new life into old standards, she was trading cries for whispers. The experiment was received with caution; many felt she had begun to be very careful with her voice and was losing the intensity that had catapulted her to the top.

At Columbia Records Barbra had insisted on calling the album *The Fourth* because she wanted to skip three, a number she dislikes. Her objection was overruled as capricious, but when she received guarded notices, she felt her superstition had been justified. "What do they want from me?" she wondered. If she pulled all the stops, she was called obstreperous; if she aimed for subtlety, she was too tame. She disregarded criticism and played the record again and again to absorb that sound once more. Time would prove her right, and the *Third Album* would come into its own as one of the cornerstones of the Streisand cult.

"Barbra does not demand total adoration," Jule Styne affirms. "But when you tell her she's doing something wrong, you have to be prepared to explain *why.*" The reviews of *Funny Girl* and the *Third Album* gave her no clues. She grew more distrustful and reserved. The chip on her shoulder was never carried with more nonchalance than in the Playbill biography she wrote for *Funny Girl.* Sentence by sentence, she alternately puffs and deflates herself with a merciless pin for every toy balloon.

> In addition to having appeared off-Broadway, on-Broadway and away from Broadway in nightclubs, on television and on the concert stage, Barbra Streisand is the recipient of *Cue* magazine's Entertainer of the Year Award. A top recording star, a talented interior decorator, dress designer and portrait painter, she also plays field hockey. Her performance in the musical *I Can Get It for You Wholesale* stopped the show and was much admired by the critics, the public and the show's leading man, Elliot [sic] Gould, who married her. Barbra is a follower of Eastern philosophy and cooking, but also favors TV dinners on occasion. Her favorite day is Tuesday, since she devotes part of each Tuesday throughout the year to stringing crystal beads which are sold in a Vermont general store. She knows how to make coffee ice cream and fix her own hair. For more personal information, write to her mother.

Diane Streisand Kind's address was not necessary to find out a lot more about Barbra. On April 10, 1964, two weeks after *Funny Girl* opened on Broadway, *Time* magazine gave her a glowing cover article. Then, in rapid succession, she was on the cover of *Life, Show,* and *Cosmopolitan.* Even self-doubting Barbra began to believe it: She had arrived.

Triumph was sweet, with an edge of bitterness. In the Playbill biography Elliott's name had been misspelled. In the *Time* article she was pictured with him in a swimming pool, her hand obliterating his face. The caption read: "Water frolicking with husband." The photo comprised a thousand words of disappointment. For the moment Gould was just "husband." His *Once Upon a Mattress* television special had been taped in March but would not be shown until June. He was inactive and despondent. Barbra bought a huge Jacobean bed for their luxurious penthouse and had curtains installed around it, to make it look as private and secluded as a Pullman berth, but even that could not stop the world from peeking into their lives and measuring the ever-widening gap in their professional status.

On April 25 her first record won the Grammy Award as Album of the Year, and she copped a second trophy as Best Female Vocalist of 1963 for "Happy Days Are Here Again." Elliott was not with her at the ceremony and there was talk about a trial separation. The truth was that he had accepted an offer to make his movie debut in *The Confession* and had left for Jamaica three days before. *The Confession* was produced by William Marshall, Ginger Rogers' husband, and starred Rogers as a bordello madam, with Ray Milland as co-star. Streisand consoled herself for Elliott's absence by telling reporters that he was destined to become "the American Jean-Paul Belmondo."

Gould had to make seven changes of planes to get back and forth from the Jamaica location and spend weekends with Barbra. Even his hectic traveling did not stop the rumors about an imminent breakup. They were compounded with innuendos about a romance between Barbra and her co-star, Sydney Chaplin. Blind items sprouted in columns, coyly asking what young superstar had fallen in love with her lead in a big musical. Chaplin was a man of great personal charm who had given columnists a field day in the late fifties when he had supposedly mesmerized Judy Holliday during their long run in *Bells Are Ringing*. The new stories read the same, as if idle gossips were merely substituting one leading lady for another, in search of a proven catch for readers.

Stars learn to grin and bear these problems as another mean trick of their trade, but it was Barbra's first encounter with the hazard and she took it badly. To scotch the rumors, she developed an attitude of hostility toward Chaplin as the *Funny Girl* run progressed. Her only bitter comment about "publicity romances" would come years later in Hollywood when she complained, "In this business if you get along with your co-star, you're having an affair; if you don't get along, you're having a feud." But this more mature point of view did not help her at twenty-two, when her marriage was as shaky as her self-confidence.

Elliott came back from Jamaica in utter disenchantment with *The Confession,* in which he played a character called The Mute. The film—later retitled *Quick, Let's Get Married*—was shelved for several years and finally had very spotty theatrical distribution in the early seventies with still another title, *Seven Different Ways,* before it was sold to television. It is ignored by Gould, who credits *The Night They Raided Minsky's* (1968) as his first movie.

Elliott's setback was soon followed by Barbra's. For the kid who never had toys, awards had become substitutes for that hot-water bottle she had played with back in Brooklyn. She had won a couple of Grammys, and now she coveted the Tony, Broadway's equivalent of the Oscar. Her *Funny Girl* was up against formidable opposition: Carol Channing's *Hello, Dolly!* In a Sunday night Actors Fund performance of *Funny Girl* Barbra faced an audience of her peers, the very people who would decide whether to vote for her or Channing. Streisand was inspired and even topped her opening-night tour de force. Channing was sitting in the eighth row of the orchestra, with floppy hat and inscrutable countenance. When Barbra exploded into "Don't Rain on My Parade," an electrified audience felt she was singing it directly at her rival.

May 24, 1964, was Tony Award night on Broadway. *Funny Girl* had garnered eight nominations, including one for Streisand. She attended the ceremony in a demure pink lace blouse atop a brown moiré skirt, an outfit that even *Women's Wear Daily* praised, selecting that ex-kook, Mrs. Gould, as one of the six best-dressed ladies in the gala.

As predicted, the award for the best leading actress in a

musical went to Carol Channing. *Hello, Dolly!* won ten Tonys and Barbra went home empty-handed. The Tony would be the only award ever to elude her. Five years later, in 1969, she was voted a plaque as Star of the Decade, but it seemed like the same kind of afterthought with which a conscience-stricken Hollywood finally honored Garbo and Chaplin. In competition, both as Miss Marmelstein and as Fanny Brice, Streisand was thumbed down by Broadway.

There was more chagrin in store the following month, when Elliott's *Once Upon a Mattress* was telecast. The success that Barbra had predicted for him failed to materialize. He was very good as the foolish prince, but it was hardly a charismatic performance in an abbreviated and dull staging of the fifties Broadway hit. Whatever praise the critics had went to the star, Carol Burnett. For Elliott no offers were forthcoming in New York. He signed to go on tour with Liza Minnelli in *The Fantasticks*.

Streisand was left alone in her cavernous penthouse. Career problems were forcing her to drift apart from Gould, so she started plans to draw him closer into her realm by joining financial forces. An intricate series of corporations was founded, under titles like Ellbar and Barbell, linking parts of their names into a legal chain that would bind them to each other in the production of a full gamut of projects in the entertainment world, from the creation of television shows to the publishing of sheet music.

Barbra was taking a cue from one of her *Funny Girl* songs: As a married lady she was proclaiming herself a corporation now, "not me, myself and I." But no matter what the legal documents said, Barbra and Elliott's situation was getting dangerously close to Fanny and Nicky's in the play. She was the successful wife of a frustrated man whose golden chance was endlessly postponed. All the juggling of syllables could not obscure the fact that Streisand was the pillar that supported Ellbar and Barbell.

When Elliott was not on the road with a touring show, he would roam Broadway, sometimes unshaven, wearing a frayed and stained raincoat, waiting until it was time to pick up Barbra at the Winter Garden. He disliked going into the theater and preferred to wait on the sidewalk. He went unrecognized by her stage-door crowds, smoking incessantly, with his foot perched on the fender of the cream-colored Bentley his wife had recently acquired. He was no stage-door Johnny; he was the husband. That was what really hurt.

Linda Gerard, who was Barbra's stand-by for almost a year, remembers that in all that time Elliott came into the theater only a couple of times. "But she was thrilled every time she was told he was downstairs. She would rush madly as she took off her makeup and changed. I kept wondering, 'My God, she can have any man she wants and she gets all upset about Elliott. Of course, he was really down at the time and no one had a crystal ball to predict his star potential. Then I really thought he had no looks, no charm, nothing. Total zero."

It was an unavoidable fact: Nobody wanted him and everybody wanted her. CBS and NBC had been vying for Streisand as a television star, and on June 22, 1964, Ellbar Productions signed a platinum-edged contract with CBS. For three specials in the next two years Barbra received a guarantee of more than a million dollars. Her minimum take over ten years would reach five million. Furthermore, Barbell would have control over the material. In plain language it meant that Barbra could devise her own shows and present herself exactly as she wanted.

With this bonanza in sight, she went on a gigantic shopping spree, filling every empty corner in her life with possessions. She surrounded herself with decorators and bought only the best for her palatial apartment. There was an Aubusson rug for the living room and five chandeliers, including one for the bathroom. She coupled exquisite taste with a sharp bargaining sense. She was once spotted at the New York Coliseum Antique Show, delicately holding a piece of Art Nouveau glass to catch its iridescent colors in the light. In her most stylish manner she asked the booth attendant for the price, then instantly toppled into enraged Brooklynese: "You mean you want two hundred dollars for this tiny thing?"

Barbra refused to be robbed blind, but by then she could

easily afford it. On July 12, 1964, her Sunday night off from *Funny Girl,* she staged her first big concert after her Broadway triumph. To the Forest Hills stadium she brought 15,000 screaming fans, for a take of more than $80,000. It was an unforgettable turn in which she lorded over an unruly crowd like a benign empress, stunning them into silence by making it clear—with just a fleeting frown—that she disapproved of hysteria. No one would be allowed to interrupt her with a "We love you, Barbra" shriek. She was not a grateful, self-pitying Judy Garland. Either you respected her work or walked out.

In the center of this maelstrom of adulation Barbra never preened. She had become a master at self-deprecation. She repeated—as she often would in stadiums—her joke about the nose, which would have been fixed earlier if she'd known she'd have a throng on each side of her face. When her diaphanous toga fluttered in the breeze, she called it "my fancy nightgown." She sang on a stand in the middle of the huge tennis court, too far from the fans who wanted to be near the magic presence. When they shouted, "Come closer," she explained that it had rained that afternoon, the grass was still wet, and she had been warned she might be electrocuted if she trailed the cord of her hand microphone in it. But even cool Barbra was drawn by the red-hot frenzy. The shouts ignited her and she finally walked on the soggy turf, getting nearer to the bleachers, in an act of mad daring that gave the audience a thrill comparable to watching El Córdobes risk his life for an *olé* in the Barcelona bullring.

The Forest Hills concert proved that Barbra was growing into more than a star. Teenagers identified with her as the underdog who had beaten parental opposition and corporate indifference to become somebody. Plain girls looked in their mirrors twice and felt that they too could be as beautiful as Barbra. Pseudo-Streisands sprouted everywhere, in their beehive hairdos, proudly displaying prominent noses and heavily mascaraed beady eyes. Behind the counters of dime stores, at the cash registers in hamburger stands, strap hanging in sweltering subways, the little girls marched, a platoon of hopeful Barbras, waiting to be "discovered" before the sun set on their fervent dreams.

Along her meteoric rise to the top Barbra had been feeding her audience on fantasies of success against impossible odds. Now the fans were legion, a starved Hydra-headed monster that kept begging for more and more, ready to devour her. The kids stood at the door of her Central Park West apartment house, waiting for hours to catch a glimpse of their redeeming goddess in the flesh. They followed her everywhere, proffering jars of chicken soup, asking for autographs.

Barbra's life was no longer her own. Biting into a spare rib in a restaurant, she would be accosted by gushing mothers who asked her to sign a napkin to bring back to their daughters, just to prove that they had *really* seen her. Streisand would wipe her sticky fingers and comply. As the pressure mounted, the star syndrome—with all its incipient paranoia—started to set in. She was seized by a very human reaction of fear. She was becoming public property, at the mercy of anyone who wanted to stop her in the street and paw her all over.

She detected that look of recognition in their eyes and fled before they pounced on her, shouting, "Hi, Barbra." She had to restrain an impulse to reply, "We haven't been introduced." Many stars have learned to fob off these attacks by saying they've been told they look like Kirk Douglas or Dustin Hoffman, but that they're not really he. But Streisand was unique. Her looks were widely imitated but intrinsically inimitable. When she was caught, there was no way out.

Once, in a traffic intersection, even the policeman on duty stopped her car and asked her for an autograph for his little niece, who adored her. "And what's the matter with you? You don't like me?" she quipped as she signed. She could still manage a smile, but her patience was getting frayed. Being naturally shy, she could not understand the aggressiveness of others. Mae West had been the idol of her adolescent years. Once when she was singing in Detroit's Caucus Room, Miss West had been playing in a nearby theater. Barbra had caught her show, applauded like mad, but would never have dared go up to the star and say, "Hi, Mae." She felt West owed her nothing beyond her performance; once she was offstage she was a private person.

Now the tables had turned and Streisand was no longer the fan but the idol. How could people be brazen enough to approach her as she never had Mae West? Around this time, when interviewers asked her the same trite question about what she disliked most, she would answer, "People who get familiar and call me Barbra as if they'd known me forever." It sounded snobbish, but it was said not in anger but in mourning for the privacy she had lost.

Barbra loved frankfurter stands and "greasy spoon" restaurants, but she could never go into one without attracting attention. When she craved French fries from Nathan's or a hamburger from the White Tower, she had to send someone—usually Elliott—to bring it back so she could gorge herself in the backseat of her Bentley. Ever since her childhood, she got a thrill from taking candy bars and saving the wrappers as trophies of her daring, but how would it look now if Barbra Streisand were caught pilfering a Milky Way? She was living in a cliché, the star's goldfish bowl, and she could not stand the transparency.

She was being watched. Everything she did was good for a line or two in the daily columns. If she sent back an overcooked steak in a restaurant, it was a black mark on the cuisine; if she walked out of a boring movie, it was reported as a slur on the quality of the performances. She felt constantly perused and criticized: Nothing she did was right. If she rented a chauffered limousine, she would be called hoity-toity, but if she drove her own car, that wouldn't look right either. Attempting to walk down twenty blocks from her apartment to the Winter Garden Theatre was out of the question: She could have provoked a street riot.

Freedom-loving Barbra was forced to retreat. Whenever Elliott was in town from his *Fantasticks* tour, they closed the curtains of their Jacobean bed and watched horror movies until dawn on a tiny TV set. Next to the bed they had a small refrigerator stacked with bricks of Breyer's coffee ice cream. On top of it was a photograph of Barbra licking a lollipop, parodying a pose from the movie *Lolita*, inscribed in misspelled baby talk: "Eleot, I wuv you." They were increasingly trapped into a secluded existence.

Worst of all, fame had not brought her security. She was once instantly depressed in the middle of lunch when a chatty waiter asked her if she had any definite plans for when *Funny Girl* closed and she'd be out of work. Barbra had read too many fan magazines back in Brooklyn and was haunted by still another cliché: the soap bubble. It all had happened so fast that, pessimistically, she was counting the minutes until everything would go bust.

The chronic worrier was just inventing phantoms. She was a coveted name and kept getting bids from the highest places. Streisand was one of the Broadway luminaries invited to attend President Johnson's inaugural gala on January 15, 1965. She arrived in Washington, far more nervous than on her previous visit to the White House, when she had sung for President Kennedy. Now she had more to lose.

William A. Raidy, a theater critic who was one of the organizers of the artistic part of that event, now remembers the occasion with a shudder:

"Barbra moved her head incessantly, trying to show the best side of her face to hundreds of cameras. Elliott held onto her elbow, sweating so profusely that I thought he might collapse from dehydration any moment. I had met Barbra when she was singing at the Bon Soir. Mme. Nicole Alphand, the French ambassador's wife, told me she adored Streisand and asked me to introduce her. The lady told Barbra that she was her favorite singer, that they played her records all the time at the embassy, and that it was a great thrill to be able to talk to her. 'Oh, yeah?' Barbra replied. End of conversation. I could have died right there. Luckily, I grabbed hold of Carol Channing and she did her whole delighted-to-meet-you number for Mme. Alphand. I still don't know why Barbra behaves like that. Is it shyness or ignorance?"

It was really mortal fear of people, of doing the wrong thing or coming up with the irreparable gaffe. Frank Sinatra once sent her a note telling her he loved her records. When they finally met at a party, she had no idea what to do or say. Sinatra sat her down on a chair and walked away to get her a glass of champagne. When he came back, instead of waiting for him to sit next to her, she stood up at attention, as if the school superintendent had walked into her class. They drank in rigid silence until he was able to put her at ease.

The anecdotes about Barbra's gaucheries multiplied. People loved hearing them and then repeating them with embellishments. By the time the story about her reply to Mme. Alphand had made the rounds it was upgraded: It was Queen Elizabeth II who had received the "Oh, yeah?" treatment. It sounded better, more impudent that way. Streisand accepted the jokes, even capitalized on them. "I am a cross between a princess and a washerwoman," she said. Put these two elements together and you get a colorful character. From the time when she dyed her hair red and painted her face white Barbra knew the formula was right. She would be anything but a nonentity.

Backstage at the Winter Garden Theatre she was every inch a princess. She had a dressing room furnished with Empire and Directoire furniture, paisley walls, a paisley-covered couch, and a chandelier. As if this display of luxury were not enough to rile an envious cast, Barbra had assumed the task of supervising everything that happened onstage. She wanted *Funny Girl* to look absolutely perfect for each customer who parted with his money for a ticket. She could not abide the slackness that erodes performances after the long-run inertia sets in.

She started sending memos, as profusely as David O. Selznick. She would notify the conductor that the trumpet was coming on too loud in one number. She sent the prop man a note informing him: "The wax flowers in the dining room set are dusty." She called for extra rehearsals to see that the chorus was perfect to the last step. When she was told to relax a little now that *Funny Girl* was an established hit, she riposted that it was *her* show and therefore it was her responsibility to have the best support possible from all quarters. She knew if the customers came out unhappy, they would blame *her* for their disappointment.

Behind the curtain at the Winter Garden Barbra claimed she knew what kind of an audience she would get just by listening to the rustle as they got into their seats. She gauged her performance to this psychological lead: She was scared of theatergoers. These people out there were not swarming in to see an unknown. They had been told she was great and she could not fail them. She wanted to adjust what she did for Wednesday-matinee ladies who came in a bus from the suburbs or for Saturday-night expense-account sharpies on their way to supper at an elegant bistro. Her swift changes of mood were unwelcome.

She was willing to try anything to brighten a performance that could go stale in her mind. William Goldman, in his Broadway chronicle, *The Season,* writes that late in the run he saw Streisand play Fanny Brice in the manner of Jerry Lewis. John Patrick, who had watched Barbra from the very first day in *Funny Girl,* went back one evening with Ray Stark to check on the show and was appalled. "She had now become confident; she wouldn't listen to anybody and was introducing tasteless things like something referred to as 'the shuffle.' Stark was so outraged at her improvisations that he threatened to go backstage and announce to the audience that the show was canceled and they could have their money back. I implored him to let the actors finish and then express his feelings privately."

There were reports about muffled reprimands from Actors Equity. Barbra was being forced to play *Funny Girl* by rote. She channeled her creative energy into the taping of her first CBS television special. Through her Ellbar corporation Streisand had artistic control of the show and fashioned it completely around herself, with no invited stars in guest spots to give her support. "If I fail," she said, "I want to be the only one to blame." The frame she chose, predictably, was autobiography. The show wildly accelerated nature's processes so that the larva could emerge from the cocoon and turn into a butterfly in a mere sixty minutes.

My Name Is Barbra, first telecast on April 28, 1965, is another installment of the Streisand story. It started with a wistful evocation of childhood. "I'm Five," she told the world in a fresh but highly disputed outburst of independence. Then there was the joy of imagining herself as every animal in Darwin's canon, from polar bear to oyster. The baby talk ended painfully with a moving panegyric to that pristine creature "My Pa." Infantile fantasies were soon deflated. As a nostalgic adult Barbra asked the question with no possible answer: "Where Is the Wonder That I Used to Know?" This loss of innocence was just a step away from the plaintive hankering for "Someone to Watch Over Me."

As audiences were wiping away tears shed over the listless waif, Streisand turned her back on unsolicited pity and returned full of bravado for the second third of the program. Shot in the posh Bergdorf Goodman department store, it presented the urchin as winner, strutting around in the most expensive regalia imaginable. She outrageously mocked every pop standard tune about destitution, from "I Got Plenty of Nothin'" to "Brother, Can You Spare a Dime?" Clad in leopard skins, ostrich feathers, crushed velvet, she sang "Give Me the Simple Life" and stopped short of showing the astronomical price tags as she proclaimed, "The Best Things in Life Are Free."

The third segment was a Streisand concert in cabaret form, including her interpretation of "My Man," the Fanny Brice number she had not been able to sing in *Funny Girl.* She used it to underline her basic differences from Fanny. Instead of a straightforward twenties version, Streisand let go with all the sobs and ululations she could muster, underlining the fact that she was not the second Brice but the first Streisand.

My Name Is Barbra was released in two installments as a double album, but number one tells the whole story in the graphic design of its blurbless jacket. The front cover is a snapshot of Barbara Joan at seven in a frilly dress, attempting a woebegone smile as if even then she could not manage to say cheese for a cajoling photographer. The back cover shows Streisand in full glory, swathed in green crepe, reclining as a tongue-in-cheek odalisque.

Both the television show and the record indicated a clean break with the past. The little girl from Brooklyn and the flabbergasting kook were to be buried, now supplanted by a refined, resplendent woman. It was the end of Barbra and the beginning of Streisand. Shortly after *My Name Is Barbra* was greeted with glowing notices and high ratings, an enterprising reporter tried to cook up a pictorial feature about Barbra coming back to Brooklyn, to be photographed on Pulaski Street, Nostrand Avenue, and in front of the Loew's Kings. She coolly refused. She had no connection with that neighborhood anymore; even her mother had moved to Manhattan.

The television show gave Streisand her first grip on Middle America, where she had been known only by people who bought the newest records and followed current events in national magazines. Now she was ready to be recognized by everyone, even those mythical cowboys she had longed to impress. Three days of work in front of a camera had given her entry into millions of living rooms, from Maine to California. After that the Winter Garden Theatre seemed tiny and constricting.

The situation backstage had worsened. Streisand knew her cancellation of a performance in *Funny Girl* would bring hundreds of angry theatergoers back to the box office for a refund. No matter how tired she felt, she'd never miss a show. Her professionalism under duress was misinterpreted. The Broadway rumor was that she was afraid her understudy, Lainie Kazan, would overshadow her. When finally Lainie Kazan got to play Fanny Brice, it was for only one night. Soon after, Lainie was given her notice and Linda Gerard was personally picked by Barbra to stand by for her. Linda now very frankly explains the incident, which sounds like a scene from *All About Eve:*

"The trouble started with Lainie Kazan. Someone told

Barbra that Lainie had said that if she ever went on, she'd have to use a lot of makeup to look as ugly as Streisand. Barbra has this tremendous talent and everything going for her, but she's always insecure. I don't know why. And, believe me, Lainie Kazan didn't help with that basic insecurity. One Saturday matinee Barbra was sick and Lainie was at last notified she would play Fanny Brice. It was her big chance, and she called the press and told them to come and watch her. Barbra found out in time and insisted on doing the matinee. But she was really sick, and the doctors advised her that she might lose her voice for a week if she did the evening show. Lainie played that Saturday night and she made every column, every entertainment page, even the news on television. She never played it again. By Monday Barbra had recovered through sheer will power, and soon after I was chosen as Barbra's standby. Of course, there was a clause in my contract that if I ever got to play the role, no one would be notified in advance."

Linda Gerard spread balm over the waves in *Funny Girl*. She found Barbra kind, warm, and generous. They were the best of friends from the first day. "We confided in each other, we were buddies," Linda remembers. "She was the most cooperative of performers. Every time she introduced new business into the show, she would tell me to watch it so that I would be perfect when I went on. I once complimented her on a new black dress she'd bought, and she smiled and said, "It's yours.' I joined *Funny Girl* in March, 1965, and her birthday was in April, so I was one of the organizers of the party the cast gave for Barbra at the Spindletop. We all chipped in and bought her a white poodle we named Sadie, for her second-act song in the show."

A story did the rounds at the time: A chorus boy was overheard saying a week after the Spindletop party, "We inoculated the dog with rabies but it didn't take." Linda Gerard is appalled to hear it and gasps, "Oh, that is so nasty! I'm sure it's not true at all. I never heard anything against Barbra. I admit I was closer to her than to most of the rest of the cast, but if there had been that kind of animosity, I would have felt it and I never did. Backstage the only conflict was with Sydney Chaplin."

Streisand's relationship with her leading man had deteriorated beyond repair. Earl Wilson's column reported that they took different sides of the stage before their joint curtain calls. It was rumored that Barbra turned her face away from the audience and exploded bubble gum in her co-star's face before the crucial first-act kiss. Linda Gerard denies it vehemently:

"I was backstage at every single show and that *never* happened. It couldn't have. Barbra is too much of a professional to jeopardize her show with such silly pranks. If anyone was out of order, it was Sydney Chaplin. He was very rude to her, onstage and off. He used to curse constantly and Barbra hated that. I never heard her utter a dirty word, even in the worst moments of backstage stress, but with Chaplin every third word started with an *f*. He did terrible things, like clearing his throat very audibly while she was singing 'People.' I used to tell Barbra not to get upset about him because he was ruining his own performance, not hers, but she felt the show was suffering, and despite the fact that he had a run-of-the-play contract, she brought matters to a head."

Chaplin demanded to leave the show and Actors Equity became an arbiter in the dispute. There was a hush-hush meeting at Sardi's Restaurant on June 11, 1965. The male co-star was given the right to abandon *Funny Girl,* though it was diplomatically stated that Miss Streisand had the highest regard for his ability. A week later Sydney Chaplin gave his last performance as Nicky Arnstein and was replaced by his understudy, George Reeder, until a suitable name was found to fill the gap.

"Once Sydney Chaplin was out of the show," Linda Gerard recalls, "there were auditions for his replacement. About twenty guys were up for the part. Top talent from New York and some that even flew in from California. I would do the scenes onstage with them and Barbra watched from the seventh row. Afterward she would ask me, 'What did they say about me?' I told her, truly, that they all thought that she was terrific. But I felt that, of all of them, Johnny Desmond had made the scenes come more alive. Barbra liked him too, and he was hired to play Nicky Arnstein. She got along very well with Desmond, and the show ran smoothly with not a single problem backstage."

Johnny Desmond stepped into the musical on August 18, 1965. A week after, Streisand had another rubdown with mass adoration at her second Forest Hills Stadium concert. This time she was not as successful in appeasing a crowd that had become belligerent and rowdy. They had listened to all her records and insisted on singing along with Barbra, swilling beer and munching popcorn. The throngs were marching to the different drum she had started banging, and now they wanted a piece of the action, however piddling. She tried to soothe them with jokes and banter, but often she could not be heard above the din. Many true Barbraphiles left in a huff during intermission.

On September 13, 1965, when Streisand won one of the five Emmys awarded to *My Name Is Barbra,* she concluded that she could reap greater benefits by giving television performances that were more widely viewed, more lasting, more profitable, and, above all, more controlled. *My Name Is Barbra* was hers forever and nothing could spoil it. But her concert audiences were getting out of hand, and she still had to give *Funny Girl* mouth-to-mouth resuscitation every evening.

"In her last three months with the show," Linda Gerard observes, "her mind was elsewhere. She was involved with her records, she was preparing her second television show, she was going to take *Funny Girl* to London next April. I got to play the part about eighteen times in that period. I will never forget the first time. Barbra was going to Philadelphia for the opening of Elliott Gould's new show, *Drat! the Cat!* She told me, 'You're going on this weekend,' and then sent me two dozen roses with a card that said, 'Have a ball.' She had all those projects of her own, and yet the thing she wanted most was for Elliott to have a hit."

Drat! the Cat! was a musical fantasy with Elliott Gould in the lead part. He had ebulliently rehearsed for what he thought was a sure bet for stardom. Broadway wags were convinced that Barbra was producing the show to save her husband from oblivion. The truth is that each had a very modest $850 stake in *Drat! the Cat!* Elliott was fuming at suggestions that Streisand had invested $100,000 to keep the venture afloat.

Drat! the Cat! was far from a vanity show. It was a charming confection, half fairy tale, half Keystone comedy. The Goulds had every right to think that it would be successful. A longer out-of-town tryout could have tightened its wispy elements into the exactly required equilibrium, but *Drat! the Cat!* had a limited budget, and it was rushed in front of the Broadway critics after a week of low-price previews at the Martin Beck Theatre. Barbra had always said that pigs were her favorite animals, and she presented Gould with a live one as a good-luck token on opening night. It proved to be an omen for the ensuing slaughter. *Drat! the Cat!* had been born prematurely. Tepid reviews did not offer the required incubator, and it died within five days.

The quick fold of Gould's musical was a brutal blow to his ego. Barbra had picked up his best song from the score, "She Touched Me," and recorded it for the second *My Name Is Barbra* album. Elliott had sung it expertly, sitting on the proscenium, feet dangling above the orchestra, with the shy character's trembling hands pressed together as if he were controlling himself by doing isometric exercises. Nothing happened: There was no catch for the audience but his utter sincerity. The song would have died with the show, but when Barbra applied her stardust to it, the forgotten number became memorable. She sang "He Touched Me" as a tender valedictory to Elliott's fine, unrecognized performance. Yet, ironically, in people's minds, it had nothing to do with him. It was later included in a portfolio record as one of *Barbra Streisand's Greatest Hits.*

In August, 1974, nine years after the fact, when he was interviewed on the Merv Griffin television show, a successful Gould was able to joke calmly about the period. He said that after Barbra had made it popular, the song was labeled in sheet music as "He (She) Touched Me." But in 1965 Elliott had a crisis of self-confidence and began his five years in analysis, because he felt that "before you can tell the world who you are, you first have to learn it by yourself."

Streisand had learned her lesson by watching *Drat! the Cat!* Now she knew how easily a good show could be scuttled by lack of precision. Annoyed at the slackness of the *Funny Girl* troupe, she called a special rehearsal with the chorus. "She's taking it out on us because her husband's show flopped," she overheard a dancer say. Streisand confessed she was more depressed than irked by "the workings of such a warped mind." Wanting to tighten her own show, she was being called a frustrated termagant. "This is a terribly bitter profession," she commented. "Everyone will call you honey, but they are out to cut your throat every time. If I had not made it by now, I would have given it all up. I couldn't have stood becoming as bitter as some chorus people twice my age."

She was through with the Broadway agonies. By Christmas of 1965 Barbra had the best possible present: She left *Funny Girl* to prepare her second television special and then take the Fanny Brice musical to London in the spring for a limited engagement. On her last night at the Winter Garden she left a stack of memos for the conductor, the stage manager, the light man, with suggestions on how to improve the show. Elliott gave her a gold-plated bagel as a closing-night present. The kids were still playing games, now a little half-heartedly.

No matter how hard they tried, when the curtain had fallen on *Drat! the Cat!* the second act of the Gould-Streisand marriage was over. The third act would continue, in endless recriminations and regret, for the next three years. Yet the perfect equilibrium in their symbiotic relationship had been shattered. They no longer had basic things to swap with each other. They merely cannibalized their memories and stayed together like Hansel and Gretel because they had gone through such perils hand in hand and were so genuinely fond of each other.

It was no use. She was too talented to be Mrs. Gould and he was too talented to be Mr. Streisand. And perhaps they had discovered that there was a cruel reverse to the lyrics of her biggest hit, the one about children needing other children, the one she had intuitively disliked from the first rehearsal of *Funny Girl.* Because, in the long run, people who need people can be the unluckiest people in the world.

10. Who Are You Now?

BARBRA'S run in *Funny Girl* had ended. For twenty-two months she had been Fanny Brice on cue every night at eight thirty. Now, temporarily, there was no one to be except Streisand. Such a difficult role! "When I'm not performing," she once said, "I don't think I have a definite personality. I think maybe I'm nothing."

The emptiness took over and she regretted *Funny Girl* as perversely as one misses a painful tooth after it has been extracted. "I felt calmer onstage than in real life," she complained. "Onstage things make sense. In life they don't." She was again cooped up in her penthouse, cooking moo shu pork, watching monster pictures on TV, walking down halls decorated with eight gold records and a laminated blowup of the page in *Billboard* magazine that showed four of her albums pushing for the top in the same week.

Among her trophies of the past there was Elliott, still looking for the formula that would prompt those indifferent millions to adopt him as they had Barbra. Ellbar Productions was mulling over a project that would supposedly launch him: an album of original songs and witty monologues under the title of *The Laundry Ticket.* It never jelled beyond wishful thinking.

Mr. Gould's name got into print only when he had something quotable to say about Mrs. Gould. He described her as a combination of Y. A. Tittle, Fred Astaire, and Sophia Loren because "Tittle is an eccentric, tenacious, competitive spirit; Astaire is the most stylish, unconsciously original man, and Loren is a gorgeous female." Cute enough, and good for three lines in a column, but hardly an ego-boosting description of a restless wife by an equally restless husband.

They tried the social whirl, disastrously. Joshua Logan gave a party for Princess Margaret, and Barbra was properly introduced to her by Tommy Steele, who had become friendly with the Goulds during his New York run in *Half a Sixpence.* Approaching British royalty, Barbra panicked as she realized that as an American citizen she could not call Margaret Your Highness since *she* was not *her* Highness at all. She stumbled a curtsy and apologized for being late by telling the princess that she had gotten "screwed up, I mean, delayed." Then she turned to a tongue-tied Tommy Steele, pointed to Margaret, and tried to break the ice with a blunt pick. "You know her well, don'tcha? I mean, you've played in shows for her sister, no?"

Later in the evening the princess told her hosts that she loved Streisand's voice. A request for a song was diplomatically conveyed to the nervous star. Barbra flatly said no and left with Elliott to have a pastrami sandwich at a Broadway delicatessen. The incident was damned as a faux pas, but Harold Rome defends Streisand's behavior: "Why should she make a fool of herself by bleating in the wrong key with the wrong accompanist just to humor Princess Margaret? Barbra was asked to do something unprofessional and she walked out like a queen. Good for her!"

Barbra justified her regal stance by stating that she could not lie, that this "truth thing" was a basic element of her public appeal. She was a princess and a washerwoman, remember? The dichotomy would prove to be at the bottom of the ambivalent relation she was to develop with her audiences. The public had made her; they felt justified in breaking her if she misbehaved. As a superstar she would tread on dangerous ground.

Streisand's agent, Marty Erlichman, had once described

her as a Chaplinesque creature whom people knocked themselves over to protect. She was too proud to accept this role of the perennially abused waif. Kay Medford, who played her mother in *Funny Girl,* shrewdly assessed the Streisand charisma in a different manner: "You can pity Judy Garland forever, but you stand in awe of this girl." Streisand resented being stroked gently like a household pet. She had the bristling power of a porcupine.

It came into full display as she started planning her second television special, *Color Me Barbra.* Even more than in her debut show for CBS Streisand was in complete control, and she held the bridle with a tenacity that made others gag. She wanted everything done her way. She even rejected the services of Paolo of Helena Rubenstein when she learned it would take him two hours to get her face ready for the cameras. She wouldn't sit still that long, so she designed her own makeup, down to the pasting of the last sequin on her eyelids.

She was driven by the demon of perfectionism. The second show not only had to be as good as the first one, it had to be better. The conception was similar: a three-paneled lavish production that opened in the Philadelphia Museum of Art, proceeded to a circus setting, and concluded with a concert before a live audience. The shooting of *Color Me Barbra* became a battlefield of bruised egos as Streisand commandeered her forces with the sternness of a general.

Barbell Productions was footing the bills to deliver CBS a finished product on time and within budget. Her own money was on the line, and she had no patience with slackers—an awesome trait in someone blessed and cursed with the Streisand stamina. In the circus sequence she jumped up and down on a trampoline for nine takes, just to get the right rhythm for a one-minute sequence. When she descended for the last time, she did not collapse as expected but just commented that if the show flopped, she could always get a job as an acrobat.

During the taping in the Philadelphia Museum she worked for a straight twenty-five-hour period, sustaining her strength on mountains of junk food, from potato chips to jelly beans. Technicians were gasping for air as she was gaining her second wind.

The recording sessions were even more exhausting. She asked the control-room director whether she was great or lousy because no one was commenting on her performance. She had to know where she was at or she'd be depressed. When there were no definite answers from the depleted crew, she clamped on the earphones and ferreted every error in timing, protesting that she wanted to be directed, but no one was offering the right suggestions because they were afraid to antagonize her.

Color Me Barbra was worth all her agonies. In the first segment she careened from existentialism to camp as she ran down the corridors of the museum, glaring at rows of masterpieces, a fugitive from encroaching "Yesterdays." She clowned in a Louis XV wig for a breathless parody of Chopin's "Minute Waltz," which she brought to the finish line only forty-one seconds overtime. In a bistro setting her elongated neck gave a Modigliani look to a Piaf-like orgy of moral declension in "Rien." Then she covertly snickered at those who compared her profile with Nefertiti's by singing "Where or When" to the famous Egyptian bust.

The talent for self-mockery was simmering. It bubbled over in the circus scene, in which she built a medley around the theme of faces: She sang "Funny Face" to a monkey, "I've Grown Accustomed to Your Face" to an elephant, then rubbed noses with an anteater, ruefully admitting, "We have so much in common it's a phenomenon." She had sent herself up with all the zoological japes; then she brought herself down with her wistful standard, "Too Long at the Fair."

The final concert-style section of the show had been the most difficult to tape. After running all around the museum and trying to get the proper reactions from the trained animals, Streisand had begun to show signs of nervous strain. She did not want people around her for the concert, but a live audience was necessary for sound effects and ambience. She had decided she hated the songs selected for her cabaret turn and spent an hour brooding in her dressing room. To a frazzled crew she was bringing back memories of Garland at her most temperamental.

Yet, once she was in the spotlight before the studio-assembled audience, all the hesitation peaked into energy. She slithered through *"C'est Si Bon"* not as an Eartha Kittenish pussycat but as a menacing panther. For the climax there was "Where Am I Going?," a Cy Coleman–Dorothy Fields number from *Sweet Charity*—the hazardous one that Gwen Verdon often omitted in matinees when the show played on Broadway. Barbra managed each intricate, larynx-bursting crescendo with the fury of her Blue Angel period. It was Barbra, the actress in song, tearing a passion to tatters in this quintessential show-business aria of disorientation. The fun show was over. After all that cute stomping with the penguins and the cavorting on the trampoline, she came down to earth with electrifying impact.

In the finale Streisand communicated a raw emotion. The response was instantaneous all over America. Viewers jumped on their seats and did something even rarer than applauding at movie theaters: They clapped their hands in front of their television sets. She had known it all along: The public loved her when she didn't fake. She had been wary of "Where Am I Going?" but once she grappled with it, it was no longer a show tune but a confession.

Where, indeed, was she going? She was fleeing the Brooklyn underdog image that had made her a star, but she still could not firmly grasp the elegance she had always aspired to. It was in-between time. Was she an anteater or a Nefertiti? Who can blame her for choosing the latter?

The ideal of glamour, so desperately sought in those photo booths at Woolworth's, again took hold of her. Once she could be bought for a chocolate mousse; now she could be won with any word that fed her obsession with beauty. She told with pride how Hedy Lamarr, one of the most gorgeous women in the world, had sent her a note telling her that she made Elizabeth Taylor look like an old bag. Her day was made when, lunching at 21, she was approached by luscious model-actress Candice Bergen, who confessed her secret ideal was to look like Streisand.

The thrift-shop outfits were gone. The monkey-skin coat was consigned to the back of a closet as a relic. Now Barbra was clad in the finest of furs, and her wardrobe reeked of class. Streisand and Mrs. Loel Guiness were chosen by the *Encyclopaedia Britannica* as examples of fashion trend setters of the sixties. Fashion *maven* Eugenia Shepard canonized Streisand as an epitome of elegance when she wrote: "She is about as kooky as Gloria Guiness, C. Z. Guest and the Duchess of Windsor or any of the all-time fashion greats were when they turned twenty-two."

The accolade was the equivalent of a papal benediction to the new Barbra. She insisted she had never been a kook because "everything they don't understand is labeled as kooky." "They" is a treacherous pronoun, both an expression and an invitation to paranoia. Many people—from the press that had elevated her to the Broadway crowd that pampered her—felt alluded to by Barbra's statements. "Who does she think she is?" became the battle cry for the enemies she was making at an alarming rate.

Barbra was skirting one of the pitfalls of stardom. Unable to stand still, she was subverting the concept she had created in people's minds. They had welcomed her as the frumpy, homely kid from Flatbush, but she would not be tolerated as the woman who could perform optical illusions and make herself beautiful. The Hans Christian Andersen story was no more than a fairy tale with a deceptive happy ending; Barbra had been loved as the ugly duckling, but she ran the risk of being detested as the swan. The Streisand anecdotes were no longer benignly amusing. Now the arrows were dipped in poison.

As young girls paraded all over in beehive hairdos and Nefertiti-anteater noses, a cruel joke started doing the rounds. There was this Brooklyn kid, one of Barbra's vestal virgins, who had gone to a beauty salon and asked to be given "the Streisand look." The hairdresser just turned his brush around and broke her nose. The story is a prime example of the nauseating humor that surrounds the Streisand image to this day. The mere mention of her name can draw epithets like "pushy yenta" from men and women who would froth at the mouth in pious liberal frenzy if you dare accuse them of an anti-Semitic remark. Paradoxically, if they are Jewish themselves, they are often twice as insidious in their attack and thrice as defensive in their retreat.

Barbra's new look was an irritant. She was no longer keeping her place. Instead of backing out, she breezed along. Powerful ego winds were puffing her sails as she arrived in France for the rite of spring: the Paris collections. Fashion shows at the best ateliers were delayed half an hour for her arrival in a $3,500-jaguar-skin jacket she had designed for herself. A mannish tie and derby completed her outfit. Sneered at or not, there she was, ready to rub knees at Cardin with the Duchess of Windsor.

Once again she was the underwhelmed realist. She found the Cardin styles too revealing. The models were walking around half naked! She bought nine gowns from the conservative Dior collection at about $2,000 each. Then she fought a Paris spring cold to pose for a spread in *Vogue* magazine. Elliott brought her chicken soup and sympathy between sittings. She angled for the camera, feverish, hoarse, and undaunted. The spiral of success had brought her back to the autumn of 1961, when she had hopefully stiffened her knees in outlandish garments for friendly photographers. Now she had a solid launching pad for her bravado. She was a *Vogue* fashion plate. The eyes were steely, the shoulders straight, the clothes stunning. "Eat your heart out, world," she seemed to be saying.

The honeymoon with the press could not last. Barbra was walking a tightrope, high up on the circus tent, ready for snipers. *Color Me Barbra* was telecast to critical acclaim on March 30, 1966. Coincidentally, the New York *Times* printed Rex Reed's interview with Barbra during the taping of the show. The iconoclastic reporter pounced on her with devastating wit.

The article was the first public expression of the hate-Barbra syndrome. Unfortunately for her, it was bright, perceptive, and to the point. It crystallized all the covert gossip about the prima donna Broadway had been fuming about for months. In a few hundred words Reed tore the poor-little-girl myth apart. Streisand was shocked when she read the piece. The reaction was similar to catching one's reflection in the mirror after a particularly rough night.

The *Times* story was the unflattering portrait of a woman in a period of extreme stress, but the faithful were horrified to read about this rude, imperious, cantankerous star who ordered people around like Marie Antoinette before the Revolution, treated chicken-soup-bearing fans like pests, and barked at guards who chided her for leaning against treasured paintings in the Philadelphia museum.

"I was tired of those 'Mickey Mouse' interviews that glorified egotistic monsters," Rex Reed now says. "She was horrible to me. I reported what I saw, very honestly. Here was this woman ordering people around and eating anything that wasn't nailed to the floor. She has never spoken to me again."

Yet the question Rex Reed raised would haunt Barbra throughout her career: Is talent—even genius—enough to get away with everything? Reed had codified, in black and white, what was being muttered behind Streisand's back for two years before his story appeared. A deferential press had kept an avuncular attitude toward the antics of the irrepressible kid, but now the lid was off. Readers lapped up the revelations with relish. After being chastised in the influential pages of the *Times*, Barbra had the option to mend her ways and be conventionally *nice* or trample her way to superstardom, no matter whose toes were crushed in the upward climb. She chose to be the most controversial performer of her era: the woman you hate to love.

After her Parisian brush with *haute couture* she toured with Elliott through Nice, Marseilles, Rome, Florence. The London opening of *Funny Girl* was imminent, and she settled down in a plush rented flat near Grosvenor Square. The Prince of Wales Theatre was still occupied by the current show, so rehearsals for her musical started in a synagogue in Soho. Elliott was with her, bearing a grudge it took him four years to reveal, when he told the New York *Post* in 1970:

"I didn't play Nicky Arnstein on Broadway because at the time I couldn't get the part. I'm more talented than all the guys who ever played Nicky put together. I'm not being immodest. Nicky Arnstein was not played. He was never written. They asked me to play him in London but I refused." When the interviewer asked Elliott how Barbra felt about co-starring with him in *Funny Girl,* he noncommittally answered, "I don't know."

It sounds like a very evasive answer for the male half of Ellbar and Barbell. As partners in a corporation the couple must have often discussed business affairs. The offer of a co-starring role in Streisand's London debut was a very important decision in Gould's career at the time. His refusal was a mistake both for him and for the show because he could have brought a refreshing, down-to-earth quality the part always lacked. Instead, the Arnstein role was played in London by Michael Craig, a proficient but woefully miscast English actor who further diluted the character's unrealized flamboyance with a stiff-upper-lip restraint.

Away from home ground Barbra was more reserved than ever with the British cast. Michael Craig told the London press that his only long conversation with his co-star had taken place during a rehearsal when, upset enough to lower her guard, Barbra had told him that things weren't going right with the show. When he assured her that rehearsals were often disappointing, she confessed that when she had started with *Funny Girl,* everything had been marvelous but that now she was getting no fun out of it anymore.

Going back to Fanny Brice was a drag, but there were compensations in assuming other transitory roles, like that of the British hostess who loved pouring tea and decorating trays with "those cute little sandwiches you have over here." One of her privileged guests was columnist Sheilah Graham. She told Graham she was the highest-paid performer in the world because the Beatles had to divide their gigantic takes four ways and Elizabeth Taylor had to spend five months of work to get a million dollars for a picture while she could reach that sum faster and with less effort.

It was true, but it was also the kind of remark reserved not for performers but for their press agents. Barbra has never paid attention to the rigid protocol of the star system. She was called "money mad" precisely at the moment when she had accepted a considerable salary cut to bring *Funny Girl* to London. She was being paid £1,000 a week, less than half the $5,000 she had been making on Broadway and less than a third of what Mary Martin had received for the London edition of *Hello, Dolly!* It was the only way to make the limited run financially viable for the producer, and Barbra wanted to succeed in London. Her aim was to widen her range as an international attraction before she started appearing in movies.

She was furious to be scolded for making financial comparisons between her drawing power and that of other stars. "If I say I'm terrific, then I'm boasting," she exploded. "If I say I'm no good, that's insincere. So what should I do, shut my mouth?" That was, of course, the last thing she would do. Barbra was tense about facing new audiences, and she untied her knots with a series of delirious pranks.

Streisand made headlines in the London papers when she ran on the grass of the Victoria Embankment for a publicity stunt. A park keeper tried to stop her, and while fifty reporters and photographers watched, she asked the man if he had a warrant to restrain her. Right after the fracas she was seething. She arrived at her big press conference with her invisible fighting gloves on.

To Jules Arbose of the staid London *Times* she said, "I hate what I'm doing. I don't even like singing. Never sing in my bath or around the house. I just do it for the money. I'd like to do the classics like Juliet and Cleopatra." Not very tactful remarks from an American musical-comedy star on the verge of making her debut in Shakespeare country. With each word she uttered Barbra seemed to be sharpening the critical fangs that could tear into her on opening night.

Producer Ray Stark was spreading balm with weary fingers and declaring, "She is a wonderful performer. The only thing she has not learned is tact." But Barbra had learned better things from those horror movies she loved to watch with Elliott. She had an intuitive knowledge of suspense and knew that the appearance of a mysterious creature had to be built up for several reels. *My Name Is Barbra* had been successfully shown on British television, her records were collectors' items, but the general public still did not know her well enough. By her antics she was pushing the situation into cliff-hanger time. Weeks before *Funny Girl* opened, the mounting anticipation for the unveiling of Streisand had accumulated £200,000 in the Prince of Wales box office for a sold-out fourteen-week engagement.

On April 5, 1966, as she stepped on the boards to scream "I'm the Greatest Star," the audience was torn. They hoped she'd be as good as they'd heard, but wouldn't it be perverse fun to see her fall on her face? The glittering opening-night list included every celebrity in town: David Niven, John Huston, Peter Sellers, Leslie Caron, Rex Harrison, and dozens of others. She worked on them like a magician. It was clear after the first ten minutes that Streisand's heady bouquet, like a good vintage wine's, could travel without fading.

Reviewers sang their prases for the visiting star. Fergus Cashin in the *Sketch* called Streisand "the most phenomenal creature of strange chemistry ever to set foot on a stage." Herbert Kretzmer in the *Express* stated, "She lives up to her legend. The girl and the myth are indivisible." B. A. Young in the *Financial Times* went even further when he wrote, "The legend erred on the side of conservatism." *Funny Girl* won the *Variety* poll of London critics as the best musical of the season. Streisand was honored at the United States embassy with the Anglo-American Award as the best American performer in that year's London season. Princess Margaret, forgetting that mild snub at the Joshua Logan party, came backstage to congratulate Barbra.

She was clearly the toast of the town, but the company at the Prince of Wales found her hard to swallow. In New York the *Funny Girl* cast had been covertly antagonistic toward the star. In London, where she was a foreigner in the ranks, the animosity was barely repressed. Barbra had started on the wrong foot, but this time it was not her fault. She had envisioned the opening-night party as a "hot dog fantasia" that would turn an elegant restaurant into an extension of Nathan's frankfurter stand in Coney Island. After a considerable wrangle with customs the frankfurters were flown from New York and arrived in the nick of time for a party that turned out to be a hit and was covered by every graphic newspaper. But producer Stark had included only the show's principals on the guest list. Streisand was accused of shunning the chorus; the boys and girls celebrated at a pub near the theater, vowing enmity to the haughty star who had supposedly kept them out of the front-page bash.

After that the cold war set in, made even icier when Barbra started sending critical memos to members of the cast after a performance failed to match her metronomical sense of precision. Her co-star, Michael Craig, came to Streisand's defense in a London *Sunday Mirror* interview, explaining that the quality of the show was her responsibility since she was carrying it with her name; she was right to insist on perfection on all levels. Yet, trying to keep things shipshape, Streisand became as detested as Captain Bligh.

Worst of all, she felt she was not making contact with the public. Traditionally restrained British audiences were not giving her the kind of ovations that made her tingle. She was again adapting her performances to the mood of the customers. She was chided for cutting songs at will, but she feared her audiences would not grasp the New York Jewish humor of *Funny Girl.* By eliminating choruses she could rush through the first act and then enthrall matinee audiences with the sentimentality of the second-act love affair between Fanny and Nicky. She tuned in for vibrations. If they came to laugh, she would be a clown; if they came to cry, she would turn on the melodrama. The public went out satisfied, but her co-workers onstage seldom knew what she was up to at any given performance, and they reeled with the uncertainty of a conga line in which the leader refuses to one-two-three-kick by rote.

Anti-Streisand forces were strong, especially in the press. They found a rallying point when her understudy, Lisa Shane, went on for an ailing Barbra. Michael Craig was chosen to announce to an enraged audience that the star was indisposed. There were boos and an avalanche of refunds, but those who stayed gave Lisa Shane a thunderous round of applause. The Sunday papers headlined her triumph, suggesting that anytime Barbra wanted to pack up and leave, Miss Shane could carry on with no substantial or financial loss.

The Cinderella story never happened. Lisa Shane could never really pack audiences into the Prince of Wales. The lame *Funny Girl* needed a crutch that only Streisand could provide. Her reason for missing performances was that she was pregnant. There was no possibility of extending her run beyond the limited fourteen weeks. On July 14, when she left, the show closed. Her pregnancy had nothing to do with it; she had never planned to stay a day longer. The rest of the year had been previously committed to a series of concerts in the United States. Yet the columns hinted that she had quit the London *Funny Girl* because she had suddenly received more tempting financial offers.

This version was given the lie in a few weeks, when she had to cancel the concert tour on doctor's orders. Streisand had been scheduled to appear in twenty cities in America, from August to October. She could fulfill only four of the sold-out engagements. The box-office results were extraordinary: $121,000 at the Newport Jazz Festival; $108,000 in Philadelphia; $78,000 on a rainy night in Atlanta. The bonanza could not be prolonged, and the tour ended in mid-August after her appearance at Soldiers Field in Chicago.

Barbra turned her back on everything to go home and prepare to be a mother. She had given up a lot of money for the remaining sixteen concerts, and the child she was carrying was announced in the press as "the million-dollar baby."

Reporters had found a catchy name. She detested it. "Why do they call him that?" she asked in anger. "Why must everything and everyone have these labels?"

For the first time in years Barbra was about to put a stop to her carousel existence and relax for a while. Before her temporary retirement she perfected her French with a special tutor in a crash course, then collaborated with Michel Legrand in one of her finest—and certainly her most daring—records: *Je M'Appelle Barbra,* a veritable coup de grace of artistic *chutzpah.*

Her mimetic powers are astounding as she does the standard favorites in the boulevard repertoire: She sounds like a dismayed, melancholy Jacqueline Francois raking up those traditional "Autumn Leaves," and she rolls her *r*'s like a militant Edith Piaf as she berates the Berlin Wall in *"Le Mur."* She then switches into the English lyrics written for several done-to-death numbers and resurrects them from the Muzak sounds that have long embalmed them in gaudy lobbies and chromium-plated elevators.

She sings "I Wish You Love" not as a sauterne-sweet song of surrender but as a string of Gypsy curses to a departing lover: When she wishes him bluebirds in the spring, she makes it sound as though she is conjuring predatory birds to scratch his eyes out, and that cooling lemonade she wishes him in July must certainly be spiked with arsenic. In the same manner, "What Now, My Love" is not sighed by a passive dove left in the cold but by a shrike who is preparing to fleece her no-longer-willing partner in the divorce court.

In these flashes of intuition Streisand brings out the difference between French pop songs and her aggressive American style. She'll be damned if she'll take all that noble masochism lying down. Compared to all this liberating frenzy, her first effort at composing is modest, almost childlike, played on the piano with just one finger and entitled *"Ma Premiere Chanson."* Yet she treasured the thirty-eight-dollar royalty check she got for the song far more than all the hundreds of thousands she was amassing.

The tiny check was deposited in her secret bank account, the one she has always kept in a Brooklyn bank throughout the years. Even as a millionairess and superstar Barbra Streisand has been unable to exorcise the devils of her early insecurity. All her *real* money would find its way to this cache, from the fifty dollars she got for writing the liner notes to one of her records to the hundred dollars she made by renting her vintage Bentley to a movie company for a day. The big sums were unbelievable, but these small ones she could put her hands on: To this day the account exists, possibly under her chosen name of Angelina Scarangella, back where she first deposited her first baby-sitting money and her earnings as a cashier in Choy's Orient and as an usherette in the Loew's Kings.

"A baby is the only thing that's going to give me roots again," she said. And her roots were never stronger than during the months when she carried her child. She had new stationery printed with "Barbara" embossed on the heading for her personal correspondence. The third *a* was back, together with a craving for the basic things she had ignored for the last decade. She started training in natural childbirth. For a precious interlude it looked as if she and Elliott could retrace their steps to that refuge the treetop and become an indissoluble unit again.

Gould was telling columnist Sheilah Graham that Barbra might give up her career if she could find happiness in private life. "I don't expect this to happen today or tomorrow, but one day she will be just my wife, quit the rat race and be content." Barbra gave every indication that Elliott was not jumping to wild conclusions but responding to her blissful quietude. She was hoping for a little girl, to be called Samantha. For five months she worked on a pink carriage cover with little pigs on the fringes.

She analyzed, picked up the pieces, and chronologized. If this event had not happened, it would not have led to the next or the next. She unraveled her life like a hastily knit garment and came up with some threads of the truth. She had started as an underachiever, then turned into an overachiever. The only way to cope with the drastic change was to open her fists and let go a little.

Barbra had always dreaded the moment when the fickle audience would tire of her. "You get built up," she had said, "and all at once the public is out looking for new kooks." Now she was less frightened. Her home and her baby would fill the gap if ever the wave of public indifference struck her. Like a runner after a record-breaking sprint, she was now collapsing into well-earned peace. Performances vanished into thin air, fame was fickle and ungraspable, but her baby was about to spell at last the true meaning of the word she had been obsessed with since her teens. He would be something *tangible.*

All else seemed shallow and unimportant. Barbra read through stacks of letters from her teenage fans. They wanted to meet her because she expressed an ideal: A word of advice from her could be the key for self-realization and success. But what could she tell them? Barbra remembered how much she had idolized Marlon Brando and the times she ached to talk to him one day and tell him they were so similar, almost the same person. Yet when Brando had kissed her and praised her when they'd met at a benefit, she had just timidly recoiled. They were not the same person at all. She had been depressed to discover how little she had to say to him. Brando had been her hallucination. A new generation now hallucinated about her, and for what? The erstwhile Martian had discovered there was nothing up there in the heights. She hoped motherhood would bring her back to earth.

The baby was two weeks late and Barbra was impatient as always. There were two false alarms when she anxiously wanted to be taken to the hospital, then to subside into a few more days of waiting. The real labor pains started at 6 A.M. on December 29, 1966. She was taken to room 507 at Mount Sinai Hospital at 9 A.M. At 3 P.M. on that day Jason Emanuel Gould was born.

He weighed seven pounds and three ounces, and his father told the world, "He looks just like her, only he has a cleft in his chin and dark hair like me. But his eyes are the brightest, bluest, flashingest—just like hers." "My God," Barbra joked for the press, "I'm a little girl myself and now I'm a mother." Jokes are a lopsided way of telling the truth, and Streisand was entering complete womanhood with a combination of tenderness and awe, like a judicious little girl with a live doll of her own.

She had always wanted to play Medea and called the child Jason because she loved that name and Emanuel in memory of the father she never knew. In fear that reporters roaming the hospital corridor might discover and commercialize "the million-dollar baby," she dredged up another name from the past and Jason's nursery crib identified him as Angelina Scarangella, that mythical Italian acting student Barbra had invented in her teens. The child had become a repository of deep-seated longings.

Barbra became a devoted mother and would not part from Jason for an instant. She hated the idea of going back to work, remembering the times when she thought her mother's absence meant that she had been run over by a truck and would never return. She spent hours talking to the child but would never sing lullabies to him because singing was what she did professionally and now she figured herself a private person. She bristled at an interviewer who asked her if Jason would become a singing sensation when he grew up. This kid would be what he wanted to be and nothing else! She had decided he would never have to fight the discouragement of a suspicious mother once he chose his vocation.

The pressures to fulfill her contracts were mounting. In the spring of 1967 Barbra reluctantly went back to work for the taping of her third television special, *The Belle of 14th Street.* Barbra's first two TV shows had been almost identical in conception. She called them "my bookends," but who had ever heard of a third bookend? This one, she vowed, would be entirely different. Fighting her ingrained fear of the number three, she embarked on the production of what was to be her first undeniable failure. As a solo star she had carried the previous specials, but this time she consented to share the spotlight with John Bubbles, a veteran vaudevillian, and Broadway star Jason Robards, who would play Prospero and Caliban to her Miranda and Ariel in a spoof of Shakespeare's *The Tempest.*

The show's theme was an evocation of the apogee of vaudeville in the early 1900's. It was a carefully calibrated incursion into the past, meant to prepare audiences for Barbra's forthcoming period movie musicals. In feathered hats and heavily corseted hourglass figure she sang old favorites such as "Alice Blue Gown," "Mother Machree," "Some of These Days," and "Put Your Arms Around Me, Honey."

Choreographer Joe Layton, who had devised Streisand's first two TV specials, had been hurt by comments that they had been overdone, so this time he strove for something "simple and in period." The result was an unvaried, almost one-note hour in which the only departures from the monotonous were disastrous, such as a chorus of monstrously fat ladies, the leaden skits with Robards, and the contrived camera tricks that had Streisand singing a duet with herself.

The Belle of 14th Street was shelved for six months and there were rumors that, at Barbra's request, it would never be telecast. Half a million dollars was riding on it, and not even Barbra's closet was big enough to hide this dinosaur skeleton. When it was finally aired on October 11, 1967, critics called it "tasteless and tedious," but they were not as harsh as Streisand, who—after watching the final tape—was reported to mutter, "Well, they can really rap me for this one." The album was never released, though she later included some of the songs, such as "My Buddy," in her LP's of the seventies.

The show was a disaster that kept Streisand away from studio-filmed television specials for the next six years. Her instant displeasure with it is a clue to her mood as she approached the ultimate challenge for Barbara Joan, the usherette at the Loew's Kings. At last she was on her way to Hollywood to make *Funny Girl.* Barbra had always felt that to be a star meant to be a *movie* star. She had taken giant steps toward this goal in cabarets, stadiums, theaters, recording studios. Now came the real, frightening thing.

Elliott traveled with her but could stay around for only a couple of days. He was getting ready to open on Broadway in Jules Feiffer's black comedy, *Little Murders.* This time Barbra would have to stand on her own. She stepped off the plane holding her baby, Jason, tucked in a blue blanket, and maneuvering her poodle, Sadie, strapped on a leash. Even behind huge tinted glasses her eyes blinked at a lightning storm of photographers' flashbulbs as she walked from the airport to the studio's limousine.

It was too late to back out. She strode on. The only words that could apply in this hour of danger were the ones she had pecked with her two fingers during that first typing lesson her mother had insisted on fifteen years ago: NOW IS THE TIME FOR ALL GOOD MEN TO COME TO THE HELP OF BARBARA JOAN STREISAND.

11. Don't Rain on My Parade

FROM the very beginning the film version of *Funny Girl* was plagued with as many troubles as the Broadway musical. Producer Ray Stark wanted Sidney Lumet to direct the movie, but they soon parted over "artistic differences." Barbra had liked *Thoroughly Modern Millie,* and she felt director George Roy Hill had the right touch for a period musical, but her suggestion was ignored. Ray Stark had his aim set for a bigger catch.

It was William Wyler, veteran director and three-time Oscar winner. After a career studded with dramatic hits he was persuaded to try his hand at directing his first musical. Wyler had a well-earned reputation for extracting good performances from his casts: A dozen actors and actresses had received Academy Awards for starring or supporting roles in his films. He was the ideal man to shape Barbra's still-unknown film potential into Oscar-winning material.

Wyler also had a reputation as a stern, no-nonsense disciplinarian who had fought legendary battles with some of the redoubtable ladies of the screen, from Margaret Sullavan to Bette Davis. "I am the only prima donna on the sets of my pictures" was one of his favorite quotes. The clash with stubborn Streisand was eagerly anticipated in Hollywood circles. If someone was going to tame this shrew, Willy Wyler could. He had the experience.

Wyler's initial confrontation was not with Streisand. The first thing he objected to was the screenplay, which he found dramatically weak. Stark secretly contacted Arthur Laurents to do a quick rewrite, but Laurents was tired of backstage musicals and refused, not before telling Stark, "There is a lot of my *Gypsy* libretto in your show. I think I've already made my unsolicited contribution." Isobel Lennart went back to the drawing board. She ended up calling her work on the movie adaptation "a deflating, ego-crushing experience."

Few believed that a show that had run two years needed improving, but Wyler kept requesting changes and would not be deterred. Eight songs from the stage show were eliminated and replaced by more visually oriented numbers such as "The Roller Skate Rag" and a parody of the *Swan Lake* ballet.

Choreographer Herbert Ross and his wife, ballerina Nora Kaye, were to stage the musical interludes. Wyler's strategy became clear: He wanted fewer numbers with more concentrated impact so he would have more running time to develop the Brice-Arnstein relationship, the one weak spot in the whole project. Wyler strove to make something more meaningful of those two characters a critic once called "as sugary and as animated as the bride and groom on a wedding cake." If there were any more dramatic possibilities to be squeezed from this prerigged contest of personalities, Wyler would do it in the movie. After all, that had been his Hollywood specialty for forty years.

"Isobel Lennart wrote me a letter I keep to this day," Jule Styne says. "She wrote, 'They're putting "My Man" in for the finale and it is the destruction of the play.' She was right, but what can you do? Every time you get a new director he wants changes, but these were not for the best. The second half of the movie was all self-pity on Fanny Brice and I think that's a bore. In the show she went on at the end, doing an encore of 'Don't Rain on My Parade,' but now they wanted her sobbing 'My Man.' They had decided to turn *Funny Girl* into a complete soap opera."

Despite all the opposition from the original creators, Wyler wanted to highlight the star-crossed love story of Fanny and Nicky. He needed a solid personality to play Arnstein. "They wanted Frank Sinatra," Arthur Laurents says, "but Barbra would not take second billing, of course." Marlon Brando and Gregory Peck were then mentioned for the role, but possibly the same hurdle stalled the negotiations. David Janssen was within an inch of signing for the Arnstein part when Wyler suggested Omar Sharif, who had scored a success as the Arab chieftain in *Lawrence of Arabia.*

Barbra was undecided and Sharif was brought to meet her. "Ray Stark told me that Sharif came in, oozing continental charm," Arthur Laurents comments. "Then Omar bowed elegantly, kissed Barbra's hand, and told her, 'In America you are the woman I have most wanted to meet.' Naturally, he got the part."

Sharif was signed as Arnstein just as the Arab-Israeli Six-Day War erupted. The choice turned into a publicity bonus for the film. Sharif is actually Lebanese, but columns were asking how this Arab could make love to Jewish Streisand while hostilities raged in the Middle East. When a shot of their first kiss was printed, an Egyptian magazine cried, "Outrageous." Sharif quipped that he never asked a girl's nationality before kissing her, and Barbra countered with, "You think Cairo was upset? You should see the letter I got from my aunt Rose!" It was clearly a publicity stunt, but fan-magazine devourers are blissfully willing to believe, then misinterpret, most of what they read. The word was out that Barbra had objected to the casting of Omar and that a feud was raging between them on the set.

The co-stars never had a moment's disagreement. The same cannot be said about Streisand and Wyler. He was a veteran of a hundred movies but she was a veteran of a thousand performances in *Funny Girl* and had many ideas on how to improve a scene. Wyler is partially deaf, so Barbra raised her voice and gestured wildly as she tried to get her points across. One memorable day, after one of her tirades-cum-pantomine, she asked the director, "Do you understand what I say?" "Just tell me some more," he calmly replied. "I guess I talk too much" was her retreating remark.

The stories about the Streisand-Wyler feud kept columnists busy. It was said that she treated him like a butler. It was also said that every time she came to him with suggestions he just turned his hearing aid off and simply advised her to "tone it down." Wyler denies all this by saying that at first she was a bit obstreperous but eventually calmed down. Years later, during the filming of *The Way We Were,* Barbra confided to Arthur Laurents that her "fights" with Wyler had been exaggerated. She had just come to Hollywood, where people did what they were told like robots, and she'd had the courage to talk back because it was Wyler's first musical and she knew what audiences could or could not take in *Funny Girl.*

According to Laurents, Barbra revealed that the one big disagreement had been about a scene in which Fanny asks her friend (Lee Allen) whether her baby is pretty. Wyler wanted her to do it one way. She insisted that no one was going to indicate the best way to deliver a line that deeply affected her emotionally. She won the point and convinced Wyler. Then she delighted him when she asked to record one of the songs live because she felt the impact would be killed by dubbing it later.

Just as she had with Jerome Robbins onstage, Barbra began to respond to Wyler's painstaking care with her performance. He said the one reason he had been attracted to the movie was Barbra, a "fascinating creature" he wanted to present in the best light. "I wanted to see if her brilliance could be brought to the screen. The true challenge of a director is to extract every nuance of greatness from a performer. She is interesting to work with. Not so easy, not so difficult. She's got ideas on how to perform. Some are good, some are not so good."

Matters improved between star and director, but it took awhile. In her first weeks in Hollywood Barbra was insecure and unhappy. Elliott was in New York playing in *Little Murders* and she stayed at home with Jason and the English nanny she had hired. She had rented a house Greta Garbo once lived in and seemed to be possessed by the "I want to be alone" spirit. She refused to go to parties and fled prying photographers by lifting a shopping bag to cover her face when recognized on the street.

What she needed was a new transfusion of mass love to spark her energy. She got it on the weekend of June 16, when she took time off from *Funny Girl* to fly to New York for a concert in Central Park sponsored by a brewery. It was first come, first served, no tab at the door. For lack of a better word it was called a "happening," described by *Webster's Dictionary* as "something that takes place, occurs, befalls." It was all that, in spades.

Streisand flew from Los Angeles on a Friday night and drove straight to Central Park's Sheep Meadow to begin rehearsals around 2 A.M. She had little time before the fans arrived. They started coming at 6 A.M., the true believers, up with the sun, ready to crouch before the altar.

Around noon the middle-ground audience drifted in. Streisand fans one and all, chagrined to find that their eight-hour sacrifice would garner them only the equivalent of a third-balcony glimpse at the star. They inched along toward the stage, dabbing sun-tan oil on their blistered foreheads. Then, as the sun started to go down, the hordes descended. Thousands were trampling down, equipped with hampers full of beer and sandwiches, to push and crawl forward in the grass.

Two ninety-foot trailers were set near the stage. Streisand spent the day in one of them, sending out deputies to check the sound, the lights, the sheet music. After the mob swept in, she dared not go out; she could have been torn to shreds for an autograph. Finally, around eight o'clock, she flew out in wings of pink organdy, a moth ready for the flames of idolatry. It was a pent-up audience. They had waited too long, and if Streisand failed to deliver, she would be facing the closest thing to a public execution since Madame Defarge put away her knitting.

Barbra stood onstage ice cold, like a stubborn stalagmite in a furnace, acknowledging the first raucous ovation by snickering, "But I haven't done nothing yet!" For someone as hypersensitively afraid of people those 135,000 perfervid souls, panting at her feet, must have been truly terrifying. She had become an icon; she proceeded to behave like one. Everything she did, good or bad, would be greeted as a miracle, with whoops of fawning adoration. The only thing she could not do was to turn around and run for her life. They were hers, but the golden coin had a disquieting reverse: She was theirs.

Barbra took the feverish pulse of the evening when she coaxed the audience into an off-key chorus of "Second Hand Rose," and then nervously said, "You don't need me here!" The throngs had not come to listen to her but to congratulate themselves on their own stamina. They had sweated for endless hours to be able to tell everyone that they'd *been* there. Each was on his private trip to the stars; she was just the spaceship.

Her performance had the precarious equilibrium of a surfer riding a tidal wave. Forget about doing it gracefully; the main thing was to maneuver the crest. She sang "Cry Me a River" as if she were covertly laughing at her own previous involvement with the lyrics. Her "Happy Days" was a gushing travesty of the original interpretation; her "People" was done as an unabashed crowd pleaser. Even the cramped idolaters in the front ranks walked out complaining that Barbra was saving her voice for Monday, when she had to report back on the *Funny Girl* set.

Whatever its shortcomings, the *Happening in Central Park* was a tremendous publicity boost. When it was eventually released as a record, the obsequious jacket lines noted that the only hitch in an otherwise smooth evening had been Barbra's: She had misquoted the audience tally and thanked 128,000 people for *schlepping* down there, but the final count had been 135,000.

Next day Sheep Meadow looked like an abandoned battlefield. The album notes tried to bestow some class on the debris and listed some exotic leftovers: empty vintage champagne bottles, a Russian-English dictionary, a jar of quail eggs, a sterling-silver champagne bucket, but also a pleated miniskirt, a Merry Widow bra, not to mention five tons of plain garbage that took the sanitation department four days to collect.

The *Happening* certified her as New York's greatest star, but Hollywood still had reservations. Coming back from all that love to all these suspicious leers was like jumping from a self-congratulatory bubble bath into a cold shower. Rampant rumors that she had had her nose fixed for the movie were the first thing Streisand encountered on her return from her hometown. Cinematographer Harry Stradling was doing a miraculous job of lighting the Streisand profile, but the results, literally, could not be believed. "I look good in the rushes and they can't take it," she said indignantly. "I didn't have my name changed or my nose fixed or my teeth capped to come here. And I'm proud of that."

Streisand had adapted to a working relationship with Wyler, but it was fraught with traces of the original animosity. It was a tightly closed pressure chamber, and she found escape valves whenever the respected tyrant was not on the set. The second-unit shooting and the musical numbers, directed by Herbert Ross, provided an opportunity to let off steam. When the company moved to an East River pier near the Manhattan Bridge to photograph the ferryboat scene for the "Don't Rain on My Parade" number, Wyler was not around, and Barbra was like the unruly child in the absence of the strong-willed teacher.

For the sequence she had to run down the pier several times on high heels, holding two bags and a bunch of roses. "Boy, I'm going to sue you," she groaned in mock annoyance to producer Ray Stark. "My back hurts, my feet hurt. This is the hardest work I've ever done. I'll probably get sick on the tugboat and I got thorns in my fingers from all those damned roses."

Barbra whined a lot to Herb Ross, but he had been her choreographer in *I Can Get It for You Wholesale* and knew how to deal with her improvisational style far better than iron-fisted Wyler. She worked like a pro in the ferryboat sequence and it was finished a day ahead of time. Even composer Jule Styne, who is very critical of the movie version, concedes: "None of the stuff they put in was better than what we had in the Broadway show. Songs like 'Cornet Man' and 'Rat-Tat-Tat-Tat' were funnier than that roller-skate thing or the Tchaikowsky ballet. But I got to hand it to Herb Ross for 'Don't Rain on My Parade.' That was brilliant."

Once the rushes for that sequence were in, everyone knew the picture would be a smash and Barbra would be a movie star. She thought so too, if they would only let her. She wanted only her left profile photographed. Once she stopped a scene and informed cinematographer Stradling that the number three baby spotlight over her head was not on. They checked and she was right. When the story came out in the press, she was reported to be a "girl monster" who was telling Oscar-winner Stradling how to photograph her.

Barbra got bored with the constant railing. Well, if they said she was a temperamental movie star, she was going to play the part to the hilt. What was the point of trying to be nice if anything she said was twisted to make her sound rude? She would talk to no one on the set for fear of being misquoted. The chorus people started grumbling: "Who does she think she is, Joan Crawford?" "Give me Julie Andrews all the time," a chorus boy told reporters. "I've just finished a movie with Julie and she was one of the gang but this one's impossible." To this day one of the dancers still damns her with a barbed comment: "She has pocket-sized delusions of grandeur." In Hollywood a joke made the rounds that when she finished *Funny Girl*, her co-workers sent her a present in an Art Nouveau-decorated envelope: a one-way ticket to New York.

She kept throwing coals on the flames. She did her own makeup and devised a portable mirror surrounded by three-way bulbs so she could match the exact lighting of every set she worked on. She claimed she'd been watching her face for twenty-four years and no one knew it better. One of the rebuffed makeup men remembers how he sat with brush and eye pencil in hand "while she messed with herself, God bless her." But Bob Schulenberg, who did the original portrait of Barbra back in 1960, says he was impressed when he saw her first movie close-ups. "She had painted a very thin white line just on the rather thick fold of her eyelids, as I'd told her to."

In Hollywood, Barbra declared, she felt like a boxer in the ring, with all those people milling around her, patting her into her corner. "They have people for everything down here," she complained. If there was a stain in her dress, she was not supposed to clean it because there was some union rule to prevent her, so she would stand in the middle of the set, mocking the stratified system and shouting "Stain person!" until someone from the wardrobe department came.

Elliott paid her a short visit and tried to soothe her, telling everyone she was not to blame for her outbursts, she was just terrified of people. Elliott's efforts reminded director Wyler of his own troubles when he was married in the thirties to the highly temperamental Margaret Sullavan, though Wyler admitted in his autobiography that Gould did his appeasing far more diplomatically than he ever had.

Elliott could not stay with her for long. *Little Murders* had had a short run on Broadway, but he was now to do *Luv* in summer stock with Shelley Winters. His time for hand holding was getting more and more limited. Gould left Hollywood, and Barbra was on her own to contend with the "hair people" and the "chair people," especially the latter after she was given a white director's chair for her poodle, Sadie, while members of the chorus had to rest between takes on crowded benches.

The hate-Streisand cult had found its most dedicated chapter in Hollywood. On October 11, when *Belle of 14th Street* was finally televised and panned by the critics, a dancer on the *Funny Girl* set remembers that it was "the best news in Hollywood since the death of Harry Cohn," though he tempers this ghoulish remark by adding, "People were saying she was paranoid but I want to be fair. That's a lie. She is, in her own way, the sanest person in the world. A paranoid person is someone who imagines he has enemies. She did not have to invent them. She *had* enemies."

Streisand was accused of demanding that all the supporting parts be cut to shreds so she could keep stage center all the time in the movie. Anne Francis, who played Georgia, a Ziegfeld girl who befriends Fanny Brice, was reported to be so good that newspapers predicted she would get an Academy Award nomination in a supporting role. Later most of Anne Francis' scenes were eliminated and she requested that her name be withdrawn from the credits. The part of Georgia was the same one that Allyn McLerie had played in early rehearsals of the Broadway musical. It had been cut out, then reinstated for the screenplay, and again it had gone down the drain as unnecessary.

Streisand was named as the hatchet woman, but it is obvious that she had nothing to do with the cutting spree that brought the film down to a manageable length. Wyler's conception stressed the love affair of Fanny and Nicky. All that stood in the way had to be pared. Streisand was no luckier than the supporting cast: Her favorite number, the *Swan Lake* ballet, was practically excised and merely used as part of a montage that showed her dancing while Nicky gambled a fortune away.

Barbra—the frustrated ballerina from Miss Marsh's dance school in Brooklyn—worked for weeks with choreographer Nora Kaye to be perfect in that sequence. She fought a losing battle to the end to get the original thirteen-minute footage restored; her proudest effort ended on the cutting-room floor. Yet she was blamed for editing performances out of a movie in which she had very limited clout. The legend survives to this day, and people will repeat, parrotlike, that Barbra masterminded everything in *Funny Girl.* Yet when she complained that the initial ad campaign was vulgar, she was summarily told to mind her own business.

Streisand was caught in a vortex of the "guess what *she* did today?" type of Hollywood rumors. The most distressing was the one that she had fallen in love with co-star Omar Sharif. He had unwittingly started the avalanche when he—or his press agent—told *Life* magazine that his first impression was that Barbra was not very pretty but that soon he had found her physically beautiful. "I started *lusting* after this woman," the quote ran, rather hyperbolically. It is the kind of hors d'oeuvre that can become a full daily meal for a columnist. Fan magazines were drooling at the banquet, asking on red-and-yellow headlines: WILL BARBRA DIVORCE ELLIOTT TO MARRY OMAR?

Gould's professional fortunes had begun to turn. Director William Friedkin had seen him play *Luv* in summer stock and had signed him immediately for a role in *The Night They Raided Minsky's.* He was busy making the movie in New York and could not fly to Hollywood to dispel the separation clouds. In mid-November the lid blew off the story when Sharif took Barbra to an exclusive fashion show at a discotheque called The Factory. Then they dined as a twosome in an elegant restaurant. Nothing else was needed to confirm that a double divorce was the next stop.

Elliott was playing Othello via long-distance phone. He called Arthur Laurents and complained that Barbra was making a public fool out of him. Then Sheilah Graham reported that Elliott was furious and had called to tell her: "She's put herself in a very difficult position. The press doesn't like her because she is uncooperative. I am a very secure person, but as a man I have certain reactions. I asked her why she had gone to that fashion show with Omar and she replied, 'Because the ticket would have cost me $250.' She is just a terribly naïve girl from Brooklyn."

Elliott still knew her better than anyone. She was flattered by the attention of Sharif, a man with a reputation as an international Don Juan. Theirs was the brief attraction of opposites: Omar, of the soulful eyes, had beauty; Barbra, of the knife-sharp mind, had genius. Their flirtation was as fast and as scratchy as a vintage record of "The Sheik of Araby," but it was reported that Barbra had said, "I'm crazy in love with Omar and I've told my Elliott about it." No amount of denials could erase the fact that Gould's pride had been wounded where it hurts most for an actor: in the glossily colored front pages of movie magazines.

The Barbra-Omar gossip was as brief as the Arab-Israeli war. There were now more disparaging items to print about her: She had been signed by producer Ernest Lehman for the movie version of *Hello, Dolly!* The Hollywood contingent had been rooting for Lucille Ball to play the role originated by Carol Channing. The Broadway faction, of course, felt that only Channing could do justice to her creation.

Barbra was now a "role stealer." But she had never wanted to play Dolly in the first place. She thought it was a part for an older woman, ideal for Elizabeth Taylor to make her debut as a musical star. It was Elliott Gould who implanted the idea in her mind: She owed it to her fans to accept the challenge and tackle the part. But, of course, Streisand owed nothing to her fans. She owed it to herself to take the risk, whatever the results. Once she realized practically everyone was against her playing Dolly, there was no stopping her.

Bitter opposition goaded her on. She had a contract with Ray Stark and his Rastar Productions; she wanted to get out of it. Stark filed suit and asked for an injunction to prevent her from working for another employer. Rastar claimed she had rejected two scripts submitted to her: *Wait Till the Sun Shines, Nellie* and a musical version of *Two for the Seesaw.* She hated the projects and was ready to go to court to escape them. They offered no challenge, and the odds for *Hello, Dolly!* were enticing: She could either be wiped out by a flop or enshrined as the star of the highest-grossing movie musical in history.

"Barbra hates gambling," Arthur Laurents affirms. "Once we were in a nightclub in London and Elliott stepped for half an hour into the casino. He came back and said matter-of-factly that he had lost $2,500. There was hardly a pause in the conversation. Barbra picked up very fast, just like Fanny Brice with Nicky Arnstein, pretending to pay no attention to what he'd just said.

"Barbra hates to bet on anything, except her career."

Hello, Dolly! presented the most daring stake thus far. The press had codified the lie that she had received $1,000,000 for *Funny Girl*, the highest sum ever paid for a starring debut in movie history. The truth is that she had done the film for $200,000, though percentages on sales of the soundtrack album and other fringe benefits finally tripled her take. On *Hello, Dolly!* she would be paid $750,000 for grabbing the plum role in the musical hit of the decade. It requires boundless sanctimoniousness to ask a star to refuse a temptation only martyrs would turn their backs on. *Dolly* was a treacherous throw of the dice, but only a soothsayer could have warned Streisand against what she later considered the biggest mistake in her career.

The casting of Streisand as Dolly met with almost universal disapproval. Producer Lehman came out with a statement that read like a defense plea in a controversial case: "I chose Streisand because of her talent. She is a great singer, a natural actress and a gifted comedienne. She has a timeless quality which means she could be the Dolly Levi of 1890 as well as the Barbra Streisand of 1967." Only the first week of rehearsals would be needed to prove how wrong he was. But even a bad risk like *Hello, Dolly!* would provide a jolt for Streisand. Her records had begun to sound dangerously predictable.

Simply Streisand, released at this juncture in her career, sounded like warmed-up leftovers from her *Third Album*. The homogenized standards were sometimes whipped into creamy sentimentality, sometimes curdled with a few drops of vinegary insight. There were few surprises in the album. The performance was, at the same time, atypical for the tried-and-true songs but typical for Streisand. A case in point is "When Sunny Gets Blue," the number that drove her early devotees crazy at The Lion and the Bon Soir. Her lingering, elastic refrain for "pitter patter, pit-ter, pat-ter," as an evocation of rain, must have been a refreshing shower in pre-Streisand 1960. In the post-Streisand era it was just another trick of her well-established trade. Even her staunchest fans began to wonder whether she had run out of golden nuggets of improvisation.

Simply Streisand would have been promising as Streisand's first album. She endearingly sings "My Funny Valentine." She fights the soupy violins with an occasional wail in "I'll Know"; she injects some nasal innuendos before succumbing to the expected schmaltz in "All the Things You Are." There are also unfortunate incursions into enemy territory: Invading Judy Garland's backyard in pursuit of "The Boy Next Door," Barbra gets impaled on the picket fence.

Simply Streisand was the right title for the album because it pointed to what was *wrong* with it. Barbra is a baroque artist, and her attempts at straightforward delivery were competent, marketable, and uninspiring, like the plans of one of mad King Ludwig's palaces restructured to the level of a drive-in restaurant. Only one cut in the record made a popular impact: her takeoff on the blustering Mounties' march from *Rose-Marie.*

In the film version of the Rudolf Friml operetta Nelson Eddy had given the number strong-jawed masculinity as MGM's baritone in residence, but it all vanished as Streisand changed the tempo into a suggestive crawl and lewdly breathed in anticipation for the arrival of those "Stout-Hearted Men." She openly imitated Mae West's insinuating phrasing, and the record, as a single, was played constantly in gay bars all over the country. Barbra was back in Lion country, nudging Mae a little bit off her pedestal as camp queen.

"Stout-Hearted Men" was a hit, but for Streisand it was one step forward, two steps back, down to that demicellar on Ninth Street. An apocryphal anecdote began to be repeated in the gay crowd: When Streisand had finally met Mae West at a Hollywood party, the valetudinarian doyenne had defended her realm by asking Barbra, the usurper, "You're okay, kid, but why don't you stop imitating me?" The joke was terrible but telling. It would be repeated even more often when *Hello, Dolly!* was eventually released. Streisand, baffled by an impossible part, took refuge in her schoolgirl idols and used West, together with Vivien Leigh and Rita Hayworth in *Strawberry Blonde,* as models for her patchwork performance as Dolly Levi.

None of the previous stage Dollys could give her a clue to the character she wanted to portray. Carol Channing had played Dolly as a spastic clown, a Judy with a lot of punch but no credibility as a human being. Succeeding Channing on Broadway, Ginger Rogers had injected some much-needed warmth to give the show a balance, to the best of her limited abilities as a singer. Pearl Bailey had revivified the conception with her own special raffish insouciance, and later Ethel Merman would close the run by roaring through the songs with brash unconcern. Mary Martin's Dolly in the London version was the closest to the Streisand possibilities, but there was still that fathomless age gap that not even Barbra's talent could bridge.

A twenty-four-year-old girl was called on to enact a forty-ish matchmaker. From this initial, untenable premise all the problems in the production arose. When the waiters at the Harmonia Gardens sang the title number to Barbra, welcoming back the long-absent Dolly, it instantly implied that she must have been a child bride to her dear departed husband and that she had been the toast of Fourteenth Street in her early teens. Marianne McAndrew, chosen to play the husband-hunting milliner, was obviously older than Barbra, and their scenes together had an added awkwardness: Barbra looked like an obnoxious kid trying to drum up dates for her spinster aunt. Nothing worked. Worst of all, Barbra was committing the capital sin of taking Dolly with levity in the skits and with dead seriousness in the songs.

When Dolly asked her dead husband to release her from marital promises and give her a sign she could remarry, Barbra took it literally and gave the facetious number the poignance of a Hamlet pleading with his father's spirit for a cue for action. In "Love Is Only Love," written specially for her by Jerry Herman as a new song for the movie version, she prepares herself for the final assault on the brusque Horace Vandergelder like a wistfully resigned maiden about to be sold into white slavery in a New Orleans bordello. Taken out of context, the interpretations are excellent, but in the midst of the inanity of *Hello, Dolly!* they were catastrophic. They blighted a rosy fable with a brush of blistering reality.

The songs were recorded first. When Streisand advanced into the performance itself, the imbalance brought down the house of cards. There were not one but two Dollys: One was a faithful widow in a baleful economic bind, ready to give up her ideals of beyond-the-grave fidelity for a comfortable income; the other was a flighty, cynical woman who manipulated people with a flick of her unscrupulous finger. When she talked, she was playing Mae West to Walter Matthau's bland parody of W. C. Fields, turning the film into a wilted version of *My Little Chickadee.* When she sang, she would take the brassy "Before the Parade Passes By" and unmask it as an anguished expression of loss of nerve and fear of aging. It certified Barbra as a superb analyst of pop music, but it left Dolly Levi not ready for a triumphant march but for the next fifty-minute session on the couch.

Director Gene Kelly tried valiantly to meld the disparate elements. He was sympathetic to what Barbra was trying to do. After all those stories about her conflicts with William Wyler he said he had gone into the set with his dukes up. But as a veteran of the MGM golden age of movie musicals Kelly knew too well that this project stood or fell on Streisand's ability to bring off her bold experiments with Dolly Levi. His misgivings—if he had any—were lulled by the fact that a lot of money was riding on the picture. The sensible thing for a professional was to try to dovetail both sides of Barbra's performance so that the seams would not show.

The rest of the cast was indignant. Many felt that Kelly was kowtowing to the dictatorial star. The Hollywood gossip mills were abuzz with stories: She was trying to direct herself as Dolly. In April, when she made a public appearance at the Academy Awards ceremony, the hostility in the theater was almost palpable. Streisand had aided her detractors by sporting a frizzy hairdo that made her look like an aspiring Colette whose home permanent had gone wrong. In her column Sheilah Graham voiced the general feeling: She did not photograph well. Barbra's nose had definitely *not* been fixed and the audience's consensus was that those reports about her odd beauty in the unreleased *Funny Girl* were just wishful thinking on the part of press agents.

The ill feelings came to the surface as the *Dolly* group went East for two weeks of location shooting in the hamlet of Garrison, New York. As befits a co-star, Walter Matthau became the leader of the anti-Streisand rebellion. One day in Garrison when Barbra was suggesting still another special touch to Gene Kelly, Matthau erupted: "Why don't you let the director direct?" Barbra turned on him with great anger: "And why don't you learn your lines properly?" She walked off the set in a huff while Matthau shouted at her, "All right, walk off! Just remember, Betty Hutton once thought she was indispensable!" His words were greeted with applause from the ranks.

Now the hostility was out in the open. It was Barbra Streisand against the world, reduced in microcosm to a troubled movie set. She did not like to have her meals with the rest of the company because lunchtime was her chance to be with her son, Jason, and feed him in her private trailer. When she had a minute to herself, she preferred to play Frisbee with the Garrison children, stumbling along in tight corset and voluminous skirt, to the dismay of the wardrobe department: There were always two replacements ready for each costume in case she had to call for "stain persons."

Matthau's outburst certified all of Barbra's sometimes irrational fears. Some people were hostile to her, so she retreated more and more into the seclusion of her trailer. The set was guarded like a concentration camp against intrusions by the press. Barbra told one of the few interviewers allowed beyond the gates, "I'm not a private person anymore. If I run someone over with my car, I could be sued for a million dollars—and they'd probably collect."

When the company returned from the stormy Garrison location to the soothingly plutocratic atmosphere of Hollywood sets, a sort of peace treaty was signed between Streisand and Matthau. *Hello, Dolly!* was blindly tottering way over budget. Before it was finished, it would go from the pink of health into bloody red, for a demented and irrecuperable expenditure of $21,000,000. The co-stars had to cooperate or Twentieth Century-Fox would sink to the tune of *Good-bye, Dolly!*

Faced with Fox's corporate disaster, Matthau temporized and told the press that Barbra had moments of likability. "She is a very compelling person, doing very well for someone so tender in years. She's very young and probably has different values that conflict with other people's. It's very difficult for anyone, let alone a young person, to become a star. They don't leave you alone, you are beset from every angle, and Barbra is not that confident." A similar statement about Matthau was expected from Streisand, but none was forthcoming.

Today, when he remembers his experiences in *Hello, Dolly!*, Walter Matthau is at his gentlemanly best, though a rictus of bitterness curdles his lips when he says, "I don't hate Barbra Streisand. I never did. She was just too young for the part and she knew it. That's why she made it so difficult for everyone involved. There's nothing more depleting for an actor than to feel he's playing the wrong role. You can be gallant about it, but she had too much at stake. I can see it now in perspective. She was a movie star, though none of her films had been released. She was insecure and she couldn't handle it."

Matthau cleverly defines Streisand's unique position in the summer of 1968 as she finished *Hello, Dolly!* Two multi-million-dollar movies had been constructed around her and no one really knew whether she was able to carry them or not. She had partially forsaken television, and a tape of her *Happening in Central Park* had been furnished to CBS by Barbell Productions in lieu of the yearly special she was under contract for. When it was telecast on August 9, the camera, that impartial and often cruel bystander, had magnified the faults inherent in this mammoth orgy of indiscriminate adulation. The impromptu performance could never compare with the clockwork precision of her first two shows. She had given away her secret; now audiences knew that she was capable of much better.

Even the fashion world was turning on her. Mr. Blackwell, a pugnacious Hollywood couturier, had included Streisand in his list of the ten worst-dressed women, describing her as "a flower child gone to seed in the cabbage patch." Barbra tried to be philosophical about the numerous attacks, but her words came out defensive when she said, "When you're a star, you're an open target. The bigger the star, the bigger the target. You just can't win."

The main question was still: how big a star? The suspense mounted as the date of the *Funny Girl* opening loomed closer and closer. She had walked away from everything else to reach the ultimate goal she had fixed for herself way up in the balcony at the Loew's King. September 8, 1968, was going to be her D day as a movie star.

Preparations were going on at fever pitch for the unveiling of the monument. A huge tent was built on an empty lot on Broadway where the Astor Hotel had been recently razed to make way for an office building. The postpremiere party would be held there, with a menu of pâté and roast beef, the two dishes over which Fanny Brice lost her control at Nicky Arnstein's artful instigation. The gala was a benefit for Mayor Lindsay's Commission for Youth and Physical Fitness. Barbra endorsed the project by telling the press, "I was always up for charity myself. I could have used some help."

The afternoon of the premiere was fraught with tension. Arnold Scaasi had designed a sumptuous gown and cape of netlike fabric, embroidered all over with silvery spiderwebs. While her hair was being tortured into a Directoire style, someone discovered her son, Jason, on the verge of defacing the dress with crayons. It was panic time. Everyone fussed and fretted, but Barbra was a calm eye in the middle of the storm. "I want to look good, that's for sure," she told her attendants. "But it doesn't really matter. What's up there on the screen is what's going to make me or break me."

The premiere was a successful social event. Streisand, buoyed by the applause that greeted her every number on screen, was in a receptive mood when the movie was over. During the party Mayor Lindsay came up to her, bussed her on the cheek, and told her, "It's a long way from Brooklyn to Broadway." "It's not so long if you take the BMT and change at Canal Street," Barbra laughingly replied. She joined the amenities like a subdued disciple of Perle Mesta. Not a flurry of anxiety marked her behavior. She was being fatalistic. The dice were tossed. The final verdict would be conveyed only by the reaction to that other person, the larger-than-life Barbra on the big screen of the Criterion Theatre.

Next day the reviews were mainly favorable to the film and enthusiastic about Streisand. She could even derive some pleasure from Renata Adler's negative notice in the New York *Times:* The critic scored the movie because it so often insisted on Streisand's plainness while she was looking splendid. Stringent Pauline Kael gave Streisand a rave in the *New Yorker*, providing the quote she treasures most from a writer: "She proves that beauty is talent." Kael was right. Barbra's attraction in *Funny Girl* went beyond the careful job Harry Stradling had done with the face disbelievers called unphotographable. She looked good because she was great.

Crafty William Wyler had prepared the movie with his inveterate talent as a star maker. He had scrubbed the edges of that scruffy oyster of a screenplay so that Barbra could shine, unhampered, like an iridescent pearl. The film started with her arrival at a darkened theater. She faced a mirror, huddling a leopard-skin coat against her face and purring to her image, "Hello, gorgeous." It was the ideal psychological ruse to proclaim, within the first two minutes, Barbra's strange ambivalence between the narcissistic and the self-deprecating.

From this feisty head start on the right track the movie bolted on like a thoroughbred, adroitly managing every curve in Streisand's rush between the not-really-ugly duckling to the not-really-graceful swan. It was the kind of optical illusion that draws audiences into mass hypnosis and creates star personalities. Wyler had made her *chutzpah* exhilarating, her brashness attractive. She was plain and fancy from one shot to the next, in a "now you see it, now you don't" conundrum. All her qualities, good or bad, were enlarged on the silver screen, so that mass audiences could empathize with her as an enormous projection of their own triumphs and defeats, sanities and follies. She was a film star.

She was also an actress. Wyler had sacrificed his moviemaker ego to convert *Funny Girl* into a Streisand portfolio. He used none of the in-depth compositions that made *The Little Foxes* and *The Best Years of Our Lives* into lasting masterpieces. The intimate scenes are visually uninteresting in *Funny Girl* because Wyler used the simplest film syntax of medium shots and close-ups. He wanted to give Streisand, pure and unadulterated, to the public. The picture was just a vehicle for her and she rode it beautifully, with a brilliant chauffeur at the wheel.

Wyler's insight had been that only Streisand could infuse the anemic love story with the sort of blood-and-guts performance he had extracted from his screen heroines in the thirties and forties. Fanny Brice's sorrow about her crumbling marriage came to life as Streisand smothered Sharif's Nicky Arnstein with the kind of total adoration that begs for total release. Wyler had often covered that territory, and *Funny Girl* was a well-disguised nostalgia trip into the time when men and women suffered bravely on the screen to purge the agonies of a matinee audience.

Wyler's heart transplant proved highly successful. The production was rich, the musical numbers were flashy, and audiences left the movie in an emotional glow. Women wept and said, "She loved him so much that she had to let him go." Men said, "He tried his best but she was more than he could handle." Nobody knew it yet, but the Streisand screen charisma was born. Such audience commitment is the stuff that popular hits are made of: The *Funny Girl* film, in its maudlin elegance, dispensed a profitable quota of tears and music. Streisand, the actress in song, milked the melodrama to the last drop when she threw her head back, sniffled in a powerful sob, and closed the show with a roof-raising anachronism: her sixties cabaret version of "My Man."

"Nobody sang like that in the twenties," Jule Styne now protests. "The only thing I'm shocked about Barbra is that she violated every code by doing 'My Man' the way Fanny Brice would never have dreamed of doing it. It was the most destructive thing." The public at large was not as exacting.

The film grossed $25,000,000 in America and went on to become a surprise hit in the foreign market that usually turns its back on Hollywood musicals. In Tokyo, Madrid, or Buenos Aires they were tolerant of all the singing as long as they could lap up the sad-glad story of proud Nicky and pushy Fanny.

Funny Girl was a smash, but Hollywood did not budge from its "show me" attitude about Barbra. All right, already, she was a star. The industry sorely needed crowd pullers like her. But they would not admit that Streisand had carried the show with her acting ability. The favorite story in movie circles was that astute Willie Wyler had nudged Barbra into a reenactment of her real-life problems, placing her performance on the level of psychodrama. They said she was so good in her last scene with the departing Nicky because she was playing—in Stanislavskyan manner—the collapse of her marriage to Elliott Gould.

Elliott's work in *The Night They Raided Minsky's* had proved that he could make it on his own. It was up to him now to reverse the classic ending of *A Star Is Born* and not drown in his wife's success but swim ashore. Hollywood had rewritten the scenario for Gould and Streisand. She was hard as nails, he was sweet as pie. He should get away from this overbearing superstar or be swept away with the tide. The couple was constantly surveyed, and Elliott could no longer take it.

On October 28 the Goulds attended the private screening of a new movie. As they walked out, photographer Anthony Rizzo shot a few pictures of them and the flashbulbs drove Elliott into a fury. He punched Rizzo, grabbed his camera, and stomped on it. The photographer filed suit against Gould, and the incident was splashed on the front pages of show-business tabloids. The clucking chorus of "tsk, tsk" grew louder. Why didn't this promising boy get out of an intolerable situation while there was still time? Now he didn't need Barbra and she certainly did not need him: She was just about to get close to $1,000,000 for her third movie, *On a Clear Day You Can See Forever.*

By the standards of a Hollywood fallen on hard times, it

was indeed a lot of money. Movie musicals were reportedly dead. Even Julie Andrews had not been saved by Mary Poppins' umbrella from her crash in the catastrophic *Star!* Musical performers on the unemployment lines wondered why Paramount was willing to invest several million in the hope that the Streisand lure could revive *On A Clear Day*, a thankless turkey stuffed with old chestnuts that the Broadway critics had roasted a couple of seasons before.

The libretto—a mélange of ESP and reincarnation—told the story of a New York nicotine addict who tried a hypnosis cure and astounded her psychiatrist by becoming, while in deep trance, a British lady of the early nineteenth century. The show was rescued from utter boredom by half a dozen good songs by Alan Jay Lerner and Burton Lane, but the ultimate effect was that of a *Search for Bridey Murphy* that had gone up the wrong psychedelic path and had landed in the middle of nowhere.

No deep Freudian analysis is needed to discover why Barbra Streisand was fascinated with the dual role. She would be a tacky, befuddled contemporary coed in one scene and a haughty aristocrat in the next. It was the princess/laundress syndrome compressed into a double-edged part. She said the dichotomy between the lowly Daisy and lofty Melinda came "very close to my schizophrenic personality: the frightened girl compared to the strong woman. It is just heaven!"

Streisand had been tired of *Funny Girl* before even the first scene was filmed. She had been justifiably wary of *Dolly*. At last she had a movie role she liked. She was determined to make it work and pull a Hollywood victory from the jaws of a Broadway defeat. Barbra got nothing but the best for *On a Clear Day*. Vincente Minnelli, whose Oscar-winning *Gigi* she admired, was selected as director. It was to be Streisand's first contemporary role and Arnold Scaasi was chosen to design the wardrobe for the modern sequences, while Cecil Beaton created the styles for the flashback into the London society of the Regency era.

Scaasi flew from New York to Los Angeles to discuss the fashion sketches with Barbra. He found her deeply immersed in her work. "We spent a whole day going over the styles she would wear as Daisy. By eight o'clock I was ready to quit," Scaasi remembers. "I had been invited to dinner at the Minnellis', so I stood up and said, 'Barbra, I must leave, I have a previous engagement.' She lifted her eyes from the sketches and very quietly said, 'Arnold, why did you come to Los Angeles?' She did not have to say another word. I immediately realized what she meant and that she was right. I was there on business, not on a social call. I phoned Vincente Minnelli and excused myself from dinner. We kept on working until past midnight. We had a job to do and we did it, no nonsense about it. That is what I admire in Barbra. She is a thorough professional, and I respond to her obstinacy because we are both Taurus. She also has this uncanny eye for detail. Once, when I sent her an embossed invitation to the opening of my collection, she wrote me a note explaining that she would be out of town on that date, and she added a postscript to call my attention to a misprint in the invitation."

Cecil Beaton was less responsive to Streisand's obdurate work ethic and her meticulous kibitzing. "She'll be producing and directing soon," he prophesied. "It's a constant battle with her and her taste—very exhausting." Undaunted, Barbra went on making suggestions and pointing out their flaws to everyone, gathering about the same amount of popularity as the smart-aleck student who raises his hand to inform the teacher that he has misspelled a word on the blackboard. She wanted to look exceptionally good in this picture, and she ran up a historic bill for $45,000 on retouching of the stills that were allowed to be released to the press.

Yet, compared to her two previous films, *On a Clear Day* was smooth going. Her co-star was Yves Montand, the seductive Frenchman who had captivated Marilyn Monroe during the filming of *Let's Make Love.* Fireworks of some sort, either romantic or temperamental, were expected from this odd couple. Columnists were oiling their typewriters, waiting for some marketable items that never came their way. Montand made the usual "oh-la-la" noises about working with talented Barbra and then subsided into mild catatonia: His performance in the film is so bland and unassuming that often Barbra seemed to be playing in a musical remake of *I Walked with a Zombie.*

Streisand took time off from *On a Clear Day* to attend the French premiere of *Funny Girl* in January, 1969. It took place at the Paris Opéra, and she was escorted by no less a show-business notable than Maurice Chevalier. Her fame had preceded her, the expectations of the public were high, and she was mobbed by thousands who wanted a close look at the star the papers were calling *"la petite juive."* The film was a hit, and it proved that Barbra's magic could work in any language, a reassuring fact in a movie business in which the foreign market was playing a vital 50 percent part in a picture's success.

Gould had not flown with her to Paris to play the part of smiling consort to the new box-office queen. He was busy rehearsing *A Way of Life*, a Murray Schisgal play he later abandoned a week before it closed during its pre-Broadway tour. There was no longer any pretense that the marriage was alive. The long-awaited announcement of their separation came on February 13, 1969, as tactfully worded as a diplomatic communiqué in which Metternich and Louella Parsons had collaborated: "We are separating not to destroy, but to save our marriage."

The double talk could not hide the facts. Barbra's private life had crumbled while her plutocratic empire was on the rise. Almost coinciding with the separation there was an announcement that she had signed a $5,000,000 deal with the new Las Vegas International Hotel, the highest sum ever paid for café appearances. She had insisted on receiving stock for the first year of her five-year obligation. The remaining four years she would get strictly cash. She was due to open in July for four weeks, at $250,000 a week.

Financially, the sky was no longer the limit for her, but she wanted something else: the Oscar. The New York Film Critics Award for best actress of 1968 had gone to Joanne Woodward for *Rachel, Rachel*, in close competition with Katharine Hepburn for *The Lion in Winter*, with not a single vote for

Streisand. When the Oscar nominations were announced, Barbra was in the running but against formidable rivals, including not only Woodward and Hepburn but also Patricia Neal in *The Subject Was Roses* as the sentimental favorite and Vanessa Redgrave in *Isadora,* who—despite the fact that she was disqualified by her politics—had actually given the indisputably best performance of that year, bar none.

The word was out in Hollywood: Detested Barbra would never win. The Academy members would just as well vote for Adolf Hitler. In her *On a Clear Day* dressing room she told reporter Dorothy Manners, "I want to win more than anything else in the world, but I can't believe I'm going to get it. It's the Jewishness in me, I guess, the pessimism. I can't win, not me. It's the agony and the ecstasy."

April 14 was the big night. Though officially estranged from her, Gould was staying at Barbra's house while he made the movie that would eventually make him a star in his own right: *Bob & Carol & Ted & Alice.* He dutifully escorted his not-quite-ex-wife to the Academy Awards ceremony.

When the best-actress winner was announced, a surprise was in store. Ingrid Bergman opened the envelope and forgot her well-learned English as she stammered in a Garboesque Scandinavian accent: "It is . . . it's a tie!" The audience winced in disbelief. Ingrid had stumbled on the first fifty-fifty Oscar since 1932, when Fredric March and Wallace Beery had shared the honor. The winners for 1968 were Katharine Hepburn and Barbra Streisand.

Reclusive Hepburn, of course, was nowhere to be seen. Streisand ran up the aisle in a revealing Scaasi number: a two-piece pajama held together by see-through gauze. As she tripped on the stairs to the stage, it seemed that she would end up showing more than was intended. But she recovered, held the statuette close to her nose, and cooed the first line from *Funny Girl:* "Hello, gorgeous." She was cool and composed, unfazed by the surprise tie, and she made a graceful impromptu speech saying that she was honored to be in such magnificent company as Katharine Hepburn. It was not at all the kind of speech the Hollywood contingent was waiting for. The Academy had bent over backward to give an Oscar to this controversial upstart for her movie debut. The least she could have done, in traditional Hollywood lore, was to dissolve in tears and blubber her thanks to everybody from her director to the grips to her mother and God, her Creator.

Next day notices were scathing. Barbra's reserve was termed disdainful, and her outfit was considered a provocation and a mockery of the solemnity of this annual parade of waxworks. Barbra did not care. It was only half an Oscar, but it gave her enough clout. Four days after the ceremony she flew to New York for location work in *On a Clear Day* and then to England for the very ornate scenes shot in the Royal Pavilion in Brighton. She cavorted around London, covered in expensive furs from head to toe, haggling with antique dealers in Portobello Road. She lorded over the sets with a Napoleonic conviction that she was the woman of destiny.

Streisand had sometimes harbored irrational fears that her audiences secretly wished that she would fall flat on her face. The night she picked up her Oscar those fears were justified. Maybe a resounding pratfall would teach Barbra the facts of Holywood life. The handwriting was on the wall. They would not have to wait long to find out.

12. *Where Am I Going?*

IN the spring of 1969 Barbra Streisand had consolidated a tidy monopoly on the media. It was time for her to pass "Go" and receive her symbolic $200 in the form of a warm recognition by her peers. When she returned from London in mid-May, she was chosen Entertainer of the Year by the Friars, a men's club for show-business personalities. Dinah Shore had been the only other woman to be selected for a similar tribute, and Barbra found herself as the honored guest in the sort of testimonial banquet usually reserved for stars celebrating their silver anniversary as topliners.

Streisand drew a record-breaking crowd of 1,200 to the Grand Ballroom of the Waldorf Astoria. The event had elements of *This Is your Life* sentimentality, guaranteed by the presence of several men who had contributed to her push to the top, from David Merrick to Harold Rome, from Harold Arlen to Jule Styne. As in the Oscar ceremony, some kind of tearful show of humility was expected from the kid who made good, but Barbra would not play the part. She was polite and grateful but never descended into breast-beating. The consensus was that she acted as if she deserved it all.

Immediately after the Friars dinner Barbra was supposed to film the last scenes of *On a Clear Day* on the campus at Fordham University, but negotiations for the use of the buildings fell through. In a hurry, Paramount tried to find another suitable campus for the sequence, but it was a time of student unrest and it was considered more judicious to wait until the summer lull to go on with the picture.

Production on the $10,000,000 movie stopped on May 21, 1969. The film would now continue beyond the expiration date of Streisand's contact, and the delays were bound to interfere with her scheduled opening of the Las Vegas International Hotel. Now Barbra, the arrogant kid who would not buckle, was cast as the Frankenstein monster of the new Hollywood: *Variety* printed rumors that she had Paramount "over a barrel" and would demand a staggering sum to appear before the cameras again. Producer Howard V. Koch denied the story; the campus sequences were finally shot without a hitch. But the fact that the rumors ever circulated is a measure of the fear with which the movie industry now approached the profitable star they had created.

With *Clear Day* wrapped up and tucked in, Barbra arrived on time for her nightclub act in Las Vegas. She had a proprietary interest in the International Hotel: When she had signed the initial contract, she had received 20,000 shares at five dollars per share; by opening night they were each worth fifty dollars. She had made a tidy profit on the sixty-story luxury hotel and wanted to give it a glittering send-off, but many things went wrong. The launching of the International placed Barbra in the embarrassing position of those matrons in wartime newsreels who try to look their best while smashing a magnum of champagne against the hulk of an aircraft carrier and instead find themselves sprayed with the bubbly.

The hotel was starting operations on a crash plan to meet a deadline. Barbra rehearsed at the nightclub while curtains were draped and light fixtures hammered into walls. The superprofessional in her was not deluded: This was going to be somewhat below her standards of perfection. Barbra wanted to appear before her audience in dungarees and work shirt, explain that the place was still unfinished, and then change into more suitable attire for the rest of her turn as soon as the public was safely in with her on the joke. The management would not hear of this. She came out flowing in gauze, and all through her first song a rain of plaster fell on her. A performer versed in the veiled hypocrisy sometimes called nonchalance would have ignored the mishap, but basic Barbra simply informed the audience, "This is not a snow effect. It's plaster."

A standard nightclub act had been written for her. It was a mistake. Barbra has proved herself to be a fine comedienne, but she is woefully inadequate as a stand-up comic. The job requires a performer with steamroller confidence to flatten the audience's defenses. Barbra can be very funny when she is assuming a role and hiding behind a theatrical mask, but not when she is pretending to be herself. Barbra as Barbra is a role that escapes her range, as demonstrated by her awkward, though blessedly brief, monologues during concerts. At the International she stumbled through arid stretches of one-way conversation, all glass jaw and limpid punch, a weak sparring partner for the tough customers.

Reviews wavered between the unimpressed and the unkind. Joyce Haber, the columnist who had labeled her a "girl monster" on the *Funny Girl* set, wrote that her patter was dreary, her repertory inappropriate, and her delivery cold. Barbra admitted the faults and tightened her act, eliminating most of the talk and concentrating on an hour of singing, concert style. Joyce Haber came back to watch the revised show and gave her a rave notice, coupling Barbra with Sinatra as the two greatest entertainers of the era.

Whether chastened or praised, Streisand hated doing her turn. When Haber visited her dressing room in the middle of the four-week stint, Barbra showed her a calendar with each day crossed out. "Only thirty-nine more performances to go," she sighed like a prisoner in mid-sentence.

Some performers derive an emotional charge from a live audience. Not Streisand. She had submitted herself to the torture in the beginning because there was nothing else. Her international success with the *Funny Girl* picture had given her a new taste for the kind of vicarious impact that did not require a nightly drain on her energy. "There's nothing better than to know that I can be taking a bath at home and at the same time someone is watching me in Brazil," she said. On the screen she could sell her image; onstage she had to sell herself. It was inevitable that the movies would pull her like a magnet.

In June of 1968 she fulfilled Cecil Beaton's prophecy that she would eventually become her own producer. Streisand, Paul Newman, and Sidney Poitier formed their own film-production company, just as Mary Pickford, Douglas Fairbanks, and Charles Chaplin had when they had started United Artists. Even the name they chose was reminiscent of that landmark rebellion of beleaguered stars against finagling money men: First Artists Productions would be their own enclave, with no poachers admitted. Each of the three partners was committed to star and produce three films for the company, with complete control over their material.

There were still some faint hopes for Streisand's return to Broadway. She gave some consideration to a musical on *Napoleon and Josephine* with Anthony Newley as Bonaparte. She demanded a limited run and final approval of the script, a one-two punch that knocked the project out before it ever got near the ring. Streisand was more substantially lured to Broadway by her dream role as Sarah Bernhardt in a musical version of the life and times of the celebrated actress. It would offer her a chance to do scenes from two of her favorite plays, *Camille* and *L'Aiglon*, which were part of the Divine Sarah's repertoire. Yet the dream could turn into a nightmare because she would have to sign a run-of-the-play contract to make the project feasible.

She backed out of playing Bernhardt onstage, but she said it was inevitable that she would play her someday in a film. "I can wear my hair in the frizziest look," she told *Look* magazine. "You know Bernhardt acted Hamlet and not Ophelia and so will I." As a token gesture to her unrealized ambition, she made herself up to resemble Sarah for her next album cover. The hair in tiny Medusa curls melded with the rivulets of a feather boa; the beringed fingers tragically clenched against overrouged cheeks; the eyes were frozen in an unnamed plea.

This was a Streisand album you could not judge by its cover, though. In spite of the deliberate quaintness of the photograph, the musical content was Barbra's first clean break with the past. The quest for contemporary answers was expressed bluntly in the title song, "What About Today?" The record was a hymn to youth, celebrated in the liner notes Barbra herself wrote and signed, dedicating the album to "the young people who push against indifference, shout down mediocrity, demand a better future, and who write and sing the songs of today."

In "What About Today?" Barbra raged against the slow-crawling future with the frustration of an existential commuter who can't wait any longer for the arrival of the gravy train. The songs were chosen from the repertories of such composers as Paul Simon, Buffy Saint-Marie, and Lennon/McCartney. A feeling of protest rang through them, from Jim Webb's antiwar elegy "Little Tin Soldier" to the question "Ask Yourself Why." Streisand was abandoning the sweet nostalgia of good days gone by for an acid impatience with the intolerable delay of youthful Nirvana.

She was sated with accentuating positives and eliminating negatives like a messed-up Mrs. In-Between. She did not want to do cabarets or Broadway musicals, but where was *Hello, Dolly!*, the film that would consolidate her beachhead as a movie star? The premiere had been postponed indefinitely because David Merrick refused to give permission for its release as long as the Broadway production was running to capacity audiences.

Merrick kept resuscitating Dolly at the St. James Theatre with a series of casting coups. First Ginger Rogers picked up where Carol Channing left off, then an all-black cast led to a very popular version built around Pearl Bailey. The show threatened to run for years, with Betty Grable, Dorothy Lamour, Martha Raye, and Ethel Merman waiting in the wings as future Dollys. Twentieth Century-Fox feared that the Streisand movie would have to be shelved until at least 1971.

The film's budget weighed heavily in Fox's depleted ledger. Merrick owned stock in the company, and he was asked to see a rough cut of the picture in hopes that he might relent. "Merrick loved it," Arthur Laurents recalls. "He came back from the coast and told me to buy some shares in Fox because they would go sky high as soon as the picture opened." A show selling out on Broadway was nothing compared to the profits from a hit movie; Merrick gave the green light for the prerelease of Streisand's *Dolly* as a Christmas attraction in 1969.

For Streisand, the movie star, one hurdle was cleared. The next was about to crumble. Ellbar's dispute with Rastar Productions was amicably settled. Producer Stark had toyed with the idea of making *The Owl and the Pussycat* with Elizabeth Taylor and Richard Burton, but nothing had come out of it. Stark finally handed Barbra the starring role in the movie version of Bill Manhoff's hit play, which would go before the cameras in the early fall.

She approached *The Owl and the Pussycat* in a state of exhilaration. Unlike her first three movie roles, this was a nonsinging contemporary part with no period costumes, wigs, or dubbing sessions. She said she had hated doing those big musicals, which burdened her with rehearsals, recordings, fittings. "Now I can make a movie in ten weeks," she enthused. "No songs, like a normal person. You do a movie in the daytime and then you go home at night."

Barbra enjoyed the respite. She arrived at sound stages rented on West Fifty-sixth Street in New York to play a straight comedy part in a very congenial atmosphere with George Segal, a co-star she liked, and Herb Ross, a director she trusted. Then she went back to her apartment to study the lines for the next day. Working with a small unit, she was relaxed and untemperamental, but she was still far from what the lower echelons of moviemaking take to heart and call "one of the boys."

Antonia Rey, a fine Broadway actress, had landed a bit part in the film. She was astonished at Streisand's entourage. "I've never seen anything like it, and I've worked with Joanne Woodward and Faye Dunaway," Antonia recalls. "She had five or six people dabbing little powder puffs all over her before she came on the set. When she did, there was a red carpet from her dressing room to the camera. She is a very private person. She seemed to accept all her retinue like a necessary evil. Some may have disliked her because she was wrapped up in her little circle and I don't know why. The woman was doing a job, a difficult one, and there was no reason for her to run around dissipating her energy and telling everyone 'Hi, there' like a public relations man. I made an enemy on that set when I defended her by saying, 'Why should she talk to you or to me? I have nothing to say to Streisand. Why should she have something to say to me?' "

The rest of the *Owl and the Pussycat* group were less understanding. Barbra spent most of her spare time reading Proust in her dressing room between takes. One day a unit publicity man found her, ruler in hand, trying to paint a Mondrian-style canvas. "That's the way they do it, don't they?" she asked. He now describes her as "a totally empty woman, a vacuum. She comes alive before the cameras, but when they say 'Cut' she recedes. There's nothing left for anybody, including herself."

A woman who worked as press contact in the film is even more critical. "She got along with those who kowtowed to her, like George Segal. They had expensive meals from the top Chinese restaurants sent in, while we, the plebeians, had to munch on a stale sandwich. The picture was shooting around Thanksgiving, and Ray Stark gave everyone in the crew a fifteen-pound turkey as a gift. You know what Streisand gave us? Two of her albums a head!"

The stories, like most of the hate-Streisand anecdotes, strive to show the star as villain, but really offer nothing more damning than the portrait of a woman who is equally parsimonious with her time and her money. Yet Barbra's enemies on the *Owl and the Pussycat* set save their strongest ammunition to blast her for an incident that occurred on a Friday afternoon. Barbra had a Monday deadline to deliver an evaluation of her own personality that would be a part of a series of autobiographical stories then being printed by *Life* magazine.

Streisand asked Buck Henry, the author of the film's screenplay, to go over her notes. Henry offered suggestions on what paragraphs to delete, what statements to tone down because they could make her vulnerable to criticism. "She was clearly incensed," the Barbra watchers say. "You could see that Buck Henry was trying his friendly best as he got smaller and smaller under her frown. She did not accept a single one of his suggestions and was very aloof to him during the rest of the shooting." The article, as it finally ran in the magazine, was very honest, refreshingly candid, and not at all antagonizing. It is clear her animosity toward Buck Henry was just in the eyes of the prejudiced beholders: Months later she would demand him as the man to do a crucial rewrite job on her next film, *What's Up Doc?*

The stories that filter from the *Owl and the Pussycat* set are interesting because they indicate how far Barbra's predicament had gone. She had strived to be an individual and had become a character. Everything she did, innocuous or not, was interpreted as part of her being "in character." She had never been more relaxed or acquiescent, but if she blew her nose into a Kleenex while talking to someone, it was interpreted as a put-down from the cantankerous superstar.

Her worst day in *The Owl and the Pussycat* came when her

mother paid a visit to the set. Diane Streisand Kind told reporters, "She had on a skimpy costume and was very embarrassed when she saw me. I'm really shocked at all those things actresses have to do today, but I guess it's part of the job." The phantoms from her puritan past were still watching Barbra. When it was printed that she would do a nude scene in the film, Elliott told a fan magazine that she would never do it because she was very shy.

Barbra was petrified on the day she had to remove her bra before she got in bed with George Segal for the controversial sequence. All nonessential personnel were banned from the set. Director Herb Ross had to coax her for an hour while she moaned, "What will my mother think of this?" Ross said that once she did it the first time it became easier for her, "but it really cost her." The ordeal was in vain because the scene was edited into a no-nipple chastity that ensured a more benign censorship rating for this pseudo-audacious movie.

Barbra was trying to liberate herself precisely at the moment when her family ties were becoming more binding. Her eighteen-year-old sister, Rosalind Kind, had been an adoring camp follower for years as president of the Barbra Streisand Fan Club. Her mama credited Rosalind with the best Streisand imitation ever, perfected after watching her older sister forty times during the *Funny Girl* run. As soon as Rosalind was graduated from Julia Richman High School, she decided on a future as a rock-and-roll singer, changing her name to Roslyn. Her first album had been released in the summer of 1969, to a hearty publicity fanfare for "Barbra's winning little sister."

Roslyn had been booked into the Persian Room at the Plaza Hotel for a mid-December opening. Diane Streisand Kind was promoting her second daughter's career as vehemently as she had opposed Barbra's. Mama was even confiding to the New York *Times* that she was also taking singing lessons in order to perhaps make her long-postponed debut sometime. When asked if she could yet be the third star in the family, she circuited the question with an ominous "Who can tell?"

The press scented a feud that Barbra denied by attending

Roslyn's first night at the Persian Room and posing with her mother and half sister for a family tableau. For better or worse, she did not otherwise interfere with Roslyn's career. Barbra was judged a little more than kin and less than kind, but in her records Roslyn sounds like a girl in good voice and high spirits, with no distinctive qualities as a popular singer. Barbra had achieved the nearly impossible by making a star of herself against all odds; it was excessive to ask her to repeat the miracle once removed.

It was a difficult time for Barbra. She wished to live for today, but her yesterdays stubbornly refused to be erased. She tried to move out of the penthouse on Central Park West, that ornate tree house now permanently abandoned by Elliott Gould. She was rejected as a potential buyer for a twenty-room co-op apartment at 1107 Fifth Avenue. She took the rebuff with quiet annoyance. Then she was turned down on her option to buy a $240,000 apartment at 1021 Park Avenue. Now she was filled with righteous indignation.

The wife of a member of the building's board of admission had blackballed Streisand because she was considered "a flamboyant type." In turn, Barbra was considering a complaint to the Commission on Human Rights because she felt the rejection of her application might have come partly because she was Jewish. The issue dissolved before it came to arbitration. What Streisand was up against was not really religious prejudice but an ingrained middle-class fear that show-business personalities would practice on the piano for hours and throw noisy parties till dawn. She had to face it: she was special and had to live accordingly. Accepting the enforced isolation, she bought a five-story town house on a residential street in the East Eighties.

The mansion needed ten times as much work as she had put into that tiny flat on top of the seafood restaurant a decade before, but she had lost the fighting spirit to knock down walls and scrub fireplaces. She tinkered with the place for a while and staged a housewarming to further the campaign of Congresswoman Bella Abzug, a spunky lady whose courage she admired. Then she gave up and sold the house before it was ever refurbished. Barbra had come all the way up from

Pulaski Street, and once she had proved her point she was bored. As much as she liked Art Nouveau, there was no lure in gilding the lily any further. When she bought another town house in the same neighborhood, the redecorating job was left almost entirely in the hands of professionals. She merely supervised the work, insisting that everyone on the staff call her, not by her star name of Miss Streisand, but by a title she had an ever-waning claim to: Mrs. Gould.

Hello, Dolly! was, at long last, opening on December 12, 1969. It was the very day when the final and most difficult scene of *The Owl and the Pussycat* was scheduled to be shot in Central Park. As Doris, the respectful prostitute, Barbra was supposed to weep and plead to Felix, the owlish intellectual, to give her a chance for marriage and respectability. The scene demanded a breaking down of sedulously kept self-defenses, the crumbling of a tough character into a last-minute humiliation. It was to be the crowd-pleasing, sentimental conclusion to a tough screenplay. Barbra must have had a hard time believing it, and she just could not play it. From the first alfresco rehearsal everyone in the crew felt there was going to be trouble.

A production manager planning an outdoor shooting schedule for a movie is forced to be part traffic cop, part meteorologist. That particular Wednesday had been selected after consulting an often unreliable oracle: the weather forecaster. It was supposed to be sunny all day, but around noon, as Streisand and Segál ran down the grassy slopes in the park—alternating roles as pursuer and pursued—the skies began to cloud ominously. And still Barbra could not summon the right emotional pitch.

"I can't cry." she told director Herb Ross. "I just can't do it." Ever the realist, she shunned glycerin tears. Take after take was fluffed. The crew looked up apprehensively at the waning sun. Then director Ross pulled a trick from the Stanislavskyan primer and gave it a twist. Instead of plunging Barbra into the past for a grim memory that would burst the dam, he astutely inverted the technique and nudged her into the very near future.

Ross apologized to his blocked star for keeping her so long

at this harrowing pace. In a few hours, at eight o'clock, she would have to face the crowds at the *Hello, Dolly!* premiere. She would certainly look tired and drawn after this ordeal. Nothing else was needed. When the cameras rolled again, Barbra cried him a river on cue, clinching the denouement that would make the picture into a hit.

Gratified by the feeling of a job well done, Barbra was at her regal best in the *Dolly* premiere, unruffled by a turbulent crowd that almost upturned her limousine and pummeled her manager in a mad effort to get near the star. She could have saved those tears she had just shed in Central Park for the next morning. That night on the screen of the Rivoli Theatre, when Dolly walked down those stairs in the Harmonia Gardens, she faced, not a chorus of smiling waiters, but a well-trained firing squad. Reviewers machine-gunned the movie.

"You can't lie to a camera," Streisand had once said while filming the musical. Now her words leaped back at her from the screen. She had approached Dolly from the outside, in quasi-Brechtian manner, showing the audience the foibles of a character she could not identify with. She had distanced herself from this bossy woman who arranges lives: the public could sense the invisible ten-foot pole between the actress and the role she did not believe in. Streisand's Dolly was wry and irreverent, like a disciple of Groucho Marx disrupting a high school pageant.

She zoomed into hilarious parody on the spur of the moment, but then, just as unpredictably, she would let everyone in on a well-kept secret: that Dolly was a pitiable, destitute widow who lived by her wits and was always a two-step away from starvation. Either way this was not the Dolly millions had adored. The Streisand version of *Hello, Dolly!* is a very mixed bag of highs and lows, but it could have been saved—at least financially—if there had been a communicable rap port between Streisand and Matthau. They seem so aloof that they create their own subliminal split-screen technique. In their obvious, blistering dislike for each other, the script's little heart shriveled like a raisin.

What was left was a white elephant that Barbra rode without the benefit of attendant clowns. Gene Kelly's superannuated choreography made the big numbers look like dismal rejects from MGM's cutting-room floor in the forties. Only Barbra, stomping on the metronome, brought the movie sporadically to life with flashes of sarcasm: when a supposedly awkward store clerk exclaimed, "I'm dancing," and leaped into a typical burst of Kelly balletomania, Streisand slyly dropped a pungent aside, "I think he's been holding out on us all the time!"

It was evident the film would never make a profit, and she defended herself by repeating that she had never wanted to play Dolly Levi in "a piece of fluff I could not respond to." As the film opened all over America, she told *Look* magazine, "I'm interested in real life, in real people and in playing Medea. *Hello, Dolly!* takes place in an age before people realized they hated their mothers, the whole Freudian thing. It was something I could not delve into psychologically but I had fun with it because I didn't have to be in every single scene for once and got a lot of days off."

These are not very tactful remarks from the star of a movie that had Twentieth Century Fox up to its collective ears in red ink. Eventually, according to *Variety, Hello, Dolly!* brought back $15,000,000 of the monstrous $21,000,000 it is supposed to have cost. Streisand had been right when she had insisted on the set that she was struggling to improve *her* picture. The film went down in the books, not as Fox's folly, not as Kelly's or Matthau's mistake, but as Barbra Streisand's first movie flop.

Every time Streisand suffers a professional setback she retreats into her personal life and struggles not to care. Now she said she was tired of the fake glitter of tinsel stardom and wanted to meet an attractive, mature, nonnarcissistic man who had nothing to do with the arts. She mentioned Pierre Trudeau, Canada's Prime Minister, as being high on the list. Trudeau obliged by dating her a couple of times in New York. Columnists began concocting the kind of scenario that MGM had neglected to film in the thirties, under the gooey title of *The Premier and the Showgirl.*

On January 30, 1970, as *Hello, Dolly!* began to show a

death pallor in half-empty movie houses, Barbra was blithe and rosy in Montreal. She attended a ballet performance, and next morning she was a distinguished guest in the gallery of Canada's House of Commons. Her presence was noted by a member of the opposition Conservative Party who jokingly asked Premier Trudeau if he could take his eyes off the visitors' gallery to answer a tricky question. Trudeau laughed and blushed, as Barbra guffawed and tapped the gallery rail. When the session was over, she visited the Prime Minister's office for a cup of coffee. To gawking reporters she said she had never seen a Parliament before, "not even on my own."

That was the end of a friendship that never transcended the level of "cute publicity" for its participants. Trudeau was even more shy and jealous of his privacy than Barbra. He quickly shied away from this brief span in the show-biz limelight. Barbra was back to the wry disappointment of being free and independent. She no longer had dependable Elliott to hold onto.

Their relationship had become strained after a *Ladies' Home Journal* interview which quoted him as saying that Barbra was really a self-centered fourteen-year-old, who constantly complained, was disdainful of men, competitive toward them, and felt they could not be trusted. Gould protested his words had been distorted and rejected the article as "a piece of rubbish, totally unrealistic." Barbra had been very upset in reading it and he was sorry because he was her friend, they had a son, and he felt Jason's mother would always be very special to him.

Despite Gould's protestations of innocence, the rift became deeper on April 7, 1970, the night of the Oscar ceremonies. *Hello, Dolly!* had received seven nominations, including a charitable one for best film. Twentieth Century-Fox was in trouble over this bedizened turkey, and the Hollywood contingent was trying to bail the company out, but not to the extent of nominating Streisand, who was conspicuously ignored. On the other hand, Elliott had risen from the doldrums and was the odds-on contestant for his supporting role in *Bob & Carol & Ted & Alice.*

Barbra got her moment onstage when she handed an Oscar to the best actor, John Wayne, for *True Grit.* Elliott never made it up the aisle; he was beaten in a last-minute upset by Gig Young in *They Shoot Horses, Don't They?* Still it was Elliott's night. He was no longer Barbra's patient escort but a star whom fans in the bleachers recognized and cheered. He had a stack of movie scripts to choose his next dozen films from. It was two-for-the-seesaw time: he was on the way up while she was being pulled down a peg by her unfortunate *Dolly.*

"Serves her right . . . serves her right." Three little words, encrusted in spite, echoed all over Hollywood. Detested Barbra was getting her comeuppance, and according to the preview circuit chitchat, there was more trouble to come. *On a Clear Day You Can See Forever,* initially conceived as a three-hour road-show presentation, was being hacked down to two hours for general release in the summer. The film was not going to make the big grade, and Paramount, after the *Hello, Dolly!* debacle, was aiming for a fast play-off before word got around that the musical lacked the dynamite charge to become a blockbuster.

All fears were confirmed when *On a Clear Day* opened in June, 1970. Minnelli's magic had not conjured the narrative flow from a disjointed screenplay, plunged further into incoherence by the elimination of miles of footage. The film seemed to be put together, not with scissors and tape in a movieola, but by machete wielders in the Mato Grosso. The cutting spree amounted to wholesale emasculation: The men in the cast ranged from ineffectual to practically nonexistent.

Jack Nicholson, fresh from an acclaimed, Oscar-nominated role in *Easy Rider,* sleepily strummed a sitar on the sidelines like a zonked-out bit player. His part had been so drastically abbreviated that no one seemed to know what he was doing in the picture: In the soundtrack album notes Nicholson is contradictorily referred to as Barbra's "step-brother" or her "current true love." Larry Blyden, a droll comedian, was miscast as Barbra's priggish fiance. Worst of all was Yves Montand. Stumped by Lerner's intricate lyrics, he missed all the hidden rhymes and murdered two of the best songs with the dedication of a Berlitz student squeezing the right pronunciation but the wrong emphasis from each word.

Streisand was again left alone to carry the show. She tried diligently. Her occasional brilliance is pathetic in these hopeless circumstances. As the maladroit Daisy she sits in self-defense, her knees close together like a do-it-yourself chastity belt, or she erupts into frantic turns that give the slapstick queens—from Mabel Normand to Judy Canova—a run for their money. Then, as she flashbacks to Melinda, the darling of the Brighton Pavilion, the mystery of her ineffable beauty is highlighted by Cecil Beaton's costumes, Harry Stradling's photography, and Vincente Minnelli's direction.

As the femme fatale she slinks like a panther hungering for the equally fatal beauty of an amoral rake, played by John Richardson. Her voice takes on the smoky timbre and exquisite diction of a Joan Greenwood as she plays the seducer seduced. Her superbly lit features are translucent as she flirts with Richardson, using her champagne glass first as a distorting monocle, then as a comforter to cool her lips, neck, and cleavage. She soon topples from erotic insinuation and ladylike grandeur as Melinda meets her scullery-maid mama, and Streisand plays the cockney upstart with the bite of an aitchless guttersnipe.

On a Clear Day was a Panavision portfolio of all that Streisand could do. She would have given her brand-new bicuspids for it when she was doing the rounds of casting offices in 1960. But now she was a star and audiences wanted to see her as a projection of their fantasies of conquest and surrender. As Melinda she was betrayed and left in the lurch by a roué. As Daisy she was sucked dry of memories by a vampirish psychiatrist who fed on the lifeblood of her alter ego. Give or take a couple of centuries, she was a two-time loser. Streisand fans concurred that the movie was "awfully pretty but kind of depressing."

This is not the response that makes lighthearted musicals into box-office hits. *On a Clear Day* cost above $10,000,000 to produce and brought back under $5,000,000. Had it been a modest song-and-dance show, it would have been profitable, but the Streisand vehicles were too expensive for a shrinking movie market. Her drawing powers had not diminished, but she was in a financial predicament as star insurance for unsalvageable projects.

A woolly Hollywood proverb was now being applied to Streisand. You are as good as your last movie, and she had had two clinkers in a row. No dazzling million-dollar musicals were coming her way. She went back to fulfilling her Las Vegas contracts, belting out her expected repertory for saloon audiences. The customers had listened to the songs so often in records that they broke into applause after a few bars of the introduction. She was like a raconteur who is about to tell a story and is rudely interrupted by a misguided friend with "I've heard it before, but please don't stop, I love it!" At the Riviera and the International she cried a river, shooed away those happy days, and identified herself resignedly with that "Second Hand Rose" who never had a thing that ain't been used. It was all profitable and frustrating.

But Streisand always bounces back with the resilience of a paddleball. Her "little" movie, *The Owl and the Pussycat,* opened quietly, with no big premiere fandango, in November, 1970, and after tallying the first-week grosses, *Variety* was again calling her "a sizzling hot property."

Bill Manhoff's two-character play had amusingly chronicled the improbable romance between an unsuccessful writer and a luckless hooker as a sort of apolitical *Born Yesterday.* Gradually delighted by the sharp intelligence hidden under her vast ignorance, "the owl" began teaching "the pussycat" words from the dictionary and ended up falling in love with his creation. In his screenplay Buck Henry had opened up the original play with the insomniac eye of an inveterate *Late Show* watcher. The film had the nostalgic aura of Frank Capra's thirties populist fantasies: it was the sort of comedy James Stewart and Jean Arthur would have essayed a couple of decades before if the Hays office had not been snooping over everyone's shoulder. *The Owl and the Pussycat* was a wry version of the Pygmalion myth, equipped with a fair lady who was never ethereal, always earthbound. The audience loved it.

In her first straight comedy role Streisand left her musical crutches behind and strode into the part with the pace and timing of a Derby winner. Her Doris was brassy, overbearing, fast-talking: the type of character one would want to choke in mid-sentence if she were sitting at the next table in a restaurant. Yet Streisand injected an element of pathos into each tirade. Doris rolled into Felix' life like a Sherman tank loaded to the turret with taffy. As she stripped off layers of bravado, Streisand made the girl more and more vulnerable and likable.

For the first time, in George Segal, Streisand found a male lead she could play with instead of against. Walter Matthau had been acid, Omar Sharif had been waxen and Yves Montand wooden, but Segal's Felix had the exact quality as the darling *schlemiel* who convincingly brought out the mother yen in Doris, the *yenta.*

Segal and Streisand worked magically as a team, illustrating Schopenhauer's theory that the ideal couple is the one in which the man's feminine components equally match the woman's masculine traits. In a hilarious inversion of the movie cliché Segal played the shy maiden to Streisand's uncontrollable seducer. The exquisite balance had a subliminal effect on the public and turned ticket buyers into matchmakers. Everyone was rooting for those two to get together. This collective desire for heterosexual harmony justified the improbable happy ending and made the film a smash.

The Owl and the Pussycat, with a modest budget that never remotely compared to the huge expenditure of previous Streisand vehicles, grossed close to $12,000,000 in the United States alone, and it was just as popular abroad. In a film market dominated by male stars the picture firmly established Streisand next to Elizabeth Taylor as the only two actresses within the ten top box-office attractions.

Funny Girl had not been a flash in the pan. Whatever it was, Streisand had it. Hollywood heaved a deep sigh and braced itself for the inevitable. She had been called imperious, rude, unmanageable, capricious, temperamental. Now there was an all-redeeming adjective to be added, in black ink, to the roster: She was "bankable."

13. *The Greatest Star*

BARBRA STREISAND had spent twenty-seven years of her life indefatigably pursuing the ultimate intangible: success. In the early sixties she had despaired because she could not hold it in her hand like a boiled egg. In the mid-sixties she had consoled herself by comparing it to a baked potato because it got crustier on the outside, mushier on the inside, and infinitely tastier after reheating it on the third day.

By the late sixties her overflowing larder of food similes was getting depleted. Professional triumph was really like those elaborate Chinese dinners she loved: After seventeen carefully chopped ingredients were added to the fried rice, one could still be hungry again in a couple of hours. She craved something more nourishing, more lasting. But before she found it she was going to have some of the fun she had denied herself throughout that decade when she had been her own sternest disciplinarian.

Barbra began to loosen up. The bourgeois shackles had been carefully soldered by Mama back in Brooklyn, but that was as far away as the Ice Age and Barbra was thawing. The Streisand shrug no longer meant "I'll show you" but "Who cares?" During Christmas of 1970 she interrupted her show at the Las Vegas International for "tea time" onstage. She pretended to puff on a marijuana joint to the considerable shock of the predominantly middle-aged audiences who could afford ringside tables: They were socially conditioned to frown on smoking the befuddling weed even after they had gulped down their third lethal martini.

She giggled at their distress. Twenty years later the yeshiva school brat was still glorying in her capacity to amaze. It was high time to defy convention since conformity seemed beyond her: She had failed at playing Mrs. Gould. Barbra was still emotionally attached to Elliott, and every time they were seen together false hopes were heralded by columnists: When he took her to see a preview of his hit film *M.A.S.H.*, the rumor spread like wildfire. A reconciliation was about to be announced.

But the Goulds were only marking time until the next, irrevocable step toward divorce. It was the winter of Barbra's discontent, but it was also the winter of *Love Story*. Barbra saw a preview of the film, and the stage was set for the next episode.

The film version of the tear-drenched novel became a four-handkerchief blockbuster that turned Ryan O'Neal into the impossible dream of female moviegoers. Tall, blond, dimpled, with the sort of clean-cut handsomeness that turns women into girls and television commercials into idylls, O'Neal was the season's Prince Charming. He would brush the last of the ashes from Barbra's Cinderella myth and establish her as Hollywood's reigning princess.

O'Neal was a prize catch and Barbra could not resist the challenge. When they started dating, stars and starlets went into envious eclipse from Burbank to Culver City. Just as with Gould in the early days, "What does he see in her?" became the battle cry of the ignored. In a paroxysm of rancor someone dubbed them "the Prince and the Frogess," a tag that was easily appropriated by others as if it had just been coined between poolside gin and tonics.

Their friendship was fraught with the manufactured publicity menace that Hedda Hopper used to wield like an evil hatpin. Movie stars are often asked to conform their lives to the absurd scenarios their fans concoct while watching their performances. It was expected that O'Neal would eventually return to his estranged wife, Leigh Taylor-Young, whom addicts of the television soap opera *Peyton Place* had cast as his ideal mate. Party hopping with Streisand was just an irritating way of postponing the happy ending. Friend and foe alike were predicting that if his fondness for Barbra broke into the news media, the faux pas would strip O'Neal of all chances of winning the Oscar for *Love Story*.

The combination of star personalities was just too explosive. Streisand and O'Neal were painfully discreet, but it was no use. They became the talk of the town when they were seen together at a party for O'Neal at the home of star agent Sue Mengers, then at the opening of singer James Taylor at the Troubadour. Hollywood—the most public city in the world—hates a well-kept secret; they inevitably balloon out of all proportion until they burst. On January 10, 1971, Streisand and O'Neal were at a party given by recording executive Robert Kraskow, then drove to the Civic Stadium in Santa Monica for a rock concert. They could not have been more prim. Kevin O'Neal was supposed to be Barbra's date, with his older brother, Ryan, tagging along as a chaperon. The very idea of trying to fool the Hollywood press was too much of a provocation.

During the early party photographer Peter Borsari had tried to get a photo of Barbra and Ryan together, but he had been adamantly refused. As they left, the enterprising *paparazzo* hopped in his car and followed them to the concert. What ensued was another version of a Hollywood ritual: the parking-lot fracas. As they were leaving the stadium incognito, a lightning storm of flashbulbs exploded. Kevin O'Neal, protecting his brother's privacy, came to the rescue and tried to wrest the camera away from Borsari. "Don't fight me, I can sue," the photographer shouted. "You can sue me for as much as you want," Kevin shouted back. "I have no money, anyway." Punches flew, lenses cracked. The episode was splashed all over the tabloids. In their secrecy Streisand and O'Neal had achieved precisely what they were avoiding. Now they were no longer an item but a headline.

Less than a month later the Goulds signed a private separation agreement. It provided that after two more years of living apart they could file for a divorce. The tree house had been chopped down to its roots. That chapter was definitely closed.

Elliott had become one of the most sought-after young actors in the movie industry. The years of inactivity and yearning were over. The dam had burst and he swam with the torrent, unable to say no to any enticing project. After *Bob & Carol & Ted & Alice* he made five movies in eighteen months: *M.A.S.H., Getting Straight, Move!, Little Murders,* and *I Love My Wife.*

Gould was in danger of overexposure, and columnists were reviving a deadly joke: "I saw a movie last night and—could you believe it?—Elliott Gould wasn't in it." Just when he should have taken a vacation, someone made him an offer he could not refuse. Sweden's Ingmar Bergman, one of the world's great film directors, was planning his first English-language venture and he wanted Elliott to play the lead.

In *The Touch* Gould was ludicrously miscast as a brooding American who exorcises his guilt over an incestuous relationship with a malformed half sister by wrecking the desiccated marriage of Max Von Sydow and Bibi Andersson. Justifiably baffled by the part, Gould trampled like an untrained bear all over the crystalline allusions of the screenplay. His role made no sense, but it did not matter; he felt inspired by Ingmar Bergman.

The Touch, on its release, would turn out to be a disaster, but Gould was the ingenuous boy from Brooklyn who had experienced Art with a capital *A.* He was no longer the lovable bumbler of homegrown movies; he had played a sinister character on a par with the ones that Barbra had hoped for him when she had called him "the American Belmondo." After exposure to the light of Bergman's midnight sun the commercial world of Hollywood movies looked dim, uninviting.

Elliott had previous commitments, and he again hopscotched from one movie to the next. He started the ill-fated *A Glimpse of Tiger* in New York, under the aegis of his partner in production, Jack Brodsky. But Gould had been in the presence of Bergman's genius, and now, deprived of his guru, he felt like Siddhartha, doomed to walk aimlessly among the fleshpots, a spiritual pariah. "I found everybody was made of cardboard," he later said, trying to explain his troubled state of mind.

Rehearsals for *A Glimpse of Tiger* were a nightmare. Gould went into tantrums and blew a whistle when his fellow performers failed to achieve perfection. On the first day of location shooting in a Manhattan subway station there was a freak accident involving an incoming train, and though no one was injured, the tension could be measured with a Geiger counter.

A couple of Gould's friends, actors David Carradine and Barbara Hershey, dropped in for a visit. Director Anthony Harvey felt they were distracting the star and ordered them off the set. Elliott flew into a rage and—in his capacity as co-producer—fired Harvey on the spot. The shooting day was finished under the impromptu supervision of associate producer Burt Harris. Next morning Jack Brodsky reinstated Harvey, and Gould exploded into unrestrained fury. His co-star, Kim Darby, claimed to be so scared that bodyguards were summoned to the tumultuous location.

After two weeks of all-around screaming less than ten minutes of usable material had been completed. Warner Brothers closed down production on the film. Then Barbra tiptoed in. Eyebrows were raised when the project was revived as a Streisand vehicle. In May, 1971, *Variety* reported that Barbra had agreed to appear in *A Glimpse of Tiger:* The story intimated that the original Elliott Gould role was being rewritten for his estranged wife.

This bizarre transsexual experiment was never fully realized because Peter Bogdanovich was assigned to direct the movie, and he commissioned a new screenplay from David Newman and Robert Benton, the writers of *Bonnie and Clyde.* The new title would be *What's Up Doc?* and Ryan O'Neal would be Streisand's co-star.

The transition from *A Glimpse of Tiger* to *What's Up Doc?* is obscure. A year later, when Gould made his one comment on the refurbishing of his film into Barbra's, he told the New York *Times:* "It makes sense, at least she made some money out of it." Yet, the connection between the original plan and the finished product appears to be little more than the gap-ing of a hole in Warner's production lineup with an entirely different crew and outlook.

As *What's Up Doc?* went into rehearsals in early July, Barbra and Elliott filed a joint petition for divorce in Santo Domingo. They were the first celebrities to avail themselves of the Dominican Republic's new liberalized law that permitted foreigners to obtain a divorce within seven days. Barbra was represented by a local attorney, but Gould flew to the Caribbean island with nineteen-year-old Jennifer Bogart, who was five months pregnant with their first child.

Elliott told reporters that he and Barbra were still good friends and that if she'd flown down to Santo Domingo he would have greeted her with a kiss. In fact, they had become increasingly distant since Jenny, the daughter of director Paul Bogart, had moved to Gould's apartment in Greenwich Village. To Barbra's chagrin, they shared the same decorator, a breach of tact star circles tend to consider almost as embarrassing as sharing the same analyst. Arthur Laurents was a loyal friend and frequent visitor of Gould, who lived around the corner from him in his new domestic arrangement. Barbra was curious about Jennifer and once called Laurents to ask him, "Is she pretty?"

She was indeed pretty, very bright, and independent-minded. When it was suggested that Jennifer and Elliott had flown to Santo Domingo for a quickie divorce that would allow them to legitimize their relationship, she coolly said, "We don't believe in marriage." Gould confirmed this when he told columnist Earl Wilson that Jenny was too smart to marry him. "She'll have my children," he explained, "but she won't get married. She thinks it's more romantic this way."

As for Barbra, anything Gould could do she could do better. As a divorced woman she had no need to sprint through parking lots to avoid being photographed with Ryan O'Neal. Both were free from the idiocies of a cover-up: He had lost the Oscar to George C. Scott and she had lost her last claim on Elliott. It was time to relax and stop worrying. Streisand and O'Neal's was a superficial but enjoyable camaraderie: a game played by experts at not getting hurt. She loved being escorted by a handsome, coveted man who was at the height of his career and wanted nothing from her but the pleasure of her company. And in *What's Up Doc?* the Streisand/O'Neal equation would result into co-star chemistry and marquee lure.

"I don't worry so much anymore," she told reporters. Streisand's obsession with beauty and artistic perfection was now superseded by a desire for youth and liberation. She gave a controversial interview to the *Rolling Stone* in which she almost pleaded to Grover Lewis: "Look, I'm considered this kind of institution thing. But I ask you . . . twenty-eight, is it that old?" There was a conscious effort to join the new generation. The gauzy gowns and elaborate coiffures were discarded. She wore jeans, tie-dyed shirts, and a flaxen mane that made her look not only up to the minute but healthier and sexier than ever. She was ready to record *Stoney End,* her first try at a rock sound.

She studied the composers of the era—Harry Nilsson, Laura Nyro, Gordon Lightfoot—and had insights into their works, just as she had with the songs of Arlen, Porter, and Styne a few years before. She found poetry in the new style of music and mined it with the obduracy of a forty-niner shaking the pan in the shallows to come up with the unadultered gold. In her intimate interpretations "I Don't Know Where I Stand" and "If You Could Read My Mind" acquire dimensions of feeling no other performer had ever discovered.

The hard-rock numbers were more difficult to tackle. She had to restrain and maneuver the usual crowd that surrounds rock stars. The album's credit list enumerates more than forty people—arrangers, musicians, mixers, and background singers. Barbra rose above them all and lorded it over like a Wagnerian soprano who knew how to keep a stentorian chorus and a blaring orchestra in their proper place. She had the lung power to attain the near impossible.

The reaction to *Stoney End* was predictably mixed. Streisand cultists of the orthodox persuasion were annoyed at being left behind by their favorite's leap on the rock bandwagon and insisted that Barbra was much better when she expressed herself more personally, away from all those supernumeraries. Yet, in a curious about-face, music critics who had never cared much for her style, such as Henry Pleasants in his anthology *The Great American Pop Singers,* gave her a backhanded compliment by conceding that she had at last found a genre that could absorb her "hollering."

It was clear that not even Barbra Streisand could please all the people all the time, but the "Stoney End" single became a jukebox hit that gave her a firm hold on the teenage audience she was trying to reach. Another of Streisand's wild bets had paid off and she was in the chips.

When she came back to movies, she was milder, more easily persuadable. There was a flicker of the old intransigence as the shooting date approached for *What's Up Doc?* According to director Peter Bogdanovich, she had reservations about the first draft of the script and insisted on a rewrite job by Buck Henry, who had given her a hit in *The Owl and the Pussycat.* Once the dialogue was revised to Streisand's taste, there was no more trouble. Young Bogdanovich had learned cinematic style by watching every classic in world cinema, and he had a way of holding the reins like an old pro. He was as inflexible as William Wyler in the handling of unruly Barbra. He informed her he was the only one allowed to display temperament on the sets of his movies. Bogdanovich knew what he was doing, and Streisand always respects a professional. In a good mood, she subsided into a devil-may-care recklessness that made her performance unstrained and infectiously funny.

The "romance" between Streisand and O'Neal—if it ever had any momentum—sputtered uphill like a wheezing cable car and left its heart in San Francisco during the shooting. Yet the highly publicized star tandem had created a flurry of expectation over *What's Up Doc?* The picture did not disappoint fan-magazine readers who wanted to see Barbra and Ryan in a clinch; it also lured a much larger audience for hefty box-office returns: With a take of $22,000,000 in the United States and Canada market, it was a mere $4,000,000 short of the *Funny Girl* bonanza at roughly a third of the budget spent on her first musical. Clinking cash registers were playing the tune while the show-business trade papers headlined: BARBRA IS MAGIC.

What's Up Doc? was half parody, half evocation of *Bringing Up Baby,* the Katharine Hepburn–Cary Grant romp of 1938. It was a second try at the *Owl and Pussycat* formula, with contemporary Streisand erupting into the pressure-sealed world of thirties comedies, this time in a deliberate updating of a classic. Ryan O'Neal tried valiantly to do a Cary Grant takeoff to the last detail, from the horn-rimmed glasses to the distressed whinny. Confronted with the inimitable, Streisand shied away from Hepburn's carefully clipped upper-class accent and snarled into the role a thousand words a minute. Her screwball heroine had more screws loose and more balls bouncing than the thirties Hepburn had been allowed to insinuate in the relentless pursuit of the fuddy-duddy professor.

What's Up Doc? congealed the pattern of what the movie public expected eagerly from Barbra Streisand. As in *The Owl and the Pussycat,* she was the irrepressible female laying siege to the repressed male. He could never escape her; she was the miniskirted Mountie who always got her man. The handsomer he was, the more titillated her fans were. She was up there on the screen, living the fantasies her fans gobbled, together with their popcorn and Coca-Cola. A niche had been found for her as a movie icon. It did not matter whether she sang or not: The main event was Barbra's capture of her prey. Audiences were learning to anticipate the denouement with the same gleeful suspension of disbelief they exercised while waiting for John Wayne to get even with the bad ones.

Barbra had no problem adapting to the pattern of this special brand of new-old movies. She had plundered a trunkful of wheezing Muzak songs and had breathed different feelings into them. She could just as well resuscitate a *Late Show* flick without the benefit of a first-aid kit. Yet her dreams of glory still haunted her. In the midst of preparations for *What's Up Doc?* Barbra announced a biography of Sarah Bernhardt as the first film she would produce for her own company, First Artists, in association with British director Ken Russell's production unit.

Russell had created several excellent one-hour biographical studies for the BBC, on subjects as varied as Isadora Duncan, Frederick Delius, and Dante Gabriel Rossetti. He would later tumble into the bizarre with his laughable Tchaikowsky biography and his abominable version of *The Devils.* Luckily for Streisand, the Bernhardt project was stalled and finally discarded. The clash of Russell and Streisand's temperaments would have been cataclysmic to say the least, but she was spared from a film that can be described—with a shudder—as "The Freak That Never Was."

Streisand's movies were running true to formula—and very profitably. The redeeming *Divine Sarah* was on ice. Her craving for experiment was channeled into a new record, entitled *Barbara Joan Streisand.* She was ready to explore new frontiers in rock music, this time in a headlong invasion of Aretha Franklin and Janis Joplin's territory.

Once again the album cover tells a story. The photograph on the front shows an openmouthed, confused girl, so undecided between a laugh or a tear that she opts for the deceptive ploy of a quizzical expression. The back cover shows the same kid grinning hopefully in the dark. Many thought there was a typographical error on the jacket because over the tentatively smiling face her name read "Barbara" with three *a*'s. With meticulous Streisand, such mistakes must be discounted. The different spellings of her name were a conscious declaration of independence from the star image she had fashioned and a return to a more naïve, freer, youthful image.

In her early days as a successful cabaret singer and recording star Barbra had said time and again that she did not want to sing rock and roll because the words meant nothing and she could not pump drama into them. Now she tried to give the lyrics some tottering stature by such excesses as the primal scream she introduces in an ear-shattering rendition of

John Lennon's "Mother." Even worse is "Space Captain," in which her powerful voice—concentrated like a ray of sun by a magnifying glass—burns the inane words to a cinder.

Barbara Joan Streisand is a record to approach with a discriminating attitude and a steady finger to drop the needle in the right groove. Between bouts with amplified guitars and relentless drums, she is at her best in the tenderness of "I Never Meant to Hurt You" and "Since I Fell for You." And she makes the electronic gadgetry work for her in a medley of Bacharach and David's "One Less Bell to Answer" and "A House Is Not a Home," singing an almost fuguelike duet with herself to prove that on her own turf no one can match Streisand but Streisand.

The record was received as a very mixed bag of successful and unsuccessful tricks, but there was no denying its shock value. It was time to apply the same pressure to her movie image. Instead of the Sarah Bernhardt picture, Barbra chose *Up the Sandbox* as her debut film within the structure of First Artists Productions. It was based on a well-received novel by Anne Richardson Roiphe: This diary of a half-mad housewife delved into the agonies of a bright college graduate who has given up her identity to be handcuffed to her baby's bassinet and her husband's sexual demands and career aspirations. In the throes of subordination her mental balance is kept precariously by the careful handling of wild fantasies as an escape valve. The harassed Susan imagines herself as a rampaging heroine just before she starts heating the bottle for her infant or the bed for her spouse.

In her daydreams Susan joins black militants to blow up the Statue of Liberty or unmasks a supermacho Fidel Castro as a covert Lesbian in fake beard and olive drag. She even dares to attack her obnoxious mother with a meringue-encrusted anniversary cake. Yet Susan simmers down to the accepted female role when she realizes she cannot go through with abortion. In the end she gains a dubious victory that seems to go no further than obtaining equal baby-sitting rights from her ineffectual husband, blandly played by David Selby.

The screenplay for *Up the Sandbox* catered to Streisand's

measured response to women's liberation, cautiously expressed when she took her stand by saying, "Job opportunities, yes. Abortion, yes. But there should be a time for mothering. If a woman chooses to stay home and be a wife and mother, she shouldn't be put down for that. A good mother is a fantastic creation." This ambivalence would enrich the film as a human document and eventually doom it as a commercial enterprise. For female militants it was too submissive; for contented housewives, too revolutionary.

Streisand had no crystal ball to foresee the reception, and she approached *Up the Sandbox* with unbounded hopes, surrounding herself with the best talent available. Paul Zindel, the Pulitzer Prize-winning playwright of *The Effect of Gamma Rays*, was given the nearly impossible task of building dramatic bridges between the heroine's id, ego, and superego. Irvin Kershner, the perceptive and underrated director of *The Luck of Ginger Coffey* and *A Fine Madness*, bravely tried to mix all the disparate elements into homogeneity.

Streisand has been often accused of masterminding her movies, but this time the reins were held by producers Irwin Winkler and Robert Chartoff. It was nominally *her* movie, presented under the banner of First Artists Productions, yet she went along with several disastrous decisions. The film never found a sharp distinction between the real and the imagined, but settled for a foggy no-man's-land. Audiences were confused as to whether something was going on in Susan's mind or in the actual world around her. With one foot in farce, the other in hot water, the character's fantasies would have worked much better on the outrageous level of high camp.

Devoid of a light touch, *Up the Sandbox* hobbled about in flat-footed earnestness. The bomb-planting scene in the Statue of Liberty was so dark and menacing that most of the mischievous fun evaporated. Worst of all, Streisand went on a costly and unnecessary location trip to Uganda to shoot the African sequence: Susan's dreamworld safari would have been ten times funnier in a fake Marx Brothers-style jungle of papier-mâché and tatterdemalion lianas.

During the trek to Uganda Streisand was faced with a disconcerting phenomenon. The women of the Samburu tribe objected at first to being photographed and had to be cajoled to play bit parts in the movie. Then, after less than a week with the film crew, Barbra noticed that the Samburus, who were used to walking five miles a day, suddenly asked for a bus to take them back to their villages. On a primitive level it was a revealing microcosm of the star syndrome: The mere fact of standing in front of a camera conferred power.

When Barbra came back from location in Africa, she decided to use her star power for a good cause. She became a dynamic force in the campaign to elect Senator McGovern as President of the United States and offered her services for a fund-raising concert in the Los Angeles Forum on April 15, 1972. The show, called "Four for McGovern," also featured James Taylor, Carole King, and Quincy Jones. The blurb for the Streisand album that was recorded live on the occasion calls Barbra truthfully—though somewhat uncourteously—the "star" of the evening.

Eighteen thousand people paid from five to a hundred dollars a seat, and Barbra closed the show proclaiming exultantly that they had raised $300,000 for the Presidential campaign of the Senator from South Dakota. Onstage she confessed that doing her first concert in around six years was exciting but terribly scary. She wished she was back "on the set." Then she explained that some stars conquered their fear of performing with drink, but she hated the taste of liquor, or with pills, but she couldn't even swallow an aspirin. To whoops of approving laughter from the audience, she pretended to puff on a marijuana joint. "You're ahead of me tonight!" she tittered. "It's still illegal?" she questioned. Then she proclaimed, "We should face our problems head on!"

The audience was in high spirits, and it was clear that Barbra was having a good time. Her enthusiasm was contagious, and it went a long way toward making a somewhat ragged performance ingratiating. Barbra basked in the instant warmth of a young audience, yet the concert should never have been released as a record that could not recapture the temperature of the moment and is sometimes as unpalatable as a hastily reheated airplane dinner.

She sang "Don't Rain on My Parade" in a vertiginous arrangement that made her sound as breathless as a sprinter trying to run the mile in three minutes. The subdued numbers like "Didn't We?" have Streisand's shuddery velvet touch, but when she tries to rise above the Eddie Kendrix singers, the hand clapping, the tambourines, and all the paraphernalia of rock and roll—without the benefit of a studio control booth—her voice evokes a different shudder: It is like chalk on a blackboard.

The concert landed her on Nixon's list of "political enemies," and it also raised some nonparanoid animosities among her fans from way back. The album's impromptu quality gave prophets of doom something to work on. It was said that this enforced hollering was tearing her voice and that she was relying too much on the relaxing powers of *cannabis:* She would probably go "the Judy Garland way" in a couple of years.

There were other portents of disaster. In Hollywood word was getting around that *Up the Sandbox* was an unreleasable hodgepodge. Looking to the future, producer Ray Stark called Arthur Laurents, the writer who had helped shape Streisand's career by directing her as Miss Marmelstein in *I Can Get It for You Wholesale.* "Ray asked me if I would write something for Barbra," Laurents says, "because he felt I knew her potential very well. I hesitated, but the offer was too tempting, so I started the screenplay that later became *The Way We Were.*

"It was rough going all the way. Barbra had changed. I had seen the changes coming, but I was not fully prepared. The first shock came when I went with her to a sneak preview of *Up the Sandbox* in San Francisco. The audience reaction was bad and she was upset. I have always told her the truth, and when she asked me what was wrong with the picture, I said I thought there was a lot of jargon that seemed picked up from an analyst's couch. She was furious and she said, 'I've never been to one, but I can give you the number of a good one. You may need him after you do this picture with me.' I had not meant it personally, just that there were too many psychiatric overtones in the script. She overreacted, but she could still balk at the advice and then take it. She came back to Hollywood and actively worked on the reediting of the movie. She made it better, less preachy."

The film was improved, but it still would not work. When *Up the Sandbox* opened around Christmas of 1972, the reviews were mixed and the audience apathetic. Fans who had loved her as the go-getting female in *The Owl and the Pussycat* and *What's Up Doc?* resented the patient, put-upon Susan who came alive only in daydreams. Streisand was more varied and resourceful than ever in the part: She had the right shading for every mood of this complex character and could be vulnerable or aggressive, valiant or defeated with just a toss of the head, a quivering of the chin. Critic Pauline Kael called it "a multi-radiant performance in a mess of a movie," a shrewd epitaph for a stillborn project.

"Barbra was baffled by the failure of *Up the Sandbox,"* Laurents remembers. "She had been told that she was star insurance and she believed it, despite the fact that no such thing seems to exist in movies anymore." Streisand could blame the financial fiascos of *On a Clear Day* and *Hello, Dolly!* on the mistakes of overproduction combined with a shrinking market for big musicals. But *Sandbox* was her own little picture. She had thought it would be a fine film and a valuable statement on the theme of women's liberation. Now her pride and joy was rejected. She was as depressed and belligerent as the mother of a whiz kid who had flunked the spelling bee over p-s-y-c-h-o-l-o-g-y.

Arthur Laurents came to the rescue. He had been close to Barbra for over a decade. In Katie Morosky, the protagonist of his screenplay for *The Way We Were,* Laurents encompassed all the facets of the Streisand he had seen evolve from a shy, nervous girl to a somewhat disillusioned woman in her artistic prime. "I had doubts that she would accept the part," the writer tells. "When she played Miss Marmelstein, she was such a puritanical kid. At bottom she still is. I had now written a story about an idealistic teenager who later goes to Hollywood, is forced to get tough to survive, starts using four-letter words, and learns to fight back to retain her individuality. When she read the first draft of the screenplay, she surprised me. She called me and said, 'You've got it. That's me!'

"But then instead of discussing the part, she wanted to know how many changes of hairdos and clothes she would go through in the years the script covered. She asked if she could wear jeans at any point in the story. I realized she was indeed the idealistic Katie put through the Hollywood grind. The Barbra I first knew was such a bright and alert person. She often asked me for reading lists and would pore over every book I recommended, but this curiosity was no longer there. I had told her once to read Solzhenitsyn, and one day while I was working on *The Way We Were,* she called me to say, 'Hey, your guy won the Nobel Prize!' 'Have you read his books?' I asked. 'No,' she replied, 'I just haven't got the time anymore. I have piles of books and I can't get a moment to concentrate on them.' I realized she had become terribly lazy and it saddened me. There was a time when you could talk to Barbra for hours on any subject and be constantly stimulated intellectually. Now she was beginning to bore me."

With Laurents' screenplay in hand, Ray Stark started looking for a co-star, the man who would play Hubbell Morrison, the handsome, elusive male the author had given Streisand as the ultimate, unattainable love object. Laurents suggested Ryan O'Neal, but Ray Stark told him that Ryan and Barbra had already made one movie together; audiences wanted a new man for Barbra to conquer. Ken Howard, who had made Thomas Jefferson into a blond sex symbol in the musical *1776,* had proved photogenic opposite Liza Minnelli in *Tell Me That You Love Me, Junie Moon.* He was next in line for the role of Hubbell, but, according to Laurents, he lost it over a tennis net.

"We wanted to see how Barbra reacted to Ken Howard, so we arranged some tennis doubles with director Herb Ross and his wife, Nora Kaye. It was Nora and me against Ken and Barbra. You've never seen bad tennis playing until you've watched Barbra on the court. Nora was letting her get away with it and I told her so. "Humor her, she's the star," Nora joked. I insisted on playing to win. We were wiping Ken and Barbra out, but she was delightful, taking the beating with a great sense of humor. At one time the ball hit one of her breasts and she quipped, 'Don't worry, I have another one.' Everything was fine until a very beautiful girl drove down to pick up Ken Howard to take him somewhere to a press luncheon. Barbra froze. Next day she told me there was no sex appeal between them, that nothing would happen up there on the screen, and that we needed that for this kind of story. I agreed with her one hundred percent and Howard was out.

"Then Ray Stark got Robert Redford, whom Barbra had wanted from the beginning. That was the start of my troubles. Redford does not want to be an actor, he wants to be a 'movie star.' The way I'd written *The Way We Were,* it was Katie Morosky's story, but Redford wanted it slanted toward Hubbell Morrison. I knew it couldn't be done, so I refused. I was taken off the project, and they brought in no less than twelve writers to reshape it, including Dalton Trumbo and Francis Ford Coppola. I took my screenplay, started reworking it as a novel, and forgot about the picture.

"It never worked out the way they wanted, so I was recalled to repair the damage and put back all the things that had been taken out. The Redford group—and that includes the director, Sidney Pollack—was disgruntled about a script that revolved inevitably around Streisand. They tried to wrench it away from her, scene by scene, but it was impossible. There are all those stories in magazines about how Barbra demands this and that, but it never happened in *The Way We Were.* She insisted on little things, like getting her good profile in the close-ups, but otherwise she was letting them maneuver things to be played Redford's way.

"I tried to shake Barbra up, telling her that she was getting a raw deal, but she would not react. She was in awe of Redford. There were ridiculous tales in fan magazines about their having a 'romance.' They're all lies. She was simply mesmerized because she found him so beautiful, and he was ever so pleasant because he thought he was stealing the movie away from her." Yet cameras can catch what the human eye misses. Her awe of Redford is evident in every shot, and it made her performance very poignant. In the end it was still *her* movie.

"When we ran the first rough cut, the Redford group hated it," Laurents continues. "They thought it was a bomb and the worst movie he'd ever made. Everyone was called in for retakes, and I advised Barbra to insist on redoing the telephone scene, the one in which she breaks down and begs Hubbell to come back and talk to her in the middle of the night. She should do it again, more frantically. Her eyes were not red enough for a woman who has been weeping for hours, and she kept covering her nose with her hands to stop the sniffling. She was surprised at my suggestion and said, 'But I look so beautiful in that scene.' It was never reshot and—if done properly—it would have won her the Academy Award. She is disliked in Hollywood, but they would never have denied her the Oscar if she really had let go in that scene. It was a set piece for her, from the very first draft of the screenplay. She did not grab the chance and it was her loss. She was just worrying about her looks."

Despite Arthur Laurents' reservations about the finished product—and his regret at the elimination of several key scenes that can be traced only in undeleted publicity stills—the writer knew what Barbra could do best and gave her a tailor-made role as Katie Morosky, the insecure girl who sets her sights on Hubbell, the college dreamboat, and pirates him because his physical beauty is no match for her saber-sharp mind.

In the film's most memorable scene a naked and anxious Katie lies in bed next to a totally drunk Hubbell. She inches close to him in an agonizing mixture of shyness and boldness. Sexually aroused but still in a stupor, Hubbell makes love to her. The camera focuses on Katie's face as the thirty-six expressions she announced in *Funny Girl* fade in and out of Streisand's cinematic face, from awe to possessiveness, from triumph to revulsion. Then, after Hubbell's quick orgasm, she is left with the vacuum of a Pyrrhic sexual victory and desperately fights for a shred of her lost identity by purring to a snoring Hubbell, "It's me, Katie."

Typical Streisand character that she is, as soon as Katie lays her hands on Hubbell, she tries to shape him into her hero. It is not important enough that after all the years of longing he finally belongs to her. He now has to climb up to her ideals of perfection. She goads Hubbell into becoming the great American novelist and the brave defender of worthy causes. He must be the male counterpart of Katie Morosky. She slowly alienates him in the same way that parents alienate their children by demanding that they become living incarnations of their unrealized dreams.

In the last, poignant scene, after Katie has lost Hubbell completely, Streisand is superb as she strokes Redford's face in a motherly caress before she releases him to go into his own world. In the throes of orgasm, sexual partners often call each other "baby." Streisand the actress illuminates this emotion in a wordless close-up that ekes out the inner meaning of *The Way We Were:* Katie and Hubbell could never make it as an adult couple because he was never really her lover but her precious baby.

The two characters can part without regrets simply because they have outgrown each other. Audiences absorbed the subliminal zinger by osmosis. It made the downbeat ending deliciously bittersweet as fans dropped the last tear into the solitary popcorn at the bottom of the carton. *The Way We Were* enjoyed a well-deserved popular success because it astutely presented a contemporary theme: the transience of love. It did not matter that Katie lost Hubbell in the end; the basic thing was that she had him for a while. Streisand, better than any other actress, could project the strain and the pleasure of holding on, then letting go.

Her mystique as a crowd-pleasing star, hinted at in her love affair with Nicky Arnstein in *Funny Girl,* was heightened by Laurents' screenplay in *The Way We Were.* As a movie icon she was the born survivor who struggles to gain and retain something but who is stubborn only to the outer limits of rationality. If you can't do it, try something else; if this subway car is full, wait for the next one because it might be empty. Indomitable spirits are often admirable bores; they don't know when to quit. They are martyrs and the era was not ready for them. To the cynical seventies Streisand offered a cunning alternative in glorious Technicolor: It was better to switch than fight.

There was also the erotic power of that scene with Katie and Hubbell in bed. Film is a fragmentary art, and long after audiences have forgotten the plot of a movie, they remember the strength of an impressive moment. In *The Way We Were* Barbra gave every smitten girl in the world the vicarious pleasure of seducing the golden boy, Robert Redford. That moment certified her as a strange new kind of female sex symbol. She was the star who could make audience identification less of a strain on the imagination, reduce wishful thinking to a demirational level. Barbara Joan—the skinny girl who had shivered at the conquering wiles of Rita and Lana in that long-ago balcony at the Loew's Kings—had at last democratized the sensual longings of the masses. "If plain Barbra can do it, why can't I?" became the hidden slogan for her spectacular success in films.

With *The Way We Were* she was back on top after that dire experience with *Up the Sandbox*. She made it just in time. Her television special, *Streisand and Other Musical Instruments*, was broadcast two weeks after *The Way We Were* opened to adoring crowds, and it met with almost universal rejection. The show had been her biggest dare: a calculated send-up of all her hallowed standards. "People" was accompanied by Turkish tambourines, kanoon, and darabukka and sounded like a hashish-induced belly dance. "Don't Rain on My Parade" was sung by a spaced-out Pocahontas to the rumble of Chippewa and Sioux tom-toms, with antelope and deer-horn rattle thrown in for bad measure.

It was a deliberate desecration of old favorites, and the show's defiance reached paroxysm with "The World Is a Concerto," a cacophonous extravaganza orchestrated with appliances, from pop-up toasters to doorbells, telephones, alarm clocks, and electric shavers. The television special was a bold, uneven, sometimes brilliant experiment, but what the public in general absorbed was an undercurrent of self-parody. The fans were not amused: This time Barbra could not draw them into sharing the joke. *Streisand and Other Musical Instruments* was received with cool annoyance: A *Variety* reviewer ventured that she seemed distressed and could not have been having a good time while preparing it and taping it in London for eleven grueling weeks.

Barbra was going through difficult personal times as her show evolved. Streisand was in the throes of a grand passion that proved to be fleeting. He was a man with no connections with show business. "I like to accompany him in his business travels," Streisand said in an interview for *Cosmopolitan* magazine. She claimed he spoiled her concentration when he visited the set of her television special, but that it didn't matter.

Streisand again insisted that this would be her last interview because she changed her mind too often and hated to be confronted with moods she had already grown out of. By the time the interview appeared in the magazine the "romance" had vanished and she was left amid the ruins with a tongue-in-cheek, thumb-against-nose show.

Streisand and Other Musical Instruments seemed like a facetious farewell performance for the "old" Barbra, but now she realized all dreams of privacy, retirement, and peace were dissolving mirages. She had to hold onto her career; it was all she had. Fortunately there was *The Way We Were* to float on. The irritating television special ran only one night, and its memory was quickly blotted out by that Streisand-Redford wry Valentine: It grossed $23,700,000 in America and was equally successful abroad. Her recording of the title song from *The Way We Were* was number one in the charts, and she was considered a formidable contender for the Oscar. But a funny thing happened on the way to the Chandler Pavilion.

Barbra was asked to sing the song onstage at the Oscar

ceremonies. She said no, then changed her mind, but by then the star spot had been given to Peggy Lee. As it turned out, Barbra would face the Oscar-cast audience only if her performance as Katie Morosky was selected the best of the year by an actress. This time she truly deserved to win, but she had a very strong competitor in Joanne Woodward, who had been previously selected by the influential New York Film Critics for *Summer Wishes, Winter Dreams.*

Streisand and Woodward have qualities in common. They are both gifted actresses but highly opinionated women, reclusive and reluctant to join the Hollywood coterie that has the final say on who is to be honored with an Academy Award. Barbra and Joanne were running neck-and-neck in that Oscar race. The suspense was mounting. The night before the ceremonies, Channel Five conducted its annual poll of the public in the program called *Your Choice for the Oscars.* Barbra won and became the odds-on favorite for twenty-four hours. But as the winner was announced in the Oscar ceremony, a dark horse sprinted forward in a photo finish: British actress Glenda Jackson garnered her second statuette for a charming but essentially lightweight performance in *A Touch of Class.* The Chandler Pavilion became a blissful realm of mixed zoological metaphors as the audience commented that in Glenda's rabbit punch the Academy had found a way to kill two birds—Barbra and Joanne—with one stone.

But what did Streisand care? Injustice was a bitter pill, but it could easily be washed down with the nectar of success. Her new album, built around the Oscar-winning theme song for *The Way We Were,* was her best received in years. It cleverly dosed the sentimentality of old favorites such as "My Buddy" and Berlin's "How About Me?" with the spiteful abrasiveness of "The Best Thing You've Ever Done." It was vintage Barbra, in a swift exorcism of the rock-and-roll demon that had lately taken hold of her. Fans breathed easily as she sensually invited them to "Summer Me, Winter Me" with a vocal suggestion of alternate applications of Coppertone and Lip Ice.

Her shoulders rose and fell again in the Streisand shrug. If she could not be an innovator, she'd be a crowd pleaser. Barbra had been deeply hurt by the public's rejection of *Up the Sandbox,* and friends say she vowed never again to get involved in a "serious" project. In this mood she stepped into *July Pork Bellies,* a screwball comedy to be produced by her long-time agent, Marty Erlichman. It was originally offered to the brilliant exiled Czech director Milos Forman, but he sniffed at the property and politely declined. The film, under the title of *For Pete's Sake,* was eventually helmed by Peter Yates, the man who had made careening cars into an automobile ballet in *Bullitt.* Yates evidently knew how to pull a fast one, and his editing legerdemain was just what a flimflam job like *For Pete's Sake* begged for.

It is Barbra's worst movie, based on an original screenplay by Stanley Shapiro and Maurice Richlin. Shapiro had made fortunes for Universal with several of those ultraplutocratic, demipornographic comedies in which the cliff-hanger was whether Doris Day was going to hold onto her superannuated virginity while being tempted by suggestive party-line calls from Rock Hudson in *Pillow Talk* or by sinful Caribbean weekends offered by Cary Grant in *A Touch of Mink.*

The new permissiveness of the movie industry had given Shapiro a chance to strip everything but the G-string away in a cynically leery film; it could classify as "family entertainment" in a pinch. Streisand would be cast as a dutiful wife who tries to drum up some money so that her husband can stop driving a taxi and finish his formal education while she is completing her rather informal one.

In her efforts for Pete's sake, Barbra borrows money from the Mafia. When she fails to meet payments, her "contract" is renegotiated and she is sold into white slavery to a madam, played by Molly Picon with the benign ghoulishness of Helen Hayes doing a takeoff on Polly Adler. Barbra is willing and able to perform her tasks, but the script's suspense is based on how she can escape, uxorial and unsullied, from the tawdriest of situations. She dons an apron and putters around the kitchen to satisfy the precoital fantasy of her first client, a meek Wall Street executive who collapses on schedule. He is spirited out of the apartment by Mafia underlings, but the implied horrors never materialize: Stanley Shapiro is a master at short-circuiting. The nice, aberrant old man is not really dead, and Barbra has not really prostituted herself.

Streisand gives the movie whatever style it has, but the best the screenplay offers her is an opportunity for slumming through the kind of slapstick that Joan Davis, Patsy Kelly, and Vera Vague patented in the thirties and forties. It is two-reeler stuff, stretched perilously into feature length. Barbra rides a bucking motorcycle, then a cantankerous Brahma bull, her eyes bulging a la Jerry Colonna and her mouth gaping a la Joe E. Brown. Pretty funny in spurts, if one can forget the sorry waste of talent.

Yet audiences laughed the film all the way to the bank. Blasted by critics, doomed by word of mouth, *For Pete's Sake* flourished undeterred, like a noxious weed, in neighborhood theaters and drive-ins. It brought in close to $12,000,000 in the United States and Canada market alone. The handwriting was on the wall in the blackest of inks. The movie was bad, but it no longer mattered: The audience got what it wanted from Streisand.

She was the strong woman, willing to do anything to protect her man. She almost literally wore the pants: Her character in *For Pete's Sake* was called Henry, short for Henrietta. In a film market where good roles for women were scarce, Streisand had survived by displaying the awesome range she had announced while she sang her credo at the beginning of *Funny Girl:* She could be sweet as pie and tough as leather.

In unisex times the public devoured her ambivalence. Elizabeth Taylor had fallen from the list of ten top box-office attractions. Liza Minnelli was struggling in the lower rungs. Among the female stars there was only Streisand, up there with Newman, Redford, Eastwood, Wayne, and McQueen.

To hold her own, she did not have to pummel or shoot, maim or stab, in the midst of a macho vogue in screen entertainment. Streisand's weapons were subliminal. Her films subtly introduced her image as the benevolent castrator whom women idolized yet men tolerated because whatever horrors she perpetrated on her mate, they were all for his own good. The equilibrium was perfect.

And now she was not bragging, but stating a mere fiscal fact, when she sang "I'm the Greatest Star."

14. How Lucky Can You Get?

"STARDOM" is a word that Barbra Streisand always detested. The friends who knew her when she was a struggling performer agree that she always fumbled it and made it sound like "stardoom." For precise Barbra the mispronunciation might have been conscious. It is impossible to tell now, more than a decade after the slip of the tongue. Yet in the mid-seventies she found herself steeped—for better or worse—in "stardoom."

In facing the dreaded nonword there were still options to be taken. She could paraphrase Oscar Wilde's aphorism about the two worst things in life: The first is not getting what you want; the second is getting it. Or she could always fall back on her favorite retort: "Oh, yeah?"

As long as she stayed within the profit margins of the big studios she could make ten pictures a year on the level of *For Pete's Sake* and keep everybody happy. Yet experiment and challenge were out of bounds. The films she wanted to star in were not readily marketable. The Swedish film genius, Ingmar Bergman, proposed a new version of Franz Lehar's operetta *The Merry Widow.* Producer Dino De Laurentiis toyed with the idea for a while but finally decided the money risk was too high, even with a star like Streisand.

"It was a marvelous screenplay," remembers Arthur Laurents, who read it, "a complete departure from all Barbra has done and a certain artistic triumph for her. But it couldn't be financed. When the project was shelved, it reminded me of one time when Barbra was complaining about something with Irene Sharaff, who was fitting one of her costumes. 'Oh, stop complaining so much, Barbra, you have everything!' Irene said. And then Barbra looked at her, so terribly hurt, and muttered, 'Oh, but I *don't* have everything.' "

For Streisand what was missing was the chance to expand and grow as an artist. There was still another film project, based on an Isaac Bashevis Singer short story, about a girl who wanted to become a Talmudic student in Poland at the time when women were barred from such lofty intellectual pursuits. The protagonist had to masquerade as a boy to invade the realm of higher learning. The picture was on Streisand's agenda for a while, then dropped. "It was perfect for Barbra," Garson Kanin says. "My only disappointment with her is that she has not fully developed her extraordinary gifts as an actress. That script was produced as a play in Brooklyn after it was discarded as a movie. It was excellent. I could not restrain myself from writing Barbra a letter and telling her she had been wrong in letting it slip through her fingers." But despite Kanin's genuine enthusiasm for Barbra's capabilities, the truth about the aborted movie was sadder. Who would lay down hard cash to make a period film, with transvestite undertones, even with Streisand as box-office guarantee?

Instead of those promising properties her next fiim would be *Funny Lady,* the last one she owed to producer Ray Stark, according to her initial contract. It was the sequel to *Funny Girl* and a further exploration of the Fanny Brice legend. "He'll have to drag me to court before I do this," Barbra snapped. But then she read the screenplay by Jay Presson Allen, who had adapted Muriel Spark's novella *The Prime of Miss Jean Brodie* into an Oscar-winning vehicle for Maggie Smith and then had won an Academy Award for Liza Minnelli with her script for *Cabaret.* "This is much better than *Funny Girl,*" Barbra admitted. "Of course I'll do it."

Streisand was in a state of elation as she started preparing for the film. After years of searching and failing she felt she had at last found love in Jon Peters, a celebrated Hollywood hairdresser. They had the kind of meeting scriptwriters in the thirties slaved after through hours of story conferences. Except that this one, in all its glorious impossibility, was real.

Barbra had seen a woman at a party wearing a short, mannish haircut—just what she wanted for the character of Henry, the heroine of *For Pete's Sake.* She found out the style had been created by Jon Peters, owner of a successful chain of beauty salons in Los Angeles. Impressed by her star name, Peters drove to her Holmsby Hills mansion, parked his Ferrari at the door, and twiddled his thumbs—or scissors—for an hour and a half. He was ready to leave in a huff when Barbra made a regal appearance and asked him if he would cut a wig for her. Peters was a star in his own profession. Asking him to reshape a wig was the equivalent of approaching Streisand to do a week of matinees at an Atlantic City pier. His answer was a definite No. Barbra had met her match.

They started dating, very carefully at first. Peters was estranged but not yet divorced from his wife, Lesley Ann Warren, who had been Elliott Gould's leading lady in *Drat! the Cat!* a decade earlier. Jon Peters was still, according to legal technicalities, not a free man, and Barbra was as usual doubly wary of premature publicity.

Peters and Streisand tried to keep one step ahead of the inquiring press. He broke an ankle sprinting away from photographers in still another parking-lot fandango. That did it. They decided to go public and gave a frank interview to *Women's Wear Daily.* Barbra played the part of gracious hostess and wondered if her shrimp dip was too heavy on the onions while Jon encouraged the hired waiter to take off his jacket as he dished out the caviar.

The secret was out. The new saga of Jon without an *h* and Barbra without an *a* had started. In the beginning their relationship was very much like the one between Barbra and Elliott twelve years before. Streisand has always appreciated men who could upstage her harrowing stories of misery and despair in the wilds of Brooklyn. Jon Peters had many a hair-raising tale to counter each one of hers.

The thirty-year-old hairdresser claims to be half Italian,

half Cherokee. He was related to the Pagano family, who had been in the beauty-parlor business for many years in California. As a child Jon never had any inclination to go into that line of work. Then he literally saw his father die before his own eyes, and the shock marked his entrance into adolescence.

Soon he showed some disquieting signs of straining at the family leash. He became a ruthless street fighter in one of the rougher sections of Los Angeles. He had what was described as a "disciplinary problem," was in juvenile court several times, and was sent to a "training school." He ran away to Europe, wandered around, and married at the age of fifteen.

The marriage did not last. He returned to Los Angeles and took up boxing, just to earn some money to go to New York and search for an easy, get-rich-quick scheme that could accommodate an unskilled youth. With eighty-seven dollars in his pocket he hit the big town and found that no doors were readily opening. Then he succumbed to the calling he had been avoiding for years. He became an apprentice in a beauty shop in New York and worked his way through beauty school by boxing after hours.

After he received his beauty-school diploma, Jon was ready to face his hometown and bring it down for the count of ten. Back in Los Angeles he went to work in Gene Shacove's salon. Shacove is the self-confessed model for the role of the irresistibly macho hairdresser whom Warren Beatty played in *Shampoo.* When he had enough clients to lure away into his private lion's den, Jon borrowed money and opened his own shop at Encino. It was an instant success, and within a year he had another shop at Woodland Hills. Then he reached the ultimate by opening the number one salon in Beverly Hills.

Somewhere along the way, ten years ago, Jon Peters for the first time basked in a star's aura when he married Lesley Ann Warren, the ravishing ingenue who played Cinderella in the television special. He made Lesley Ann look like a modern, sophisticated woman by cutting off the long hair that gave her the appeal of a fairy-tale princess. The new image failed to sell. She stopped getting starring roles and had to settle for parts in minor movies and television series like *Mission: Impossible.* But she was content with Jon and their son, Christopher, who was born in 1968.

While Lesley's star was on the wane, Peters was becoming a luminary in his own field. He had 300 employees in his beauty empire and was developing the business acumen of an awesome entrepreneur. Besides the three shops he owned, Jon's firm manufactured all the beauty supplies used and sold in them. He bought a wigmaking factory in Japan and distributed its product all over the United States, with Peters' label on each wig.

At his salons Jon's collection of "heads" (hairdresser lingo for clients) was impressive. Stars and starlets waited their turn to receive Peters' glamour touch. His skill as a stylist was fabled, and his reputation as a ladies' man soon eclipsed that of his mentor, Gene Shacove, to the point where people who know them both swear there is more of Jon Peters in the Warren Beatty character in *Shampoo* than of Shacove, who initially inspired the Robert Towne screenplay. (After all, Beatty himself was once one of Peters' "heads," and he may have been remembering some special traits when he collaborated in the Towne script.)

Rumors were floating around Hollywood that golden girls such as Jacqueline Bisset and Leigh Taylor-Young were not immune to the Peters charm. At this point in his irresistible assault on success Jon met Barbra. They quickly entered into the same symbiotic communication she had had with Elliott Gould, but with a significant difference. Barbra, the shaper of men, was trying to mold Jon into her image of the perfect male; Jon, equally strong, was teasing her toward his ideal of the perfect female. He wanted her to be free of her old hang-ups and turn her into a more natural creature, liberated and fully attuned to what was going on around her.

"She is like ten different women and I love them all," Jon said. "I get all the ego nourishment I need from him," Barbra said. And Streisand was again involved in one of those mutual-admiration societies she had fallen into—and out of—all through the years.

Barbra began spending more and more time at Peters' Paradise Cove ranch, ten acres of land hidden in the middle of one of the canyons near Malibu. The ranch was an incredible combination of pioneer roughness and creature comforts. Peters loved to build things with his own hands and had made a Jacuzzi whirlpool bath out of an old wine vat. He had a couple of corrals and a large riding paddock for jumping horses. For Barbra he rebaptized one of them and called it Cupid. He presented it to her as a gift and then sat back to applaud her growing equestrian prowess.

Hopelessly urban Barbra had sprouted in the sidewalks of Pulaski street like that memorable tree that grows in Brooklyn, pushing through cement. Her mother had given up sending her to camp because the child had an asthma attack as soon as she was within a mile of a grassy knoll. Now at Paradise Cove she had found her own parcel of Eden: Jon had a special garden for her, and she was able to grow orchids without a sneeze or a wheeze. A healthy color tinged her cheeks; she no longer had to use a blusher.

"I think I'm younger than when I started to be successful," she told *Newsweek*. "I was so carried away that I bought a second-hand Bentley and went through a period loving status things. Now I wear T-shirts and dungarees. It's as if I've taken up where I left off at eighteen . . . back to my thrift-shop goodies."

Streisand posed in her sumptuous Holmsby Hills home for a color spread in *House Beautiful*. There she was, surrounded by her Muchas and her Schieles and her Art Deco bric-a-brac. The story had a decided air of "good-bye to all that." She was no longer collecting stuff, no longer bound by possessions. Barbra preferred to spend hours on end at the Paradise Cove ranch, watching Jon build a guest house around a 700-year-old tree.

His energy and drive awed even a dynamo like Streisand. Jon got up at six A.M. to direct his crew of ranch hands on the day's chores. By nine A.M. he dashed away to his Beverly Hills shop to design hair styles for twenty different women. Barbra was left behind to feed the pet lion Jon had bought as a three-week-old cub. She also did her own laundry, baked her own bread, and took her son, Jason, and Peters' son, Christopher (who had become fast friends), to the nearest public beach: no chlorinated Los Angeles swimming pool was going to give the kiddies a premature taste of the artificial.

As with every man who has crossed Streisand's path since she has reached "stardoom," the inevitable question popped with Jon Peters. "What does she see in him?" people asked. Sue Mengers, Barbra's agent, put it clearly and succinctly when she replied, "He makes her happy." In this mood of bliss Barbra approached the filming of *Funny Lady*.

The fearsome, cantankerous Barbra had almost disappeared. Oscar-winning cinematographer James Wong Howe had been cajoled out of semiretirement to photograph her: They got along famously and exchanged Chinese delicacies between takes. Co-star James Caan had insisted on billing over the title with Streisand; she never quarreled with it. She even came to the studio when her presence was not required to feed Caan off-camera lines for his close-ups. She accepted being showered with talcum by Caan in a scene that could not have been very pleasant to repeat six times. Though scared to death, for a production number she circled an airport in a biplane through heavy fog.

Of course, the going was not all that smooth, not with Streisand at the helm. She had her usual fights with producer Ray Stark, mainly because he wanted Fanny Brice, his late mother-in-law, played more sympathetically. Barbra insisted on playing Fanny as a tough lady who hid her inner softness under a carapace of flinty wisecracks and never aimed to be "lovable" at the cost of her own personality. "I'm not playing me anymore," she declared. "I'm completely relaxed." And nobody was going to force her to tone down the character into benevolent blandness.

The most difficult sequence was at the Los Angeles Swim Stadium in Exposition Park, which was doubling as the giant swimming pool for Billy Rose's Aquacade rehearsal hall in Cleveland. The water was heated to 86 degrees before Barbra dared to dip a toe in it. Then she wanted it at precisely 92 degrees. Stark balked at the huge expenditure of having to heat more than a million gallons of water to the temperature required by the star.

Barbra was furious and uncomfortable. The sequence, scheduled for two days' shooting, went on for a week. She tried all sorts of improvisations, like lifting her water wings to make an enormous bust. By then director Herbert Ross, a veteran of Streisand skirmishes, knew how to handle his star, so he diplomatically told her, "I can't see your face that way, but it was a good idea." She did not concede, but the scene ended on the cutting-room floor anyway.

Funny Lady was the last movie Barbra owed Ray Stark. When it was over at last, she gave the producer an antique mirror on which she had written in bloodred lipstick "Paid in Full." Yet she also sent him a plaque that added, "Even though I sometimes forget to say it, thank you, Ray. Love, Barbra."

Everyone involved was convinced the movie would be a smash, but Jon Peters was telling the press that Barbra could not go on playing Ray Stark's mother-in-law. Streisand took his cue and snorted, "So what's going to be next . . . *Funny Grandma?*" Peters was intent on creating a new, youthful image for his paramour. There was a shudder of dread in the media when he was announced as the producer of her next record, *Butterfly*.

Peters went to work to find the best material for Barbra. There were discarded cuts, doctored orchestrations, and a flurry of anger at how the credits were allotted in the album, with some key names dropped in a rather embarrassing oversight. Again a Streisand album cover tells a whole story, this time about her new phase. She is pictured all over it embracing and nuzzling Peters. With his piercing eyes and a black beard, he gave gossip writers miles of copy: He was described in sinister terms as Barbra's Svengali or the film empress' Rasputin.

These tales of impending cataclysm vanished as soon as *Butterfly* hit the stands and sold into gold-record status within a couple of weeks. It is Streisand's best entry in the contemporary-music sweepstakes. She sounds finally relaxed in the new genre, not pushing as hard as she did with *Stoney End* or *Barbara Joan Streisand.* There is a devil-may-care, here-goes-nothing attitude that fits the style of the numbers. There is also an open sexuality that is unprecedented in her career. She can sing the naughty "guava jelly" with a subliminal wink for each suggestive phrase.

The duo had a hit. Now it was unavoidable. Jon Peters was in control, and despite all the snickers, the "Fighting Hairdresser" definitely had something on the ball. If he could produce a gold record, why not an Oscar-winning movie? And so the mad caper of *Rainbow Road* started, in all colors from angry red to envy green to coward yellow and lavender blue. The story about the creation of this film project is so rich in good old back-stabbing Hollywood melodrama that a studio head is quoted by intimates as saying, "Why in the hell don't they dump the script and make a movie about what happened backstairs while it was being whacked into shape?"

For starters, a talented couple of writers, John Gregory Dunne and his wife, Joan Didion, had the idea of refurbishing the movie classic *A Star Is Born* by placing it in a rock-and-roll milieu. Basically, the story was about a waning movie idol, Norman Maine, who finds himself upstaged by the rise of the bit player he married, Vicky Lester. She ascends to Academy Award-winning heights while he sinks into an alcoholic stupor and finally commits suicide by drowning. Dunne and Didion tried to parallel the story with the similar collapse of a tired rock-and-roller and the emergence of his mousy wife as a nova.

After the Dunnes had worked on it for fifteen months, the script was taken to producer John Foreman at Warner. The film was definitely "on," and Mark Rydell, a multifaceted producer-writer-director-actor, fell in love with it. Rydell would do the picture if he were allowed to make changes in the screenplay and, of course, if he could find a dynamite co-star package to portray the ill-fated couple.

After this the internecine fighting becomes so confused that it could be followed only by military maps drawn by Napoleon and Kutuzov. At one point or another countless star combinations were rumored to be on the verge of signing for *Rainbow Road:* Elvis Presley and Liza Minnelli, Diana Ross and Allan Price, Carly Simon and James Taylor, Mick Jagger and his wife, Bianca, Cher and her then husband, Sonny. The list goes on and on.

Then Barbra Streisand and Jon Peters saw the screenplay. They adored it—with reservations. Mark Rydell bowed out, together with Dunne and Didion. Now Jon Peters would be the producer and the film would be directed by Jerry Schatzberg, who had impressive credits such as *Panic in Needle Park* and *Scarecrow.* Jonathan Axelrod, son of playwright and scriptwriter George Axelrod, was hired to rewrite the film and make it, in vague terms, "more funky and with it." Arthur Hiller and Hal Ashby were approached as possible directors in case Schatzberg did not work out.

Barbra and Jon had seen the Judy Garland version of *A Star Is Born* but not the Janet Gaynor–Fredric March version. When they screened it at Holmsby Hills, they wanted their film much closer to the 1937 movie. Jon Peters announced that he would not only produce but also make his debut as director of the project they were no longer calling *Rainbow Road* but *A Star Is Born.*

Strangely, Barbra and Jon came up with an idea about reversing the roles. She would play the established singer on the decline and the male character would be the aspiring performer who finally eclipses her. The trouble was where to find a well-known male star who could make a climb from rags to riches credible. Peters tentatively volunteered and told Axelrod that he himself would play the part. That is precisely when Axelrod bailed out. He claims that what he had gone through was like the old Ben Hecht horror stories about Hollywood and prophesied that the picture would turn out to be "the *Myra Breckinridge* of 1975."

Undaunted, Barbra and Jon called in Robert and Laurie Dillon, who had done the script of *99 and 44/100% Dead,* a gangster farce that arrived in rigor mortis at the box office. As late as March of 1975 Barbra was calling her old friend Garson Kanin, who talked to her—and Jon Peters—on the phone for two hours and then politely declined to wield the forceps and play obstetrician for a star who was having so much trouble aborning.

The idea of reversing the roles—and of Jon co-starring—had been dropped. (Barbra later claimed it was a joke in the first place.) Now Peters was after Kris Kristofferson to play the lead. But Kristofferson would not sign until he saw a finished screenplay. Yet Peters' extraordinary stamina in putting together this film was not overlooked in Hollywood, capital of the never-never land of Chutzpah. David Begelman, the president of Columbia Pictures, announced he had a deal with Jon to produce—and probably direct—a picture called *Eyes*, about a woman who dreams about her own murder.

Just before the opening of *Funny Lady* reluctant Barbra agreed to face penetrating television reporter Barbara Walters on the *Today* show. It was the duel of the Barbaras, and Streisand won it by a toss of her somewhat scraggly mane. She launched into a defense of Peters, equating his problems as a producer-director with her own as a fledgling Hollywood personality. He had not paid his dues, they had never seen his work but . . . how could you prove you could do something unless they gave you a chance of doing it? She made Peters sound like a combination of Orson Welles–Peter Bogdanovich. For all anyone knows, she may be right. For years she has had a natural talent to pick winners.

With the release of *Funny Lady* she proved again right. She received fine reviews from critics who were previously unimpressed, and not only for her singing. This time people had to admit that she had a dramatic talent that went far beyond the belting of a song.

Funny Lady is an unwieldy package held together with the Scotch tape of Streisand's talent. If *Funny Girl* was a fairy tale on the level of Cinderella, the second stanza of the Fanny Brice story is more akin to Rapunzel. The love affair between Fanny and Nicky Arnstein in *Funny Girl* bore only the slightest resemblance to the truth. *Funny Lady* goes it one better by completely fantasizing the complicated ménage of Fanny and Billy. The film is an outrageous combination of backstage musical and soap opera, a delirious mélange of *Footlight Parade* and *As the World Turns.*

It was a tough nut to crack, but Barbra had an insight while preparing for the role: "This script is about losing one's fantasies and illusions and getting in touch with and appreciating reality. It is really about learning to accept yourself. That's what I've started to do in my own personal life." And that, in terms of audience identification, is what she brings to the movie.

The screenplay has Miss Brice marrying her brash producer, Mr. Rose, on the rebound from elegant Nicky Arnstein, whose attraction she finds difficult to resist. Fanny then drifts into a long-distance marriage with slobbish Billy, as they both pursue conflicting careers. Briefly, Fanny falls again under Arnstein's spell.

There were legal hurdles to clear before the film reached the screen, and they are reflected in the choppy continuity. Eleanor Holm, the Olympic swimmer who snared Billy away from Fanny, was offered $5,000 to allow herself to be portrayed as a money-grabbing Circe. Nicky Arnstein had died and was no longer a potential plaintiff in libel suits. In contrast with his "doomed gentleman" image in *Funny Girl*, he is presented the second time around as a preening cad and expensive gigolo. Omar Sharif, in a ruthless cameo, wheezes his despicable lines through that supposedly fetching gap between his front teeth: He tells Fanny that if he walks out on his fortyish wife, he can come back to her with a sizable share of the loot.

Thoroughly disillusioned at his combination of materialism and narcissism, Fanny discards Nicky and flies back to Billy, contrite and chastened. Unfortunately, she finds him in bed with Eleanor Holm, who is his new star for the Cleveland Aquacade. Brice, the two-time loser, heads once more for the divorce court. In a nostalgic coda after the Fanny-Billy fiasco they meet again. He tries to hustle her into starring in his new show and the film ends ambivalently, with a suggestion that Fanny might come back to the stage in Billy's

Seven Lively Arts. In real life Rose and Brice's paths never recrossed, either romantically or professionally. Her final comment on her ex-husband occurred when she told producer Max Gordon, as they walked by Billy's lair in the Ziegfeld Theatre: "Up there on the fifth floor is the most evil man I have ever met."

But never mind that *Funny Lady* whitewashes some ugly truths. It works as a Streisand vehicle. The stage numbers are diverting but not very imaginative. Her sure-fire songs ignite the proper response, but the important thing about the film is its quality as a tour de force for Streisand as an actress. She holds the pieces of this scrambled jigsaw puzzle of a movie with her bravura scenes. She can lay down her defenses and humilate herself before Arnstein, begging him to come back until her face congeals in a moment of insufferable embarrassment as she notices a brand-new wedding ring on his finger.

Then, when a worthless Nicky tries to wield his magic on her again, Streisand retreats within herself as she tells him how impressed she was with his seven toothbrushes during their first night together at a Baltimore hotel. Nicky tries to recover lost ground and kisses her, but Fanny is petrified, unyielding. After the crucial kiss Streisand gives Sharif a cross-eyed frown—full of anger, self-pity, and regret—as she recoils to mutter a line no other actress would be able to put across without giggles from the audience: "And in all these years I've only been in love with a set of toothbrushes."

She tops this display of injured pride and battling womanhood with her breakup scene with Billy Rose. In a train station, after she has caught him in flagrant adultery with Eleanor Holm, she tries to patch things up. Ever the modern screen's epitome of the practical woman, Streisand tentatively offers: "Let's negotiate. I'll forget if you forget." But when he is ominously silent to her plea, Barbra uses her actress' intuition and populist charisma to squeeze heartbreak out of a pedestrian line that rings very true: "I'm in trouble, right?"

The film's coda is her ultimate triumph. The confrontation between the old-timers would have been ludicrous in less skillful hands. There are Streisand and Caan, both aged by well-applied talcum powder on their temples. She maneuvers Caan into poignancy by playing against the grain of the scene, with no cheap sentimentality, but with the wry intimacy of people who have left animosity behind and together can at last laugh at themselves in the comfort of being middle-aged, safely—and perhaps regrettably—beyond passion.

Funny Lady cannot be taken seriously. The chronology of the Brice-Rose tandem is as haphazard as a biography of Napoleon and Josephine in which she would come back to commiserate in St. Helena just before he rode into Waterloo. The script is a skein of fabrications straight out of a thirties Irving Thalberg movie starring Norma Shearer, whom Streisand oddly resembles. But the audience responds to her in an almost palpable give-and-take. In the previews for *Funny Lady* they went wild, applauding not only her songs but her dramatic scenes. In the first sneak preview in Denver, when Streisand told Omar Sharif off, a woman actually stood up, tears streaming down her face, and shouted, "Right on, Barbra!"

The film's opening was staged in Washington, where Barbra gave one of her now rare live concerts at the Kennedy Center, televised under the title *From Funny Girl to Funny Lady*—a giant commercial for her new movie. Between numbers she reassured the black-tie audience of her approval by telling them all—from President Ford down—that she thought they'd be stuffed shirts but that they were really nice. After the concert she was the superstar of a gala at the Iranian embassy, where she danced with Ted Kennedy and was served a special plate of exotic delicacies by Ambassador Zahedi.

Immediately afterward Barbra went to London, where *Funny Lady* had been selected for a royal command performance in the presence of Elizabeth II. Barbra faced—and fazed—the Queen of England by asking her point-blank: "Your Majesty, why do women have to wear gloves to meet you and the men don't?" "Well, I don't really know," Her Majesty replied. "It's just tradition, I suppose." As the Queen moved down the curtsying line, Barbra turned to Jon Peters and said, "Well, I guess I still don't know." Then she told the press, "I think it's the men's sweaty hands that ought to be covered, not ours."

Barbra was still doing her blunt-but-regal bit. Her audience loved it. Despite mixed reviews, *Funny Lady* lined them up at the box office.

The star magic is still there, stronger than ever. But so is the dilemma of the actress *manquée*. That a woman capable of such intensity of feeling would be forced to squander it in enameled claptrap is an American tragedy, whatever the tabulation in dollars and cents. Streisand should go on to play the extraordinary roles she once felt she was born to enact, but could she? The most depressing aspect is that her cultists might not let her.

She is at the same time buoyed by adoration and strapped by it. She will be enshrined as Barbra as long as she remains Barbra. It is the Marlon Brando disaster all over again. Or even worse, the Tallulah Bankhead catastrophe. Tennessee Williams wrote *A Streetcar Named Desire* for Bankhead and she refused to play it. When she finally did at the end of her career in a New York City Center revival, the audience tittered at her most moving lines, anticipating the star's eruption into "camp." Bankhead finally gave up and played the remainder of the run for easy laughs, with a throaty delivery that sent a predictable and tawdry shiver up to the second balcony. One wonders what would be Streisand's fate if she ever essayed one of the classics she dreamed about in her eager youth. If she played Medea, would the audience expect her to belt to Jason, "Come on, bleed me a river?"

Barbra claims that Jon Peters has given her a new taste for adventure. "What the hell," she says, "we're both taking chances and it's the only way to grow. What excites me is the element of risk. After all, the worst we can do is fail. But on the other hand, we'll have more fun playing around."

But playing around with *A Star Is Born* is not what Barbra

Streisand was all about to begin with. And even if that movie gets off the ground, the next Jon Peters project for her is another Doris Dayish comedy, *Suppose They Meet,* about a women's lib executive who tangles with a male chauvinist pig of a millionaire. Money in the bank, to be sure, but what else?

Meanwhile, her stalwarts keep begging her to go back to what she has abandoned. Arthur Laurents offered Barbra a triumphal return to Broadway in a revival of *Gypsy.* "She is now the right age to play Rose, who was actually in her early thirties when her daughters were doing kiddie acts in the vaudeville circuit. Barbra not only refused my offer but was downright offended at my suggestion. Angela Lansbury got the role, the acclaim."

Barry Dennen, the man who first saw the glory that would be Barbra, is equally disenchanted. "It is difficult to quarrel with that kind of success, but if people only knew what she was capable of. . . . After she *schlepped* through *Hello, Dolly!* I wrote her a telegram with just three words: "What a pity." But I never sent it because it would not do her any good now."

After years of Streisand's procrastination her prize role as Sarah Bernhardt is going to Glenda Jackson. It grieves Marilyn Fried, the roommate who went through all the agonies with Barbra when she wanted to be a great artist. "She has settled for more," Marilyn says, "but it is really less. She will never be happy until she fulfills her promise."

Pauline Kael, the critic who could always be counted on to defend Streisand, gave *Funny Lady* a scathing review, claimed that she had fallen "out of like" with the star and concluded by saying, "Has Streisand lost sight of the actress she could be?" She has betrayed her aspirations and betrayed *us* who believed in her. That's all you hear from the people who nurtured her talent: She has so much more to give. It is a *ritornello.* But they are all talking about Barbra the actress, and who knows what Barbra the woman really wants? She has discarded many dreams along the way. But what are private dreams compared to her capacity to purvey mass dreams, those that money can buy for the price of a ticket?

Barbara Joan Streisand has made millions happy, for a little while: in the reels of a movie, the grooves of an LP. If she wants to sit back and survey it all like a sated empress, she's entitled. She owes absolutely nothing to anybody; she has done her bit. Against all odds she has become the greatest star, the living escape valve for myriad repressions. Who cares if it lasts or if it evaporates in another decade? At least she made it once and that is enough for a lifetime. It is history.

And if the magic ever begins to falter, get ready for the Streisand comeback. She is now in transitory bliss, lulled by success. But a bee lies sleeping in the palm of her hand. She said it once: "if you clutch it long enough, it stings . . . it stings!" When it does, she will clench her teeth, cross her fingers for luck, and get ready to face, and vanquish, still another Lion.

397268	Mike and Bernie Winters **SHAKE A PAGODA TREE**	60p
398302	Mike Yarwood **AND THIS IS ME!**	50p
300140	Jimmy Young **JY**	50p
300000	**ERIC AND ERNIE: THE AUTOBIOGRAPHY OF MORECAMBE & WISE**	50p
	FILMS	(all are illustrated)
398485	W. A. Harbinson **BRONSON**	50p*
398418	James Juneau **JUDY GARLAND**	80p*
398426	Des Hickey and Gus Smith **LAURENCE HARVEY: HIS PUBLIC AND PRIVATE LIFE**	75p*
398116	Malachy McCoy **STEVE McQUEEN**	75p
398027	Groucho Marx and Richard Anobile **THE MARX BROTHERS SCRAPBOOK**	75p*
300248	Anthony Quinn **THE ORIGINAL SIN**	75p*
	MUSIC	(all are illustrated)
397462	Larry Pryce **QUEEN: AN OFFICIAL BIOGRAPHY**	50p
0426	Tandem **GENERAL**	
165985	The Duchess of Windsor **THE HEART HAS ITS REASONS**	60p*
12992X	Jake La Motta **RAGING BULL**	35p*

*Not for sale in Canada